IGNACIO ELLACURÍA

IGNACIO ELLACURÍA

Essays on History, Liberation, and Salvation

Edited with an Introduction by

Michael E. Lee

Commentary by

Kevin F. Burke, SJ

ORBIS BOOKS
Maryknoll, New York 10545

Founded in 1970, Orbis Books endeavors to publish works that enlighten the mind, nourish the spirit, and challenge the conscience. The publishing arm of the Maryknoll Fathers and Brothers, Orbis seeks to explore the global dimensions of the Christian faith and mission, to invite dialogue with diverse cultures and religious traditions, and to serve the cause of reconciliation and peace. The books published reflect the views of their authors and do not represent the official position of the Maryknoll Society. To learn more about Maryknoll and Orbis Books, please visit our website at www.maryknollsociety.org.

Library of Congress Cataloging-in-Publication Data

Ellacuría, Ignacio.
    Ignacio Ellacuría : essays on history, liberation, and salvation / Edited with an
  Introduction by Michael E. Lee ; Commentary by Kevin F. Burke, SJ.
       pages cm
    Includes index.
    ISBN 978-1-62698-022-8 (pbk.)
    1. Liberation theology.   2. Theology, Doctrinal.   3. Theology—Latin America.
  I. Lee, Michael Edward, 1967–   II. Title.
  BT83.57.E454 2013
  230'.2—dc23
                                                                    2012049630

In memory of

Dean Brackley, SJ (1946-2011)
who joined his fate to that of the Salvadoran people.
His life and service truly represent
the finest translation of liberation theology.

Contents

Part III. Saving History

Introduction

Ignacio Ellacuría:

A View from the North

Michael E. Lee

Inevitably, it is the starting point. San Salvador, El Salvador. November 16, 1989. For many in the English-speaking world, if they have heard the name Ignacio Ellacuría, they know it because of the night on which he, Julia Elba Ramos, and Celina Ramos, and five other Jesuit priests, Ignacio Martín Baró, Segundo Montes, Amando López, Joaquín López y López, and Juan Ramón Moreno were murdered on the lawn of the Universidad Centroamericana José Simeon Cañas (UCA). Some from this group were victims of circumstance: their deaths occurred because they were at the wrong place at the wrong time. However, in the case of Ellacuría, we have what Martha Doggett calls "a death foretold."[1] Ellacuría's life and work ended abruptly and brutally on that November night, not as an aberration or happenstance, but as an inextricable outcome of his life and work.

This volume presents twelve essays that introduce Ellacuría's theological thought, and in doing so, hopes to contribute to a fuller understanding of his life, his work, and his death. Greater familiarity with Ellacuría has significant historical value in relation to, among other things, Roman Catholicism and liberation theology, Latin American philosophy, the Society of Jesus (Jesuits) and its educational vision, and the Salvadoran civil war and its role in the twilight of the global Cold War. Above all, nearly twenty-five years after an assassin's bullet took his life, this volume seeks to present Ellacuría's thought not simply as an archival object of the past, but as an ongoing challenge for the present and future.

In Ellacuría there exists an extraordinary confluence of intellectual insight and lived witness. For English-speaking readers of Ellacuría, particularly from the United States and Canada, the United Kingdom, and other nations whose economies make them part of the global "North," his challenge lies in how that intellect and lived witness came together as commitment to and solidarity with those majorities of the "South" that daily experience grinding poverty, unthinkable repression, and death before their time.[2]

Though Ellacuría's thought is worth a full-fledged intellectual biography, this introduction will focus on two key elements in order to help contextualize and illuminate the essays found in this volume. First, an account of Ellacuría's intellectual formation and central ideas helps locate him on the terrain of contemporary thought and, in particular, as a significant figure of that movement known as liberation theology. The inner dynamism between Ellacuría's philosophy of historical reality and his historical soteriology (theology of salvation) represents his distinctive intellectual contribution, and because so little of it has appeared in English, it also signals how, for many, a figure killed decades ago can serve as a "new" intellectual voice.

Secondly, a narrative of Ellacuría's life and work at the UCA in the last decade of his life (1979–89) illustrates how Ellacuría's imposing philosophical framework and theological ideas did not remain in the theoretical realm but came to take flesh at the university that he led. The Salvadoran civil war served as the crucible that tested Ellacuría personally and challenged the UCA as an institution to make manifest ideas like the "preferential option for the poor" and "a university at the service of the national reality." The manner with which Ellacuría and the UCA sought a negotiated end to the conflict, while countering the propaganda of the Salvadoran military dictatorship and the U.S. government that supported it, gives witness to a university president who did more than just think abstractly about the relation of religion and politics. He was a theologian, priest, and public figure who wrestled with his faith tradition to respond in a faithful-critical manner to a situation of almost unimaginable violence and repression.

Ellacuría's Formation

Most commentators narrate Ellacuría's early development by mapping out the series of teachers or mentors he encountered through his formation as a Jesuit priest and his academic training. Ellacuría was born in Portugalete, in the Basque region of Spain on November 9, 1930, and entered the Jesuit novitiate in Loyola as a seventeen-year old boy in 1947. For the next twenty years, opportunities to study in Ecuador, Austria, and Spain alternated with periods of work in El Salvador. Influences during this time include the Jesuits Miguel Elizondo, his novice master in El Salvador, and Aurelio Espinosa Pólit, a professor of humanities whom Ellacuría encountered as a scholastic in Quito. It would be his next two teachers, however, who exerted a more direct influence on Ellacuría's intellectual formation: the German Jesuit theologian Karl Rahner, and the Basque philosopher, Xavier Zubiri.

Ellacuría encountered Rahner while completing theological studies in Innsbruck in 1958 on the way to priestly ordination in 1961. It was a pivotal time in Roman Catholic theology, the years just prior to the Second Vatican Council. Rahner, who would emerge as the most important theologian of the postconciliar era, led a generation of theologians and philosophers who were creatively rethinking the stilted interpretations of Thomistic thought that characterized the neoscholasticism of the previous century. In contrast to that theology that so sharply distinguished natural and supernatural orders, Rahner emphasized the already-graced character of the world and the human person. The human being, as a "hearer of the word," was constituted with an openness to receive God's grace, and that grace, more than merely a thing to be prayed for or earned, was nothing less than the very self-communication of God.[3]

The implications for Ellacuría were clear: false dualisms that separated human history from salvation history, or a "pure" human nature from graced human nature, had to be overcome. Rahner's notion of grace provided Ellacuría an important principle of unity, but it did have its limitations as well. While Ellacuría recognized the richness of Rahner's theology for the modern individual, he also strove to push that theology beyond an individual framework and explore its social and historical consequences. Under the tutelage of his next mentor, Xavier Zubiri, Ellacuría developed such a philosophical framework by rethinking the nature of human intellection and the central importance of historical reality.

After ordination to the priesthood, Ellacuría went to Madrid and asked Zubiri to mentor his doctoral studies. Zubiri, a far-reaching thinker who studied mathematics, theoretical physics, philology, and who had attended the lectures of Husserl and Heidegger, had withdrawn from public academic life, quitting his chair in philosophy in Barcelona in 1943. However, he had continued developing his thought and offering seminars in Madrid. At the time that Ellacuría arranged to do doctoral studies under him, Zubiri was publishing a major work, *On Essence*. In it, Zubiri began to develop a critique of Western philosophy along with his constructive proposal that *reality* (in contrast to "being" or "essence") should constitute the central object of philosophy. The close working relationship between Zubiri and Ellacuría initiated during this time would continue for the next two decades until Zubiri's death in 1983. Indeed, Zubiri petitioned Ellacuría's superiors to allow him to remain in Madrid as his collaborator. However, though Ellacuría was permitted to return to Spain regularly to assist Zubiri, he was needed much more in Central America and the fledgling Jesuit university in El Salvador.

After completing his doctorate, Ellacuría returned to El Salvador as formation superior for the Central American Jesuits and as professor of philosophy and theology at the UCA. The late 1960s and early 1970s saw the first fruits of Ellacuría's long years of development. He joined the board of directors at the UCA, began publishing various essays in philosophy and theology, and played a key role in the way that the Jesuits discerned their mission in Central America. Although the Jesuits traditionally tended to educate the wealthy elite in countries like El Salvador, Ellacuría and a new generation of Jesuits embodied a sense of mission that would be summed up in the Society's 32nd General Congregation (1975) as "the service of faith and the promotion of justice."[4]

In 1975, Ellacuría, relieved of his duties as formation superior, entered into the period marked by his mature writing and his ascending leadership at the UCA. The promotion of justice was no fanciful motto during these tumultuous political years. When President Molina caved in to pressure from wealthy oligarchs and scuttled the first attempts at agrarian reform in 1976, Ellacuría published a stinging editorial entitled "¡A sus órdenes, mi capital!"[5] Not only did the Salvadoran government pull financial support from the UCA, but the campus was bombed several times, and the violence began to escalate. In 1977, the Jesuit Rutilio Grande, whose pastoral work involved forming some of the earliest Christian base communities in El Salvador, was murdered by a paramilitary group that threatened the assassination of all Jesuits who did not leave the country within thirty days. Ellacuría, who was in Spain when Grande was murdered, would not be permitted to enter the country for nearly a year.

Though 1975 signaled the beginning of Ellacuría's mature writing, it did not mean the end of his "formation." In the wake of Rutilio Grande's assassination, a surprising figure emerged in the Salvadoran Catholic Church, the new archbishop, Oscar Arnulfo Romero. Though initially supported by the oligarchy and papal nuncio as a conservative traditionalist who would "rein in" the liberationist elements in the church, Romero became an outspoken critic of the systemic injustice in the country and a bold defender of those who faced repression in their struggle for justice.

In Romero, Ellacuría saw embodied in a powerful way the vocation of the Christian and the mission of the church in a world of injustice and social conflict. Although he held the most important ecclesiastical position in the country, Romero's office door was open to the hundreds of *campesinos* who would trek to the capital to tell him of their sufferings, of fathers who disappeared, of children who were killed. Romero's pastoral letters and homilies attempted to shed the light of the gospel on questions such as violence, poverty, and the nation's spiraling political crisis, but they also allowed those realities to reconfigure the meaning of such concepts as sin, idolatry, and conversion. Romero embodied the mission of the church both in his firm devotion to prayer and the Eucharist and through the creation and support of diocesan offices for the documentation of human rights abuses and the legal defense of victims. In Romero and the archdiocese that he led, Ellacuría experienced firsthand the transformation engendered by a firm commitment to the preferential option for the poor. Ellacuría would carry forward the lessons learned from Romero as he assumed the role of rector (president) of the UCA in 1979. Before detailing that remarkable last decade of his life, let us turn to some of the central ideas that mark his thought.

Philosophy of Historical Reality

Ellacuría's constructive philosophical vision builds upon the basic diagnosis of Western philosophy that he inherited from Zubiri. Western philosophy has misapprehended the basic act of human knowing by dividing sense and intellect, and this division has two disastrous consequences: (1) the intellect, divorced from reality, can now only arrive at reality through "concepts"; and (2) reality itself is reduced to a thing or entity that loses its openness and dynamism.[6] Rather than perpetuate a division between ideas (beyond reality) and sense-data (that we perceive), Zubiri treats human intellection as a "sentient intelligence." He assumes that humans are "installed in" reality in a basic way.[7] Humans apprehend real things that have an "itself-ness" to them. As real, all things are interrelated. Reality, then, possesses a primacy, which implies that "existence, " meaning," "being," etc., all emerge within and from it. Moreover, reality itself places an ethical demand upon human beings to which they must respond.

Ellacuría intensifies Zubiri's insight regarding this inherent demand upon human beings by bringing out the historical dimension of reality. Reality possesses a basic materiality: from matter, to living things, to human beings. Similarly, materiality insures that all things are profoundly interrelated. So when humans, with their sentient intelligence, actualize reality, their actions (or praxis) open and close all sorts of possibilities for opting and creating new forms of reality. These possibilities and the ways of life they imply are handed on from generation to generation much like DNA, so that history is a "traditioning" of possible realizations of the real. From simple personal actions to complex social structures, history represents the highest realization of reality.[8]

Three important implications of this carefully elaborated philosophy appear in the essays presented in this volume. The first is that philosophy must engage in ideology critique. Whether narrating Latin American history in a way that unmasks the legacy of colonization or documenting the reality of repressive violence in the face of deceptive propaganda, Ellacuría's philosophy insists that concepts cannot, in fact do not, remain in an abstract realm of ideas. Rather, they are historically conditioned. Therefore, to be accurately interpreted and employed, they must be *historicized*, that is, seen in the manner that they manifest in history. Seemingly benign ideas like private property or national security, when historicized, can be revealed as tools that further injustice and repression.

Second, as Ellacuría's philosophy necessitates ideology critique, it follows that such critique is done best from that location where the fullness of reality makes itself present. For Ellacuría, this is the *world of the poor*. However, his approach to the world of the poor is neither abstract nor paternalistic. Rather, the priority of the poor is epistemological and practical. It is epistemological because no account of knowledge or truth can escape the fact that the majority of humankind is poor. The poor bear the weight of prior historical decisions and actions, including the real economic and cultural structures that have emerged in our world. For that reason, they clarify the reality of the world and the ethical demands that historical reality places upon all people. The epistemological principle that *one cannot know the truth of the world outside of the world of the poor* became practical in the research of the UCA. Ellacuría's theoretical work emerged in concert with the UCA's efforts to research and document the reality of poverty, oppression, and repression of the poor majorities of El Salvador.

A third implication of Ellacuría's thought comes from the *open* nature of his emphasis on the material roots of historical reality. Rather than viewing reality or history as a closed system, Ellacuría described his philosophy as an "open materialism" that views reality as dynamic, open-ended, and transcendental.[9] Not only are ever-new forms of reality always possible, but from a theological perspective that adopts the philosophy of historical reality—all of intramundane reality is linked intrinsically to the reality of God. At the same time, this dynamism and openness possess a special qualifier: the higher forms of history never bypass the material—reality's "more" always includes prior and lesser forms. This ensures the unity of history. It also serves as a principle of historicization and curbs any inclination to idealistic or escapist logic that would attempt to ignore or bypass historical reality.

Ellacuría's Theology of Liberation

As noted above, Ellacuría's studies with Karl Rahner were influential, particularly as they coincided with the shifts leading to the Second Vatican Council. As much as Vatican II signaled a culmination of extraordinary developments in biblical, historical, and systematic theological reflection, it also initiated a truly global Roman Catholicism where voices from non-European, "nondeveloped" nations could be heard. In this context, Ellacuría stood as a major figure in what was among the most significant of postconciliar theological developments—liberation theology, particularly as it emerged in Latin America.

Mid-twentieth-century Catholic theologies such as the approach developed by Rahner can be characterized as a creative rethinking of neoscholasticism in light of modern philosophical horizons. However, the latter third of the twentieth century saw this project itself undergo a creative-critical rethinking. In particular, Latin American theologians analyzed anew the import of modern theological categories in light of those for whom modernity was simply the continuation of centuries of colonial domination—the millions of those on a "Christian" continent whose lives were marked by poverty and oppression. They concluded that in this context, to announce the gospel of Christian salvation with integrity required that it truly be "good news for the poor." That is, it must be tied to their liberation from poverty and repression. For Ellacuría, with echoes of Zubiri's diagnosis, the key lay in overcoming theologically the dualisms latent in Western philosophy, dualisms that reduced faith, God, grace, salvation, and Christian discipleship to privatized concepts divorced from history and removed from the real challenge to live the gospel.

Although he wrote on a number of theological themes, at the heart of Ellacuría's theology is a concern for that most basic yet comprehensive idea in Christian theology: salvation. He not only composed a number of essays that consider the notion of salvation (soteriology) directly, but even his essays on Christ and the church find their way back to the question of salvation. Ellacuría cannot accept either the bifurcation between history and an exclusively other-worldly transcendence, or between the historical liberation sought by oppressed peoples and the Christian salvation preached by the church. For Ellacuría, the solution involved not reducing Christian salvation to historical, sociopolitical liberation, but rather, emphasizing an incarnational transcendence that recognizes in liberation the historical foretaste of the fullness of salvation. Using a negative contrast, Ellacuría insisted that while one must never *reduce* salvation to sociopolitical liberation, one cannot speak of salvation *without* it. Put positively, Ellacuría speaks of a God who transcends *in*, not away *from*, history, and of a salvation history that is a salvation in and through history.

Ellacuría's achievement lies in how he develops Rahner's insight regarding the historicity of faith by linking it to his philosophy of historical reality. For example, while Rahner creatively distinguishes transcendental and categorical poles of human subjectivity and speaks of historicity as an important existential of the human experience of God's gracious self-offer, Ellacuría goes further by specifying that historicity in terms of history, a history that is personal, social, and structural. Human freedom is not simply a characteristic of subjectivity, but is related to the opening and closing of possibilities inherent in the "traditioning" process of history. As such, when Ellacuría recognizes a duality to history, it is not between a divine history and a human history, but between a history of grace and a history of sin. Thus, Ellacuría preserves Rahner's insight that the transcendental is never experienced outside the categorical. He also retains Aquinas' view that grace works through nature. But he intensifies both these insights by specifying the location of human beings within history.

Understanding the weight of the terms "salvation" and "history" in Ellacuría's thought allows one to perceive correctly the ways that he critically reflects on and locates other theological topics. It would be easy to misunderstand Ellacuría's claim that at the basis of his Christology is the historical Jesus. Yet, his interest is not in the attempt by the biblical "quests" for what can be said about the Jesus of Nazareth behind the gospel portraits. Rather, Ellacuría asks what those gospel portraits look like when they are historicized. In Ellacuría's pithy contrast, the difference emerges between the questions, "Why did Jesus die?" and "Why was Jesus killed?"[10] The latter question invites the disciples of Jesus to enter into the central drama of his ministry: his preaching of God's Reign and his prophetic actions toward those whom he healed, those whom he criticized, and those whose power and authority he threatened. This in turn forces one to reckon with the issue of who supported Jesus and who opposed and persecuted him, a matter that keeps the answer to the former question from being a mere flight of ideological fancy. One cannot make dogmatic claims about the meaning of Jesus' death apart from understanding the historical reasons for his execution on a cross.

Likewise, Ellacuría's reflections on church (ecclesiology) stem from his historical soteriology. He frequently draws upon Vatican II's image of the church as the sacrament of salvation, but he "historicizes" this language to conceive of the mission of the church in historical terms. In Ellacuría's eyes, the church realizes its sacramentality by announcing and manifesting the Reign of God in history. His emphasis on the Reign counters those ecclesiologies that would valorize the church as a goal in itself. Ellacuría's historical turn exhibits the same openness latent in his philosophical materialism and his view of sacramentality. While Ellacuría affirms the "more" of history, one cannot see that "more" outside of history. Certainly there is "more" to the historical Jesus of Nazareth or to the Christian church than meets the eye, but again that "more" cannot be grasped outside of what is seen, outside of a concrete, historical praxis.

Perhaps Ellacuría's favorite biblical image for the church is that of the "leaven" that "makes the dough rise." It indicates the kind of discipleship demanded of believers. Far from the triumphalist view of a church that stands above and outside of the world, or of a sectarian view that pits the church against the world, Ellacuría sees Christians called to transform the world through their taking up and continuing Jesus' mission of proclaiming and actualizing God's Reign in history. That this involves being part of struggles for justice is one of the signs of the times, but it would be a mistake to see in Ellacuría's spirituality a mere activism. Responding to the ethical demands of reality is a philosophical principle that finds theological articulation in the preferential option for the poor. Believers participate in the history of grace, the one history of God and humanity, in the Spirit-led transformation of the world to more closely resemble the reign, and the reality of the poor is where this truth can be most fully realized as good news.

Ellacuría's Last Decade

Ellacuría's philosophy of historical reality and his theology of liberation represent valuable contributions in their own right. However, both assume special significance in view of the remarkable way that Ellacuría utilized them to address the issues of systemic injustice and oppression in El Salvador. In particular, the commitment made by Ellacuría and the UCA to work for a just end to the Salvadoran civil war, a commitment made on behalf of the poor majority of the Salvadoran population for whom the war was especially devastating, reflects the commitment to reality articulated in his philosophy and theology.

Admittedly, there is no simple or automatic correlation between thought and action (scurrilous characters in history have generated great ideas). However, Ellacuría takes his place with others in the past century, such as Mohandas Gandhi, Dorothy Day, Dietrich Bonhoeffer, Martin Luther King, Jr., and Archbishop Romero, whose words resonate deeply because of the remarkable witness that accompanied and validated them. In the last decade of his life, Ellacuría historicized his own philosophical ideas, giving witness to what the preferential option for the poor looks like when taken up by a university.

No account of Ellacuría's thought or his tragic death is complete without considering the final decade of Ellacuría's life (1979–89), one in which he assumed the top leadership position in the UCA just as El Salvador was descending into the madness of civil war. During this tumultuous decade, Ellacuría and the UCA would focus on accurately assessing the reality of a country in a political context where propaganda and the fog of war reigned. This fog resulted from the many, radically different accounts of the ethical and moral demands of the situation. Diametrically opposed versions and assessments of events poured in from all quarters, and even those who specifically identified themselves as "Christians" could be found on opposing sides of the conflict.

Ellacuría wrote in a context where the spectrum of options for the "faithful" Christian ranged from supporting the oligarchy and military in its defense against "communist subversion," to participating in the attempt to forge a new society through armed revolution. Add to this spectrum a third position that would remove religion entirely from worldly, political questions, and one sees the great challenge that occupied Ellacuría personally as a theologian and institutionally as president of the nation's Jesuit university. What was the optimal way to seek truth and knowledge so as to reveal the historical reality of El Salvador and participate in a path that would lead to the good news of life and justice in a situation rife with injustice and death?

The difficulty of Ellacuría's situation becomes more apparent when one realizes that one of the most powerful political voices in the Salvadoran conflict came from outside—namely, the United States and more specifically the Reagan administration that assumed power in 1981. From the coup that overthrew Gen. Humberto Romero's government in October 1979 to the assassination of the Jesuits in 1989, Ellacuría and the

UCA collided with U.S. foreign policy and the Salvadoran government it sustained by (1) offering radically different assessments of the problems in El Salvador and (2) calling for a negotiated settlement rather than a military solution to the conflict.

Shedding Light on the Fog of War

In November of 1979, Ignacio Ellacuría became president of the UCA, filling a vacancy in the post left by Ramon Mayorga, who, along with Guillermo Ungo and over a dozen UCA staff, left to be part of the civilian component of the junta that had displaced the repressive government of Gen. Humberto Romero the previous month. Although many people, including Archbishop Oscar Romero, harbored hopes that the junta would survive and begin curbing, if not ending, the horrendous violence perpetrated by the military and various death squads, those hopes began to wane as the violence actually increased and the junta unraveled.

At the time of the October 1979 coup, Ellacuría and the editorial team at the UCA's journal *Estudios Centroamericanos* offered critical but tentative approval of the regime change.[11] Though he saw the coup as a positive sign of change, Ellacuría knew too well the power of the military and other interests. Hence, his optimism about the ability of the junta to carry through its promised reforms was guarded. The junta represented a tentative center, one that Ellacuría tried to support. Even that center was dangerous territory. While the Right saw support for the coup as sympathy for Communist subversion, many on the Left viewed the coup as one more betrayal of the popular movement and a distraction from real revolutionary change.[12]

In the very month that Ellacuría became rector of the UCA, Jeane Kirkpatrick published the article, "Dictatorships and Double Standards,"[13] which so appealed to President-elect Ronald Reagan that he asked her to join his cabinet as U.S. Ambassador to the United Nations. In the article, Kirkpatrick lambasted the Carter administration's conduct in Iran and Nicaragua and laid out a rationale for supporting authoritarian regimes such as that in El Salvador in terms of U.S. interests.[14] Kirkpatrick's article was shortly followed by a monograph by the so-called Committee of Santa Fe, which included Roger Fontaine, Reagan's principal foreign policy adviser on Latin America. Their document, *A New Inter-American Policy for the Eighties*, portrayed Latin America as under attack by the Soviet Union and echoed Kirkpatrick's rejection of détente or containment as adequate policies.[15] Thus, at the same time that Ellacuría was analyzing the coup as a hopeful first step toward civilian rule, just structural change, and the end of violent repression, U.S. foreign policy was setting out a course that would tolerate military dictatorships and government repression as the only alternative to communist advance.

Under Reagan's secretary of state, Alexander Haig, containing the threat of Soviet expansionism served as the template for foreign policy and the lens by which to see all events in El Salvador. When four American churchwomen were brutally raped and murdered in December of 1980, the Carter administration had initially suspended military aid. However, the decision was reversed after the Salvadoran government promised an investigation of the murders. The investigation was a sham. As a bewildered, Carter-appointed U.S. Ambassador Robert White would discover, the new Reagan administration had no interest in pursuing the truth behind the murders. Alexander Haig falsely claimed that there was evidence that the women had run a roadblock and were killed in an exchange of fire. Kirkpatrick disparaged the women as "not just nuns," but "political activists on behalf of the Frente."[16]

After rejecting an offer by the guerrilla's political-military leadership to open private dialogue, Haig issued a State Department white paper in 1981 called *Communist Interference in El Salvador.*[17] In it, he consolidated the foreign policy view that he had been advancing in incremental ways since taking office, namely, that "the insurgency in El Salvador has been progressively transformed into a textbook case of indirect armed aggression by Communist powers."[18] Framed as a microcosm of East-West conflict, the "great line in the sand" was drawn against Communist aggression in tiny El Salvador.

In the same month as Haig's white paper and the approval of military aid to bolster the fight against "Soviet intervention" in El Salvador, Ellacuría met with the leadership of the Jesuit Central American Province and concluded that the Salvadoran conflict "hasn't got a military solution. Nobody is going to win this war."[19] The meeting took place in Nicaragua, where Ellacuría had been shuttling back and forth from Spain since death threats had exiled him from El Salvador three months earlier. As civilian casualties climbed to over 20,000 in the time since the 1979 coup, Ellacuría was convinced that a real solution to the war could not be achieved through a military victory by either side. Nor could it be achieved by a political process that naively ignored the power of the military and the influence of the United States. What was needed was a "political-military" solution based upon dialogue and negotiation with the priority being the "objective needs of the national reality and the just demands of the people."[20]

Even though Reagan's State Department would never agree to negotiations, particularly if it meant recognition of the FMLN-FDR as anything other than a "terrorist organization," U.S. policy did undergo a shift. In the wake of rising domestic opposition to Haig's bellicose rhetoric, the State Department toned down its confrontational anti-Communist rhetoric and began calling for democracy and free elections. Yet, it is now clear that these elections primarily served a public relations role. As an alternative to negotiation they correlated nicely with the Low Intensity Conflict (LIC) strategy that the Salvadoran military was pursuing.

Military aid to El Salvador began to be tied to regular presidential certification reports on the Salvadoran government's progress on human rights, the first of which occurred in January of 1982.[21] A document of only six pages, it claimed that progress was being made on human rights and agrarian reform and denied that death squads were linked to the government's security forces. Relying on reports from the embassy on political murders, the Reagan administration claimed that fewer people (5,331) were being killed in 1981 than in 1980 (9,000), and fewer were killed monthly in December of 1981 (349) as opposed to January (665).

In contrast to these fabricated numbers, the UCA's Center for Information, Documentation, and Support for Research (CIDAI) in addition to similar findings by the Catholic Church's Legal Aid Office (Socorro Jurídico) and the Salvadoran Human Rights Commission, counted an increase in killings from 1980's 9,826 to 13,229 in 1981.[22] When confronted with the large discrepancy, Assistant Secretary of State Thomas Enders claimed that the UCA had an "ideological bias." Yet, no amount of bias could invent the news of a massacre the night before the certification report. In a small village of the Morazán province called El Mozote, reports surfaced of a search-and-destroy operation the previous month by the Atlactl battalion, the rapid response unit trained by U.S. advisers. Survivors listed the names of close to 800 dead, over half of them children under fourteen.[23] As for elections, in two issues of *Estudios Centroamericanos*, UCA researchers concluded that the reported "massive turnout" was inflated in an attempt to discredit the FMLN.[24] U.S. Ambassador Deane Hinton called the UCA's conclusions "bullshit" and added, "It would take a professor in an ivory tower who didn't go out to vote because the guerrillas told him not to, to come up with a theory like that."[25]

While the LIC strategy pursued by the military was criticized by the UCA, so was the change in strategy enacted by the FMLN. While still holding out hope for a popular insurrection, the FMLN, by 1984, had begun to turn to a war of attrition, characterized by damage to infrastructure and political kidnappings and assassinations. In an article that May, Ellacuría noted a growing chasm between the rhetoric of the guerrillas and the reality of the people they claimed to want to liberate.

> The impoverishment of the mass revolutionary movement that began in 1981 has continued in the subsequent years. Today the memory is distant and there is a great tiredness; the illusion of a rapid change in the situation has faded. . . . It must be said that in El Salvador there are two realities: the reality of the war which is lived by very few, and the everyday reality that is lived by the vast majority.[26]

In the same month as Ellacuría's article, Ronald Reagan spoke to Congress in a prime-time television address and offered his own somber assessment of El Salvador. As he had done two years previously, Reagan drew upon all of his charisma to frame the battle in Central America as a battle against "Cuban and Nicaraguan aggression aided and abetted by the Soviet Union." He challenged critics by asking, "Will we defend our vital interests in the hemisphere or not? Will we stop the spread of Communism in this hemisphere or not?"[27] Congress answered in the affirmative when it subsequently passed the Broomfield proposal that authorized all of Reagan's requested aid and did so without any binding conditions. That, along with Napoleon Duarte's electoral victory, would cement the U.S. policy of massive economic and military aid to the Salvadoran government in an effort to achieve a military victory in the war, a war that would last another seven years.

A Personal and Institutional
Option for the Poor

While 1985 saw the consolidation of Reagan's Salvadoran policy in the United States and tactical shifts in El Salvador by both the military and the FMLN, the UCA was also in the process of introducing new ways to fulfill its commitment as a university. Commentators would note the role that Ellacuría assumed in negotiating the release of President Duarte's kidnapped daughter Ines, but perhaps of more lasting impact was the founding that year of the UCA's Human Rights Institute (IDHUCA) headed by Segundo Montes, and the Forum on National Reality (La Cátedra de la Realidad Nacional), a brainchild of Ellacuría that entailed a series of lectures and symposia on the pressing issues of the day, providing a public space for debate possible nowhere else. These two research arms of the

UCA, along with the Institute of Public Opinion (IUDOP) that would be founded the following year with Ignacio Martín-Baró as its head, were the most visible manifestations of the distinctive mission that the UCA had been developing since Ellacuría had become rector—an explicit commitment to serve the national reality of El Salvador. That mission grounded the positions taken by the UCA during the war. It also provided spurious "evidence" for why these intellectuals were so dangerous and why they needed to be eliminated.

In examining the self-understanding of the UCA and its mission, what stands out is that in addition to the traditional tasks of the university— teaching and research—the UCA dedicated itself to the task of "*proyección social*," a social projection in which the university is not seen as an end in itself but "projects" its knowledge beyond the campus to the wider society.[28] This social projection then forms a circular relationship with teaching and research, such that each one informs and is informed by the others. All were integrated around the commitment "to understand and to serve" the national reality.

Along with the important institutes founded by Martín-Baró and Montes, perhaps the most visible way the UCA confronted El Salvador's national reality happened through the University Forum on the National Reality (Cátedra de la Realidad Nacional). Though the work of the Center for Investigation, Documentation, and Support for Research and the highly esteemed journal *Estudios Centroamericanos* had been contributing to a greater understanding of the national reality for years, the forum was exceptional in creating a space for exchange where honest assessments of the situation of the country could be made. For foreign journalists and other newcomers, it was often a shock to see a Catholic priest who could speak so intelligently about the sociopolitical and economic circumstances of the nation. The forum provided the venue for highly visible lectures and debates in which Ellacuría would take questions on any subject that related to El Salvador's reality. This forum, along with radio and television debates and his numerous editorials put Ellacuría and the UCA at the forefront of the national debate.

The work of social projection embodied in the Institutes and the forum sprang from a commitment to serve the national reality and, given the reality of poverty and oppression, to transform the society. To some, that commitment might appear to compromise the objectivity of research and the pursuit of pure intellectual inquiry. However, the UCA countered these objections by pointing out that, precisely as a social force interwoven in the very fabric of the society in which it exists, a university must make explicit commitments in order to objectively assess the national reality.

Although there were critical voices in Congress and the wider public, including new voices of moderation within the Reagan administration (symbolized, for instance, by the replacement of Al Haig with George Schulz as secretary of state), U.S. policy on El Salvador and the decisions ultimately carried out in view of that policy remained largely unchanged. They were guided by an anti-Communist ideology that excused the structural injustice at the root of the war and willfully ignored the violation of human rights by the armed forces and death squads. This disastrous policy would ultimately be exposed and painstakingly documented by the United Nations Truth Commission after the war.[29] It is one of the tragic ironies that November of 1989, when the UCA murders occurred, is also the month that the Berlin Wall, the enduring symbol of communism, would come down.

Legacy for the North

In the end, the enduring legacy of Ignacio Ellacuría is not as a voice from the margins. Ellacuría was a white, male, European-born, highly educated, Roman Catholic priest and university president—a background of privilege far different from the destitute, uneducated Salvadoran peasant women who bore the weight of injustice, repression, and the war.[30] It could be said that Ellacuría's work served to thematize and elaborate theoretically the situation of those marginalized people and to confront those who perpetuated and benefited from their suffering. Yet, there is something more to his legacy. Precisely because it comes from a situation of privilege, Ellacuría's life, work, and death address and challenge more directly the situation of those in the North who enjoy advantages that are historical, geographical, and demographic in nature.

Ellacuría could have remained in Spain and enjoyed a comfortable career as an intellectual there, but he spent the majority of his life in El Salvador, where the endless hours of work and tensions of the war meant unrelenting stress and physical exhaustion. He could have restricted himself to writing philosophy and perhaps achieved some fame in that arena, but instead he complemented his philosophical work on the historical reality of the poor with political writings and debate that would earn him calumny in the press, bombings at the UCA, and periods of exile from the country. He could have written safe and sanitized theology that contented itself with harmless pieties or dualistic thinking far removed from the concerns of this world. Instead, Ellacuría pursued a theology that boldly asserted the incarnational dimensions of a faith lived out in the quest for justice in the world. He also continually defended liberation theologies from unjust criticisms, whether ignorant mischaracterizations or malicious caricatures, even if they came from the highest ecclesiastical circles.

In his writing, in his life, and even in his death, Ignacio Ellacuría offers a powerful legacy, one that challenges those from the North in a particular way. As an intellectual, he demonstrated that the pursuit of truth does not involve a false detachment or neutrality in the face of a suffering world but a detachment from unreality that ensues when the historical reality of the poor becomes the center of inquiry. As a human being, he evinced a commitment that meant putting all of his energies at the service of the poor majority of his country. Finally, as a Christian and martyr, Ellacuría revealed a contemporary example of what the New Testament calls "kenosis," the self-emptying attributed to Jesus in becoming human and offering a model for self-sacrificial love. Eschewing a pietism or ecclesiocentrism, Ellacuría's spirituality bears witness to a contemplation of God's presence in the complexity of historical reality: a contemplation that seeks to attain love by the transformation of the world in conformity to the vision of God's will for human and earthly flourishing.

Liberation theology's greatest gift may be its articulation of marginalized voices, a theological articulation that has been called the "irruption of the poor" in history, however broadly one may conceive the term "poor." The other side to this theological coin is the challenge posed to those who do not experience material poverty—those who benefit from historical structures that for many mean death before their time. Ellacuría's legacy involves seriously confronting that challenge and discerning the forms of conversion, intellectual and practical, that it entails. It is hoped that this presentation of Ellacuría's thought in English can encourage that confrontation and that discernment to accomplish what Ellacuría described in his last major published essay: "We have to turn history around, subvert it, and send it in a new direction."[31]

*   *   *

The twelve selections here represent only a fraction of Ellacuría's theological, much less his wider intellectual, output.[32] Inevitably, for every essay included here, there are several other essays that could be considered essential and worthy of inclusion. Moreover, the desire to provide a theological reader useful for study and teaching meant leaving out many of his philosophical, political, or university writings.[33] However, it is hoped that the essays included here provide a solid orientation to Ellacuría's thought and will spur others to bring more of his work to the attention of the English-speaking world.

The chapters in this volume range from the highly sophisticated scholarly essays polished for publication to transcriptions of lectures that Ellacuría delivered. Taken together, these pieces deploy Ellacuría's central concepts and reveal the inner dynamisms that run throughout his work on a range of theological topics including theological method, Christology, ecclesiology, soteriology, spirituality, and the theology of God. How to organize them?

A chronological ordering does not yield much for two reasons. First, while Ellacuría's thought matures over time, the developments are not so startling as to denote "shifts" in his ideas or "periods" to his thinking. As we have noted, Ellacuría does have specific times of formation under various mentors, but his mature thinking, from 1975 to his death in 1989, stands out more for its consistency than radical shifts of concepts or terminology. Second, the window of these productive years is relatively small. So, while readers may note certain modifications, for example, the change in tone of his writing before and during the Salvadoran civil war, the span of almost fifteen years represented in this volume is such that a chronological layout of the essays does little to contribute to a fuller understanding of these writings.

Although any thematic arrangement of the essays necessarily imposes an artificial structure on Ellacuría's thought, this volume takes as its organizing principle the schema for human intelligence suggested by Ellacuría himself in his seminal essay, "Laying the Philosophical Foundations for Latin American Theological Method."[34] There, skillfully playing with the multiple connotations of the Spanish verb "cargar," Ellacuría describes a threefold structure for how human beings engage real things as: (1) becoming aware of reality (*el hacerse cargo de la realidad*); (2) shouldering the weight of reality (*el cargar con la realidad*); and (3) taking charge of the weight of reality (*el encargarse de la realidad*).[35] As three dimensions of the human encounter with reality, and not a linear process, they indicate how human "knowing" is more than just a noetic process (becoming aware), but involves ethical demands (shouldering) and the need for action or praxis (taking charge) as well.

As the basic structure of the book came together, it also became clear that certain terms were emerging as central to Ellacuría's project—history, liberation, and salvation. By taking these terms and understanding them in light of Ellacuría's methodological framework, the three parts of the book came into focus. Part I would consist of essays that emphasize becoming of aware of historical reality and how that awareness affects the intellectual disciplines. Part II would include those essays where Ellacuría considers liberation and how its demands illumine the historical and ethical dimensions of what Christians call salvation. Finally, Part III would comprise essays in which Christian praxis, whether personal or ecclesial in nature, is central as both applying and informing the tasks of becoming aware of and shouldering the weight of reality.

This volume opens with the essay, "The Latin American Quincentenary: Discovery or Cover-up?" It demonstrates that for Latin Americans any account of their historical reality is bound up with the history of colonialism. Only by understanding this context can one realize the full import of the notion of "liberation" that emerged so powerfully in Latin America in the second half of the 20th century. While the second essay, "On Liberation," unpacks the significance of its title term, the following two essays, "Laying the Philosophical Foundations of Latin American Theological Method," and "The Liberating Function of Philosophy," situate liberation within the dynamics of historical reality and indicate how the confrontation with that reality and the struggle for liberation should orient and animate the disciplines of theology and philosophy respectively. No commentator on Ellacuría does justice to his thought without understanding the role of historical reality in his theology and philosophy.

The essays in Part II reveal the inner dynamism and structural unity that Ellacuría sees between historical liberation and what Christians call salvation. Not coincidentally, many of these essays respond directly to the critics of liberation theology, especially the Vatican and its charge that liberation theologians reduce salvation to "mere" historical liberation. The trio of essays, "The Christian Challenge of Liberation Theology," "The Historicity of Christian Salvation," and "Salvation History," offer a tour-de-force refutation of that accusation by fusing the thick Zubirian-inspired (and not Marxist) notion of history with a view of human liberation as the manifestation of the Triune presence of God. Closing this section is the essay that features one of Ellacuría's most important contributions, the image of the suffering and marginalized today as a "crucified people." As the gospel authors powerfully interpret Isaiah's "Suffering Servant" hymns in light of the experience of Jesus Christ, Ellacuría performs this very "traditional" move by bringing these images together with the ones who bear the weight of historical sin today. In doing so, Ellacuría challenges abstract and juridical notions of divine redemption and challenges how Christians view themselves within the economy of salvation.

Part III contains essays that elaborate on the historical manifestation or incarnation of salvation in both personal and institutional modes. "The Church of the Poor: Historical Sacrament of Liberation" shows the ecclesiological power latent in a key image from Vatican II: church as sacrament. However, far from grounding a claim for ecclesial triumphalism, Ellacuría conceives of the church's sacramental character as a challenge to make manifest in history the saving and life-giving will of God in its praxis. Crucial to this ecclesial praxis is the task of theology clarified in the essay, "Theology as the Ideological Moment of Ecclesial Praxis." With echoes of Zubiri's notion of reality, Ellacuría locates theology within a differentiated structural unity of ecclesial praxis and a wider historical praxis. While so much of Ellacuría's reflections are structural in character, it would be a mistake to claim that he overlooks the role of personal faith. "Christian Spirituality" both affirms and elaborates the role of spirituality and indicates the importance of Ignatian spirituality in Ellacuría's thought. The concluding essay on Monseñor Romero brings the volume to a worthy close by describing the one who in many ways embodies for Ellacuría what lived Christianity should look like today.

Short commentaries are included before each one of the essays. Functioning as a kind of prelude, each commentary provides contextual details and highlights central ideas prominent in the given essay. These commentaries richly indicate how Ellacuría's context influenced his work, and how he responded to that context in a brilliant fashion. This is not to suggest that one can ignore these essays or write them off as coming from a "different context." On the contrary, as it has become clear that all theologies are contextual, these essays not only provide important content to consider but also an important example of how to carry out theology today.

*   *   *

Bringing this project to completion has meant relying on the patience and generosity of so many. I would like to acknowledge first the contribution of my collaborator, Kevin F. Burke, SJ. This volume sprang from his vision, and were it not for his generous administrative service for others, he would have been co-editor. As it is, his introductory commentary on each essay strikes me as one of the great strengths of this volume. Between those commentaries and his own scholarship, he is an enduring resource for those who wish to plunge into Ellacuría's thought.

Speaking of patience and generosity, there is no greater exemplar of these virtues than Robert Ellsberg, Publisher of Orbis Books. His constancy and cajoling, wit and wisdom were all essential to this volume's seeing the light of day. Thanks also to Margaret D. Wilde, J. Matthew Ashley, and Anna Bonta for their translation work, with thanks to Orbis Books for the use of Phillip Berryman's and Robert Barr's translation. Their contributions were a foundational part of the arduous process of getting Ellacuría's dense, philosophical, neologism-filled prose into an English accessible to a wide readership. If readers present and future discover errors or distortions, let it fall on my limitations as the builder, not on the wonderful building blocks provided me.

I am very grateful for my wonderful colleagues in the Department of Theology and the Latin American and Latino Studies Institute at Fordham University. Their creativity, insight, and collegiality are source of encouragement and inspiration. I am indebted to the Office of Faculty Fellowships & Internal Grants for its Summer Faculty Research Grant. Closest to home, let me thank my wife Natalia and our boys William and Benjamin who by now might think of this volume as another member of the family.

Finally, this book is dedicated to the memory of Dean Brackley, SJ. In 1989, he left his position in Fordham University's theology department to step in for his slain brothers at the UCA. For over twenty years, Dean modeled a remarkable hospitality in El Salvador for countless delegations making pilgrimages and learning the stories of the remarkable country, its resilient people, and its heroic martyrs. If there is any great "translation" of El Salvador's liberation theology into English, it is in lives of remarkable witnesses like that of Dean.

Notes

[1] Martha Doggett, *A Death Foretold: The Jesuit Murders in El Salvador* (Washington, DC: Georgetown University Press, 1993).

[2] It is important to note how even "Northern" countries possess within their borders populations whose living conditions are closer to "Southern" ones.

[3] Karl Rahner, *Hearer of the Word*, trans. Joseph Donceel (New York: Continuum, 1994).

[4] See Decree 4 of *Documents of the Thirty-Second General Congregation of the Society of Jesus, Dec. 2, 1974–Mar. 7, 1975, An English Translation* (Washington, DC: The Jesuit Conference, 1975), 17.

[5] *Estudios Centroamericanos* 337 (1976): 637–43. It is also found in Ellacuría's collected political writings, *Escritos políticos: Veinte Años de historia en El Salvador, vol. 1* (San Salvador: UCA Editores, 1993), 649–56 [henceforth EP].

[6] Problems Zubiri coins as the "logification of intelligence" and the "entification of reality." See Xavier Zubiri, *Inteligencia sentiente* (Madrid: Alianza Editorial Sociedad de Estudios y Publicaciones, 1980).

[7] Diego Gracia and Robert Lassalle-Klein view this move as a corrective to the phenomenological tradition of Husserl and Heidegger. See Lassalle-Klein's "Ignacio Ellacuría's

Debt to Xavier Zubiri," in *The Love that Produces Hope: The Thought of Ignacio Ellacuría* (Collegeville, MN: Liturgical Press, 2006), 88–127.

[8] For an informative exposition of Ellacuría's key philosophical concepts, see David Gandolfo, "Human Essence, History and Liberation: Karl Marx and Ignacio Ellacuría on Being Human" (Ph.D. diss., Loyola University Chicago, 2003).

[9] See the excellent work by Héctor Samour, *Voluntad de liberación: el pensamiento filosófico de Ignacio Ellacuría* (San Salvador: UCA Editores, 2002).

[10] Ignacio Ellacuría, "¿Por qué muere Jesús y por qué le matan?" *Misión Abierta,* no. 2 (1977): 17–26.

[11] See, for example, "La revolución necesaria," EP II, 819.

[12] These radio addresses were subsequently published in *El Salvador: Entre el terror y la esperanza* (San Salvador: UCA Editores, 1982). They also appear in the EP volumes.

[13] Jeane Kirkpatrick, "Dictatorships and Double Standards," reprinted in Marvin E. Gettleman et al., *El Salvador: Central America in the New Cold War* (New York: Grove Press, 1981), 15–39. Orginally appeared in *Commentary* 68, no. 5 (1979): 34–45.

[14] Kirkpatrick, "Dictatorships," in Gettleman et al., 36.

[15] As noted in William M. Leogrande, *In Our Own Backyard: The United States in Central America, 1977–1992* (Chapel Hill: University of North Carolina Press, 1998), 55.

[16] See ibid., 63.

[17] U.S. Department of State, *Communist Interference in El Salvador,* Special Report No. 80, February 23, 1981.

[18] As cited in Leogrande, *In Our Own Backyard,* 86.

[19] As recounted in Theresa Whitfield, *Paying the Price: Ignacio Ellacuría and the Murdered Jesuits of El Salvador* (Philadelphia: Temple University Press, 1994), 151.

[20] He laid these ideas out in Ignacio Ellacuría, "Solución política o solución militar para El Salvador?" *Estudios Centroamericanos* 390–91 (April–May 1981): 295–324; EP II, 951–96.

[21] U.S. House of Representatives, Presidential Certification on El Salvador, vol. 1: Hearings Before the Subcommittee on Inter-American Affairs of the Committee on Foreign Affairs, 97th Cong., 2nd sess. (Washington, D.C.: Government Printing Office, 1982), 2–9.

[22] Numbers are quoted from Barbara Crossette, "Salvadorans are Accused of More Massacres," *New York Times,* March 8, 1982.

[23] Mark Danner, *The Massacre at El Mozote* (New York: Vintage Books, 1993).

[24] "Las elecciones y la unidad nacional: Diez tesis críticas," ECA 402 (Apr 1982): 233–58; "Las elecciones de 1982. Realidades detrás de las apariencias," ibid., 573ff.

[25] Raymond Bonner, *Weakness and Deceit: U.S. Policy and El Salvador* (New York: Times Books, 1984), 305. Bonner notes that months later, Hinton would reject Ellacuría's idea of forming an independent commission, including one or two people appointed by the U.S. Congress, to investigate the charges. Instead, he claimed that those who ran the election should supervise any investigation. Ellacuría rejected this notion on the basis that those who could be involved in the fraud should not be the ones to investigate themselves.

[26] Ignacio Ellacuría, "Visión de conjunto de las elecciones de 1984," ECA 426–27 (Apr–May 1984): 315.

[27] Ronald Reagan, "Address to the Nation on United States Policy in Central America, May 9, 1984," *Reagan Papers, 1984,* book 1, 659–65.

[28] See Charles Beirne, SJ, *Jesuit Education and Social Change in El Salvador* (New York: Garland, 1996).

[29] U.N. Security Council Annex, *From Madness to Hope: The 12-Year War in El Salvador. Report of the Commission on the Truth for El Salvador* (1993).

[30] For a powerful account of their testimony, see Renny Golden, *The Hour of the Poor, The Hour of Women: Salvadoran Women Speak* (New York: Crossroad, 1991).

[31] Ignacio Ellacuría, "Utopia and Prophecy," in *Mysterium Liberationis: Fundamental Concepts of Liberation Theology* (Maryknoll, NY: Orbis Books, 1990).

[32] The four volumes of his collected theological writings include over 113 essays. See *Escritos teológicos I–IV* (San Salvador: UCA Editores, 2000, 2002).

[33] Along with his philosophical monograph *Filosofía de la realidad histórica*(San Salvador: UCA Editories, 1999) Ellacuría's collected writings published by UCA Editores include: *Escritos filosóficos* I–III, *Escritos políticos* I–III, and the single-volume *Escritos universitarios*.

[34] Chapter three in this volume.

[35] For further discussion of these terms see, Michael E. Lee, *Bearing the Weight of Salvation: The Soteriology of Ignacio Ellacuría* (New York: Crossroad, 2009).

Part I

The Reality of History
through Latin American Eyes

1

Latin American Quincentenary

Discovery or Cover-up?

(1989)

Ignacio Ellacuría's provocatively titled reflection, "Quinto centenario de América Latina ¿descubrimiento o encubrimiento?" was written not as a book chapter or even as an essay for publication in an academic journal. Rather, it originated as a transcription of a lecture that Ellacuría delivered in Barcelona, Spain, on January 27, 1989. He fully intended to write a fuller essay on this theme, but that desire was interrupted by the brutal historical event of his assassination later in the same year that he gave this address.

What is the relevance today of an anniversary celebration observed two decades ago in recognition of a historical event that occurred five centuries previously? The question is a fair one, but as soon as one encounters the opening paragraphs of this essay, one understands that Ellacuría is approaching this now-distant historical anniversary in a way that subverts our usual ways of thinking about anniversaries and the events they commemorate. He enables us to reconsider not only the "meaning" of a particular historical event but the reality of concrete history itself. Indeed, the nature of the "celebration" of the fifth centenary of the "discovery of America" provides Ellacuría with a point of entry for naming and interpreting not only what happened 500+ years ago but for assessing the ongoing history of what ensued as a result of the voyages of Columbus and his companions. This "point of entry" leads us to the heart of our human reality precisely as historical reality. In that regard, this seemingly out-of-date and innocuous topic is actually charged with the profound urgency of our divine-human history so in need of salvation-liberation.

Ellacuría's lecture serves multiple purposes within this current collection. It introduces his brilliant grasp of the human responsibility for making and thinking about history. It gives us a glimpse into what themes were on his mind in the months just before his tragic death, including several that receive further development in other places—utopia and propheticism, the "civilization of poverty" in contrast to the "civilization of capital," his nuanced assessment of violence and peace, etc. Finally, this essay exemplifies Ellacuría's enormous capacity to bring his systematic philosophical thought to bear on historically particular events.

The Quincentenary of the "Discovery" as Seen from Latin America

To discuss the quincentenary of the discovery from a Latin American viewpoint presupposes, first, a theoretical framework for understanding that historical event. Obviously from the viewpoint of Spain and less critical sectors, the quincentenary will be presented once more as a hymn of praise to a great accomplishment. Deep down, one gets the impression that those who commemorate it from this grandiloquent viewpoint are mainly interested in self-aggrandizement: "what a great thing we have done!" It is an opportunity to retell and celebrate the glories of this great thing they have done.

But the truth is that in Latin America the quincentenary as such, in practical terms, is of interest to no one. And that, as I see it, is the best thing that could occur. The problem is that we are going to receive a deluge of writings, celebrations, and programs from the outside, and in light of this situation, we will have to take part, we will have to turn ourselves to the voices that can critically understand this matter. Naturally we hope that our critique will not be destructive, but what we cannot tolerate is that, through the commemoration, what happened then be repeated today.

The Same Story Repeated with Different Characters

Commemorations tend to be different from reality; yet the same things have been repeated mechanically for the past five centuries. What could happen, and in fact is happening, is that the present "conquering representative" of the Western world—which is now the United States—could do again to the so-called new world, within the possibilities of our time, what Spain and Portugal did in the past. For that reason our struggle is not against what happened five centuries ago; rather we seek to gather the experience of that past in order to say to them—to the North Americans especially, and also to the Europeans as members of the same Western-Christian civilization—that their current approach to Latin America, and the third world in general, has not changed much in the past five hundred years.

To put it briefly, this approach by the current Western powers toward the third world countries is characterized by the *covering up* of a fundamentally dominating and oppressive reality with a lovely ideological curtain that is only a mask. They are thereby falsifying the reality. And it must be unmasked.

What has occurred in the past five centuries is domination on the part of some peoples, some cultures, some languages, some religions, etc. As we see it, it follows that what we must do in the quincentenary (and all the others that will come) is an act of liberation.

We should not adopt an absolutist position, saying that these five hundred years of continual domination have done no good; that would be to conceive of the process of domination and liberation in clearly differentiated terms of black and white. Reality is never that "clear and distinct." But on the whole, we cannot deny or ignore the fact that after five hundred years, other countries are doing in Latin America what Spain did then. I repeat: this must be unmasked.

The One "Discovered" Is Always the Oppressor

Five Centuries Ago . . .

What really happens in the mutual relationship that was established between these two groups of nations? In my view, what happens first is that the "conquistador" or dominator *is uncovered*. Thus, five hundred years ago, with the "discovery" of the so-called new world, what was really discovered was the reality of Spain, the reality of Western culture and also of the church of that time. They were uncovered, inadvertently seen in their nakedness, because what they did to the other side was to "cover it up." In reality it is the third world that discovers the negative, and the most real, aspects of the first world.

From the viewpoint of the third world, on the occasion of this quincentenary, it would be interesting and fruitful to listen to the confession of the first world. That of course is unlikely to happen. So we believe that if the prophet does not speak truth to the first world, the first world will not be able to see and discover its own reality; on the contrary, it will go on telling the third world what to do.

If we look closely, what the conquerors said at the beginning of the conquest is that they had come to make Christians of the indigenous peoples. But that is obviously not what they came for. The affirmation was a great lie, even when justified by the best theological reasoning, even if some people sincerely believed the justifications. The truth is very different: Spain went to America to dominate, to conquer, to expand its power and its sources of wealth. It went for that purpose, carrying ideological or ideologized baggage that was represented, especially at the beginning, by the Roman church. Thus, it is the (hidden) sociohistorical structure of Spain that was uncovered as a powerful human force. Also uncovered was the fact that the zealous search for wealth and power was the main engine of this force: that was the real motive of the individuals who came to Latin America.

On the other hand, this force was controlled by an expansionist power (which we rightly call the Spanish empire), with policies represented by the established political regime. All this was legitimated by a "Christian" ideology, which certainly contributed a series of humanizing values— among the wave of people who arrived in Latin America, there were people whose intentions and actions really did go against the overall dynamic of the process—but in fact they were always subsidiary to the effective attainment of the collective, national goals.

. . . and Also Today

Today too we can truly say that the first world is coming, globally, in the same way and with the same intentions. And it comes today, too, in ideological clothing whose only purpose is to spread a "lovely" curtain over its real intentions.

The powerful nations of today say they are coming to the third world to make us "democratic." But their "generous proposals" conceal a very different political and economic project. To discover and unmask the real truth of that project, we do not need to look inside the borders of the dominant Western nations, but rather outside their borders—to the places that manifest the underlying effects of that Western project and its purposes, of which the primary representative and bearer is the United States.

In fact the United States may be democratic, up to a point, within its borders—as long as it maintains an antidemocratic position at the international level. Thus, the democracy it defends is false, deceptive, and means absolutely nothing as a universal value. But the truth of its political, economic, and cultural system is most clearly visible, not in the place where the benefits of that system are reaped, but in the place that must be conquered and dominated in order to maintain the structure of power.

We can illustrate this in different ways. For example, is it credible to think that the United States really cares about democratic elections in

Nicaragua? The truth is that it doesn't care at all. Rather, if Nicaragua were its special ally, the United States would let Nicaragua have whatever political system it wanted. The fact is that for a variety of reasons, the political system that best suits capitalism and protects its interests is "this" type of "democratic" system.

Another illustrative case is El Salvador. As part of the agreed-on search for peaceful solutions to that country's internal conflict, the guerrilla forces [FMLN] have offered to participate in elections; but they have asked for time to prepare a slate of candidates. The government's reply was no, that would be against the Constitution, which provides for a presidential term of five years; therefore it would be unconstitutional to grant the guerrilla forces the extra three months they requested. In this context, fortunately, the church has spoken a rather prophetic and positive word: "peace is more important than the Constitution." This was perceived by the "constitutionalists," the "legalists," and the "democrats" as a kind of "heresy." But behind this whole "legalistic trap" of the Constitution, we can see that the whole problem lies in the fear of the powerful and the oppressors. Seeing that the FMLN proposal could threaten the North American project and the ARENA [ruling party] project of winning the next elections, they withdraw and refuse to accept the proposal. Clearly what they are seeking is not a political solution that really responds to the needs and will of the people, but rather a new conquest of power.

I think these brief examples can help us to understand the present reality of this quincentenary and the perspective from which we are viewing it.

The Church Too Was and Is Discovered

The church was an important element in the wider process of "conquest" five centuries ago. Although the church with its missionary and evangelizing zeal projected the "American mission," it also ended up legitimating a project designed by others.

The effects of this legitimation were not always and everywhere negative; the church's action often helped to improve the existing reality. In some places the church struggled in important ways against this dominating and crushing process. Certainly there were ecclesial elements—especially in the religious orders—which gave primacy to the service of the faith over the service of the crown, to evangelical concern over unchristian passions and interests, to the defense of the Indian over the legitimation of the exploiter. Thus, even then, more than occasionally, the preferential option for the poor was being made present. We cannot say that this option was always assumed by the whole church, by the whole hierarchy, by all the religious orders, but it was not an occasional or merely perfunctory occurrence.

But in any case, the action of the church in the process of conquest and colonization was always secondary and incidental; it was never the initiator of what was done. That initiative was always taken by the economic and political interests.

This leads us to a deeper discovery: all ideologies, when they are ideologized, seek to cover up something evil by "cloaking" it with something good; this need to present something good can be utilized to do good things. Thus, the empire takes the church along to legitimate its process, and the church puts a "good face" on the process (although on some occasions, not even that).

So we can also say that good things were discovered in the church, but also some very serious evils, such as its propensity to identify with power and wealth (a permanent temptation for the church), and its subtle tendency to prefer and prioritize its "institutionality" over its "mission" (also still a very present reality). In large part, the church was carried along by this reasoning: "right now I cannot carry out my mission, which is to proclaim the kingdom of God in accordance with the message of Jesus, because to do so would put the ecclesial institution at risk, and that must be avoided above all. When the time is right, I shall carry out my mission."

The film *The Mission* offers an interesting example that illustrates this historical question regarding the mission of a group of men with respect to the institutionality of the country that was leading the colonization and also of the institutional church. What precisely was the reason for the expulsion of the Jesuits from the Paraguayan reductions? Why did the Roman Curia and the supreme authorities of the Society of Jesus itself give the order to withdraw from that mission, from that proclamation, from that concrete realization of the Christian faith in the midst of history? There is only one possible answer to these questions: they did it because the Jesuit mission in Paraguay was putting the universal institution of the Society of Jesus at risk.

Not only in the past, but also today, the church in Latin America faces the temptation of prioritizing its institutionality over its mission, and it continues to struggle against that temptation.

I think, for example, of what is happening to us in the Central American University "José Simeón Cañas" (UCA). We have often chosen to protect its institutionality over its mission. It is also true that we have often put our institution in danger of being bombed, of being shot at. Just now when I left El Salvador, a bomb exploded very close to the university. For that reason I sent a note to the newspaper saying that I was leaving the country, so they would not bomb my companions while I was away. We are not going to be silenced by bombs. I am not saying that we are putting the institution at great risk, but we have risked a little, and repeatedly. Once we wrote a book defending a strike; that cost us US $200,000 because the government threatened to cut off our subsidy if we came out in defense of the striking teachers. We supported the strike in the full awareness that we were losing funding and weakening our institution.

Along the same line I want to point out that the church in El Salvador receives no funding from the [U.S.] Agency for International Development because that money is corrupt; it is money given deceptively to carry out the war in El Salvador or to support North American policy. We could count on millions of dollars from that agency to do good things, but if we preached and carried out our liberating mission among the popular and marginalized groups, they would immediately cut off those funds.

I want to pose a final, recent example. In a way, we have also experienced the temptation I mentioned in the field of theology. In this case the temptation for theology is to offer a Christian reflection and *praxis* that is not historicized or inculturated in the Latin American context. And a Christian theology that is not historicized and inculturated in the place where it is also becomes oppressive. In this regard I must also say that the controversial "theology of liberation" has sought—with varying degrees of success—to give a Latin American reading of Christianity, of a Christianity that came to us laden with "Europeanism."

So I repeat, by way of summary, the insight that we have been developing up to this point. What happened with the first entrance of Europe into what today is Latin America, led by Spain and Portugal, was "the discovery of the conqueror" and a "violent, violating cover-up of the people they found there," of their cultures, their religion, their persons, their languages. Everything that was there was covered up, violently so. This profound cover-up gave way to a "new culture," to a "new race," to a "new religion," etc.

From this viewpoint, what remains to be done is the discovery of what was covered up, that is, to enable the resurgence of the "new world," not as a repetition of the "old world," but in its true "newness."

The essential question now is, is that possible? Is it purely utopian? Is there really a solution for the problem of our "old world"?

Solution in the North, Problem in the South

From my viewpoint—and this may be at once prophetic and paradoxical—
the United States is much worse off than Latin America. Because the United
States has a solution, but in my opinion it is a bad solution, both for them
and for the world in general. In Latin America, on the other hand, there are
no solutions, only problems; but as painful as they are, it is better to have
problems than to have a bad solution for the future of history.

Obviously Latin America has a terrible problem: Latin America is itself
a problem. The great challenge is to resolve that problem but not with
the solution the United States is offering. By this I do not mean that everything that country has and offers is evil and negative, but rather that
the solution it offers, taken as a whole, is not a good one. It is not good
because of the Kantian principle: a solution that cannot be universalized
to the whole world is not a human solution.

Since the United States' solution cannot be universalized to the whole
world, it is not a human solution; it does not serve humanity. If everyone
had a U.S. standard of consumption—of meat, electricity, petroleum, etc.—
we would exhaust the existing resources in twenty years. So from a concrete, measurable, ecological perspective on world reality, that is not and
cannot be the solution. It is at best a solution for them, which can make
them feel happy and proud. Meanwhile we and the whole third world are
left with a great problem.

That great problem can be expressed in the popular Spanish phrase:
"*Lo han dejado como a un Cristo*" [they turned him into a Christ]. The
third world in fact has been turned into a Christ. It is what we have often
called, from the viewpoint of faith, "the crucified people." But as I said, as
painful as it seems, it is better to have a great problem than a bad solution
for the problem. Because although we don't know how, faith tells us that
this people with problems, this "crucified people," is where Christ is really
present; it is where he wanted to be. Thus, from this believer's perspective,
there is great potential for solving the problem; it is not hard to formulate
the problem abstractly, but it is very difficult to carry out the solution in
real life.

Civilization of Capital and Civilization of Work

Our problem is that the dominant civilization of our day—both in the
East and in the West—is the civilization of capital. That civilization is shaping the world and has turned the great majority of the world (four-fifths

of humanity) into "Christ." In the face of that dominant civilization, we must struggle to build a new one: the civilization of work. That is the great challenge ahead of us.

We must understand this clearly. The important thing is that the destiny of humanity not be controlled by the internal laws of capital. Because these laws, though not immoral, are amoral; and they follow a certain dynamic that pulls along everyone involved in it. We can say that capitalists do not create capital, but capital creates capitalists and pushes them to do what they are doing in the West and also in the Soviet Union. Because the defining issue is not the possession of capital in private or in collective hands. That is an important point to distinguish, but it is not the fundamental issue. Fundamentally, they are both civilizations of capital. And we all know that in its very development, capital does many things that are not only useless and deceptive to humanity but that also oblige most of humanity to live in a certain way, in a problematic way.

In this regard we want to struggle for a civilization of labor, in which it is labor that moves history: not labor to produce capital but labor to develop humanity. The pope [John Paul II] has also spoken along these lines in his encyclical *Solicitudo rei socialis*. There he very clearly supports the priority of labor over capital: that is the measure of a just or unjust political and economic order. Any order where the dynamic of capital prevails over the dynamic of labor is an unjust order, an order that shapes a structural sin, which generates other sins. In contrast, a civilization where the dynamic of labor prevails over the dynamic of capital is an order that really focuses on Christian inspiration.

By the Way of Violence?

The struggle for that "newness" in El Salvador (the country I know best and will talk about here) has emerged forcefully by means of violent processes, especially as reflected in the guerrilla revolutionary movement—of which by the way I am not a blind and uncritical admirer, since there are also great problems in its position—as a force rising up in protest against the invasion, colonization and oppression of the Salvadoran people.

I have always maintained that all violence is wrong. But I also hold that some violence is worse than others; this is clear. Every act of violence is wrong, but sometimes it may be unavoidable. In this sense the "theology of liberation," for example, has insisted that the gravest violence and the very root of all violence is structural violence, that is, the violence of the civilization of capital, which keeps the immense majority of humanity in absolutely inhuman biological, cultural, social, and political conditions. That is fundamental structural violence. Thus, to say that the theologians are defending violence and that the theology of liberation propitiates violence is an error. This is the theology that has most systematically denounced structural violence—which no one describes as "violent," because people see it as normal, a reflection of the established order, etc.—as the fundamental violence against which we must struggle to eradicate it with the least possible violence.

Certainly the response to structural violence has usually been revolutionary violence. I don't think we should necessarily identify "revolution" with "violence," but sometimes—and specifically in the case of El Salvador—there has been recourse to guerrilla violence to combat what was seen as structural violence. It certainly is not Christian, and it probably is not ethical, to make a cause, a value, an ideal of violence. But the fundamental problem that remains is to see to what degree that violence is unavoidable. I repeat, revolutionary violence is wrong in itself, but in many cases it may have become unavoidable.

In this sense, we in El Salvador have tried first to combat the existing structural violence with all our nonviolent forces. Thus, the "institutional" work of our university is focused on struggling against the country's structural violence, based on creating the conditions to enable the liberation of the oppressed popular majorities. With varying degrees of success, the potential of our university is addressed to that end.

From that standpoint we have related to other groups, like the guerrilla forces, which are combating that violence in other ways. Specifically, I have personally held long and critical conversations with one of the most prominent guerrilla fighters, commander [Joaquín] Villalobos. In one of those conversations I said the actions they had taken—they had recently killed some town mayors—were absolutely intolerable from a Christian viewpoint, and counterproductive from a political viewpoint. I also said that other actions they were taking in El Salvador (like setting bombs in the homes of military officials, gas stations, etc.) in order to spark a popular insurrection—or as they say, a "social explosion"—seemed off the mark to me under the present conditions of the country.

We have also been fighting to ensure the least possible harm to the least number of people. When we secured a declaration from the FMLN military leadership that they would not harm civilians, we considered it a great advance. We shall try to advance further toward an end to the war, through the proposals we have made for negotiations.

But at this moment, although I believe there is little future for armed struggle in El Salvador, we cannot ask the FMLN to stop making war against the army—even to stop its sabotage—without other initiatives. What we can tell them is that negotiations are needed, we need to seek peace, because the way of violence has nothing more to offer in El Salvador.

So as you see, our objective and our struggle are to bring about an end to the war and to structural violence, and meanwhile, to try to reduce the harm done by all types of violence in the country. We think this is an approach much more pacifist than violent.

Our Martyrs Are the Seed of Hope

In all this, we have been able to see the heart of the situation in which we move. The same thing is happening today in El Salvador, in Central America, as happened during the "conquest" five centuries ago. External powers, allied with internal elements, have been shaping a civilization of capital and ideologizations to cover up what is really happening. That is our situation today.

But in that situation new forms of rebellion have been emerging, not purely rhetorical or political but real, laborious, painful, even martyrial, both within the church and in other social and even political movements. This means that there, in this rebellion, we see a seed of hope that can bear new fruit. Certainly in El Salvador, in this situation we have been living, the seed of liberation has been and remains present, both among the popular majorities—who have not lost hope—and within the church.

Keeping alive that seed of liberation has cost a lot of blood; many priests, religious, and lay workers have been assassinated. They too are the legacy of a church that throughout these five centuries has not only planted bad seeds in Latin America but also contributed great struggle and fruitful blood on behalf of simple people. To put it simply, they are our martyrs.

In the framework of this hopeful—and martyrial—struggle for liberation, I want to recall the exceptional case of Archbishop Romero. I remember that whenever a priest was killed in El Salvador, he said, with both resignation and hope, "It would be sad if when so many people are dying, no priests were being killed." He used to say—although they didn't give him much time to speak, because they killed him before his time—that the preferential option for the popular majorities and the poor of the earth must be a fundamental element in the work and preaching of the church. If in recent times there has been a man who was not afraid to risk the institutionality of the church in favor of its mission, it was Archbishop Romero. Naturally all the powers isolated him, threatened him, and attacked him until they killed him. The most radical people see his successor, Archbishop Rivera y Damas, as rather more moderate and less progressive, acceptable to the Holy See, etc. I won't go into that discussion here. Clearly Monsignor Rivera never speaks in the same prophetic tones as Archbishop Romero. But I will say that this ethical, prudent, and measured man has never even been elected president of the bishops' conference. It says something about our church, that it is even afraid of Archbishop Rivera!

In any case, I want to affirm the following. All the blood of martyrs that has been spilled in El Salvador and throughout Latin America, rather than causing discouragement and despair, is infusing a new spirit of struggle and new hope in our people. In this sense we may not be a "new world" or a "new continent," but we are clearly and verifiably—not by outsiders but ourselves—a continent of hope. That is a telling sign of a coming change with respect to other continents that do not have hope; all they really have is fear.

—Translated by Margaret D. Wilde

2

On Liberation
(1989)

For obvious reasons, the concept of liberation plays an important role in the philo-sophical and theological lexicon of Ignacio Ellacuría. Less obvious, perhaps, is the fluid, evolving, and contested nature of the term in El Salvador and throughout Latin America, and, above all, in ecclesial discourse throughout the world, during the years of Ellacuría's theological activity. Already viewed as a controversial subject in Catholic ecclesiastical circles in the 1970s, "liberation" took on an even more polemical aspect after the Vatican Congregation for the Doctrine of the Faith (CDF) issued its "Instruction on Certain Aspects of the 'Theology of Liberation'" in 1984. "On Liberation," like many of Ellacuría's late writings, advances a profoundly Catholic response to various misrepresentations of liberation theology and what theologians mean by "liberation." At the same time, it responds to and critiques various contemporary versions of political and social liberalism for their ideologically limited accounts of human freedom and liberation.

Ellacuría juxtaposes the centrality of the theme of liberation for Christian life and thought with the relative paucity of treatment of the term throughout the Christian centuries. He draws several important lessons from this. First, the theme does not appear initially as a biblical or dogmatic concept. It enters into our theo-logical conversations through the mediation of life itself, above all the lives of people of faith who are victims of historical oppression. In other words, Ellacuría treats the idea of liberation as "a question of historical reality posed to people of faith." Before its appearance as a nuanced academic concept, Ellacuría argues, liberation functions as "a historical task, and within history, a socioeconomic task." Second, this crucial theme of liberation, too long theologically neglected to the detriment of the Chris-tian movement, was rescued for magisterial discourse by Latin American liberation theology. Third, Ellacuría views the concept of liberation as an extraordinarily dense and rich concept, deeply related to themes of freedom (understood in all its depth), personal conversion, social-historical transformation, justice, salvation, and holiness.

Liberation is a concept that represents the very essence of the revealed message and God's salvific gift to humanity. That message and that gift may be viewed from other points of view, but if they are not viewed from the perspective of liberation, they remain substantially reduced and often mischaracterized. "The hope for liberation . . . touches upon a fundamental theme of the Old Testament and New Testament."[1] "The gospel of Jesus Christ is a message of freedom and a force of liberation. In recent years, this essential truth has been an object of reflection on the part of theologians."[2] "The Church of Jesus Christ makes these aspirations its own, exercising its discernment in the light of the gospel, which is by its very nature a message of freedom and liberation."[3] This theme of freedom and liberation, "which is the center of the gospel message"[4] should be examined with great attention, precisely because of its centrality and essentialness. "It certainly belongs to the traditional heritage of the churches and ecclesial communities."[5] There again, it is also sustained that "the powerful and almost irresistible hope for a liberation by the people constitutes one of the principal signs of the times"[6] and is one of the great challenges of our time to disciples of Christ.[7]

Notwithstanding this importance of liberation, the magisterial and theological attention that has been given to it officially on the part of the church has been rather slight, practically null, until very recently. When *Libertatis conscientia* wishes to demonstrate the opposite, it has recourse to Vatican II's *Gaudium et spes* and *Dignitatis humanae*, to the papal encyclicals *Mater et magistra*, *Pacem in terris*, *Populorum progressio*, *Redemptor hominis*, and *Laborem exercens*, to *Evangelii nuntiandi*, *Reconciliatio et poenitentia* and *Octogesima adveniens*, to various talks of John Paul II, to the Bishops' Synods of 1971 and 1974, and to Medellín and Puebla, and the Bishops' Conference of France.[8] This whole series of references cannot conceal its recent character and many of them are already subsidiary to what liberation theology has produced, itself moved by the renewing spirit of Vatican II. The truth is that the great theological treatises and most well-known dictionaries of theology have until very recently overlooked this essential problem of the Christian faith and theological anthropology. This neglect is that much more surprising considering that the related concept of freedom has enjoyed great prominence. It has had to be the theology of liberation, produced in Latin America as ecclesial praxis and theoretical reflection, to retrieve something so essential for the faith and ecclesial praxis; something that although it was not formally negated, had been unknown, forgotten, and at times implicitly rejected.

The Christian Retrieval of Liberation

Liberation theology, which has so vigorously introduced the theme of liberation into the magisterium and into the reflection and the practice of the church, has discovered this theme outside of itself and outside of the church, at least in a first moment. It has discovered liberation not so much directly in hearing the cry of the people and oppressed classes, but in the sociopolitical movements for liberation that have effectively taken up that cry and have articulated it in distinct forms of political struggle.

Within those movements, one cannot be ignorant of the significance of those movements that are Marxist inspired. Acknowledging this fact does not make liberation theology or liberation itself dependent upon the ideology of those movements. Not every origin becomes a principle; nor is every process assumed unchanged into the structure. However, the call to attention stems from the ethical and political commitment on behalf of the oppressed by those who are not directly or explicitly animated by the Christian faith. This commitment that has been attempted in other parts of the world had not provoked a new theology; nor had it served to recuperate the newness of the Christian message of liberation. This does not cease to be a question of great significance for the life of the church.

Although the church was never very alert with respect to movements of decolonization, when this liberation was from supposedly Christian colonies, it has been alert in a more relevant way with respect to the suffering of the working classes. Though when the church finally occupied itself with this magisterially, it did so in the realm of social doctrine or teaching, that is, in a realm separated from theological reflection and pastoral praxis. The dogmatic theologians, for their part, and even the biblical theologians never came to see the enormous Christian and theological wealth inscribed in the very fact of liberation. They considered the term too political and not very theologal, perhaps important for some moral aspect, but irrelevant for the development of dogma. The explication of this fact is, in part, the task of the sociology of knowledge, but also that of a theological epistemology that does not overlook the possibility that God reveals Godself to whomever, especially to those who in the eyes of the world are not exactly the most academically wise.

Liberation, then, is not, in a first moment, something read in the scriptures or received in the tradition that is referred to a determined historical situation. It is, better, in a first moment, a question of historical reality posed to people of faith. People of faith, pastoral as well as theoretical, bishops, and priests, as well as laypeople, begin to hear the cry of the oppressed, and this cry directs them to God and the message of revelation. It obliges them to reread the scriptures to discern in them what can be offered to men, women, and the peoples that cry for their liberation.

The Marxists had already given their response. Some self-styled Christians, who identified the common good with the maintenance of tranquility and the established order, had also given theirs. A new generation of Christians, more incarnated in the poor and in the popular struggles, also began to elaborate their own theory and their own praxis of liberation. Liberation theology, creative matrix of the new Christian concept of liberation, begins to be elaborated. Impelled by the new spirit of Vatican II and a rereading of the Old and New Testaments, it seeks to respond to the demands of the most oppressed from the word of God.

Liberation is, meanwhile, a historical task, and within history, a socioeconomic task. That was the demand, and to that there was need to respond. The demand was not light, nor was the response simple. In the structural-historical element of the socioeconomic, there was debated, in large part, the very destiny of the human being and humanity; however, the reality of God in the face of human salvation was also debated. The original precedent of this concept was in the Exodus. The experience of an oppressed people that in its oppression-liberation discovers God the liberator, which is revealed foundationally and fundamentally in a determined historical experience, is given now to a new oppressed people. For the Israelites, God is God the liberator, who took them out of the socioeconomic oppression of the Egyptians, and starting from this historical liberation, the Israelites would go on discovering the always-greater richness of God and the always-greater fullness of salvation-liberation. The people believed when they heard that the Lord would take care of their oppression (Exod. 4:31). The revelation to Moses has that specific character, "I have seen the oppression of my people in Egypt, I have heard their cries against their oppressors, I have noticed their suffering. And I have come to liberate them from the Egyptians, to take them from this land in order to lead them to a fertile and spacious land. . . . The cry of the Israelites has come to me, and I have seen how the Egyptians oppress them" (Exod. 3:7–9).

That salvation has to do with sin; that liberation ultimately is liberation from sin, would come gradually through the fundamental historical experience of an oppressed people to whom God wishes to give freedom through the historical process of liberation. Seen from the end, it would appear that the origin of the process of revelation and salvation could be left behind. Once one has arrived at the fullness of Jesus Christ and the revelation of the New Testament, it could seem that the Old Testament had already passed, that the collective should be abandoned for the personal, exteriority for subjectivity, the historical for the transcendent. The reality of oppressed people, its profound symbolic similarity with that of the Israelites in Egypt, the renewal of Christian life made by base communities that suffer oppression in their own flesh and want to participate in liberation, make that similarity stand out. The distinct confessions of faith of the Jewish people, which were substantially historical stories of the salvific acts of God for God's people need to be recovered. Jesus did not come to abolish the Old Testament, but to fulfill it. This fulfillment could be unexpected, could overcome the historical expectations of a specific people, but it could not reconcile itself to a situation of oppression in which the majority of humanity reproduces almost to the letter the historical experience of the Israelites under the oppression of the Pharaohs.

Medellín saw this very clearly:

Just as Israel of old, the first people (of God) felt the saving presence of God when God delivered them from the oppression of Egypt by the passage through the sea and led them to the promised land, so we also, the new people of God, cannot cease to feel God's saving passage in view of "true development, which is the passage for each and all, from conditions of life that are less human, to those that are more human."[9]

The citation of Paul VI (from *Populorum progressio*, 20–21) makes reference to material and moral deficiencies, to oppressive structures, to the meeting of basic necessities, to a more just order leading to the recognition and acceptance of God given in the faith. "A deafening cry pours from the throats of millions of men and women, asking their pastors for a liberation that reaches them from nowhere else."[10] Therefore, the appeal to an integral liberation cannot constitute a forgetting or overcoming of the fundamental experience that consists, on the one hand, in the living of social, economic, and political injustice as an evil that affects the dispossessed and oppressed and that constitutes a sin that negates God and the divine life, and on the other hand, in the active liberation from that sin of injustice as a Passover in which God the liberator is made present. Integral liberation, as Puebla declares, precisely because it is integral, cannot forget that it should overcome the structures of sin and not just sinful intentionality.[11]

Paul himself presented salvation essentially as a liberation from sin, from death, and from the law. Clearly, none of these three liberative dimensions of salvation has a mere individual or exclusively individual sense. Sin, death, and the law doubtlessly affect the interiority of individuals, but they also affect their totality and fullness. Moreover, they affect people, in this case, the Jewish and Christian peoples.

It is fine, then, to speak of liberation from sin, once one keeps in mind the totality of sin and the depth of its essence. Of course, there is original sin (natural), personal sin, and historical sin (social). These do not have the same personal or interior transcendence, although none of them fail to possess some because they proceed from persons and affect them. Liberation from original sin begins with the incorporation into Christ in baptism, but it culminates only when the person takes on the life of Christ, and with it, its death, its crucifixion, and its resurrection (Rom. 6:1–23). This liberation from sin does not automatically mean liberation from the consequences of sin, from the great concupiscence of humanity that is at the origin and many times the principle of many other sins and oppressions. Liberation from original sin is thus a progressive and historical liberation. So is liberation from personal sin, not just in what it has *opus operantis*, as action of the one who commits it, but what it is *opus operatum*, objective action (Zubiri), so that no sin, not even the most individual or interior, fails to have repercussions of some manner over the configuration of the person and the course of history. This liberation from personal sin is, above all, the work of God the savior, but it also presents itself at the same time as a liberation of the sinful person as an active being in history.

Liberation from historical and social sin, as the sinful and sinning configuration of structures and historical processes, is also a process in which God and the human intervene conjointly because of the very social and historical character of that sin. Insofar as sin is social and historical, it is not attributable directly and immediately to any human in particular, but this does not keep it from being positively the concealment of God's truth and the intention to annul the fullness of life that God wants to communicate to humanity. It is in this dimension of sin where the necessity for the transformation of structures occurs precisely, in that these structures are the effect of sin and cause of new sin.

However much these triple sins, the original, social, and personal, only analogically begin consideration of the concept of sin, they do not cease strictly to be sin, needing divine salvation in the form of liberation. In effect, they are dominators and oppressors of the human being and of humanity. They are the negation of the divine image in the human and are the fundamental obstacle between the human and God, between human beings, and between humanity and nature. Stated in classical terms, they are the fundamental disobedience to the design of God for humanity, history, and nature; they are the negation of the faith in all of its rich fullness (Severino Croatto) and in time the negation of love. Sin should not be understood primarily as an offense against God that has been made personally, but rather as the real straying from, or real annulment of, the divine plan as it is glimpsed in nature and as it manifests itself in salvation history.

Liberation from sin is closely connected to liberation from death and liberation from the law. Death is, in some sense, the effect of sin, and the law is its cause. There is no integral liberation without liberation from death and the law in connection with liberation from sin.

The death that Paul speaks of is at once both a theologal and biological death. The human being is called by God to life, above all the divine life. Yet this life is not possible without the life of each person, the integrity of each person's life. For that reason, resurrection is necessary, one with the fullness of liberation from sin, death, and the law, not stemming from a presumption of the immortality of the soul, but the revivifying strength of the Spirit. However, definitive death, as a consequence of natural (original) sin, emerges in many forms in history. The overabundance of sin in history carries with it an overabundance of death in history, in which the struggle between life and death, both understood in all their fullness and extent, is made present. Liberation theology, following the most profound theologies in this line of thought, contemplates God as the God of life and, consequently, contemplates sin as an agent of death. In light of this, one of the best ways to struggle against sin is to struggle against death in all its forms, but initially in the form of human survival. Because of misery, hunger, lack of basic necessities, and sickness caused by oppression and repression, the majority of human beings die before their time, that is, life is taken from them, and with it, the very possibility to be the glory of God (*Gloria Dei, homo vivens*). To whom this occurs, because of social sin, because of structural injustice, they are the ones who should be called the poor par excellence, and they are the ones to whom God's preferential love is directed.

From this does liberation from death, in all its forms, become an essential part of the Christian message, above all when with death the integral development of the person is taken away and the very possibility to live or the capacity to live in fullness. Liberation from death will appear in its total and definitive form only after death, in the enjoyment of an eternal life, but where the emphasis is not so much on eternity, but on life, life in which there would be no oppression, crying, sickness, division, but rather fullness in the communication of God who is life and love. However, this definitive liberation should be anticipated now. It is empirically evident that if the sin of the world and the causes of sin disappear, human life, from its biological roots to its fullest culmination would appear for the majority of human beings in a much richer form. Life, as liberation from death, is thus one of the essential elements of liberation.

Finally, there is, according to Paul, liberation from the law, the great midwife of sin. That the Pauline texts speak specifically of the Jewish law does not prevent one from developing the liberation from any law imposed on human beings along the same lines. This does not mean preaching anarchy, or diminishing the necessity of law, at least as a necessary evil. Yet in the church, and, above all, in the life of the people, the law becomes a restraint from which liberation is needed. When in the church the law and the Sabbath are put above humans—and in the concrete and effective, not just the abstract and universal—instead of placing the human above the law and Sabbath, one sees a return to the practice that Paul and Jesus himself criticized. Yet the problem appears, above all, in the structuring and governing of nations, where many times the law is the institutional justification for the habitual practice of oppression and repression. Structural and institutional injustice, as forms of social and historical sin, are that law that is the fruit of sin and carries with it the power of death. It is that law that in great part makes for a world in which there is an exploitative life for some and an exploited life for others. It is this law that legitimates social sin, proposing unreachable ideals negated in practice while protecting the established disorder favorable to a few and disadvantageous to the great majority. This law rules not only in the social-political sphere but also in the moral, where the letter is imposed upon the spirit, where legality is imposed on justice, where the defense of one's interests is imposed over solidaristic love. All of this goes against the revealed message of the Old and New Testaments, where it appears with total clarity, the different hierarchy between the principal and secondary, between the fundamental and the instrumental, between the generous, well-intentioned heart and the formal law, between grace and the law.

Liberation from sin, death, and the law is thus an essential part of integral liberation as it is seen from the Christian faith. Therefore, liberation is not, as some would like to object, a liberation from social evils that because of moral reasons must be attended to, as one should dedicate oneself to profane works that are demanded by faith. When the discussion over whether the promotion of justice is an essential or integral part of the faith or whether it is merely a fundamental demand of it has taken place, it has run the danger of framing the question idealistically or dualistically. Without confusing them, faith and justice are inseparable dimensions, at least when both are given in their fullness within a world of sin. Christian faith in its fullness is not only the conveyance of God, the acceptance of God's revelatory communication, and the putting in motion a supernatural dynamism, but it is a new form of life that necessarily includes doing justice. For its part, doing justice is already a form of knowing God and giving oneself to God, although perhaps without sufficient explicitation and clarity. In any case, it is more evident that there is no faith without justice than that there is no justice without faith. One should also not forget that the human may be saved without explicit faith, while there is not salvation without justice. What is certain, on the other hand, is that the full truth of justice, and consequently, of justification is not reached except by faith. For example, only from faith can one affirm that the preferential option for the poor, the partiality in favor of the most needy, is from (Christian) justice. That this is accepted from the revelation of Jesus or is learned by hearing the voices of reality through whom the God of love speaks is an open question that does not negate the mutually determinant version of full justice and full faith.

Sin, death, and the law are closely connected. These three fundamental dimensions equally make present the things of God and human things, individual things and collective ones. Not to see in sin, the law, and death more than their theologal dimensions is, in the majority of cases, to favor an abstract vision of these things. In the worst cases, it means favoring an ideologized, interested, and deforming vision. However, at the same time, a purely secularized reading of sin, death, and the law deprives these fundamental realities of their own reality and transcendence. Into these two extremes, many have fallen, and it happens frequently. When abstraction is not negative, but only methodological, it can be useful, always positively affirming the mutual openness of each of the two spheres. When abstraction is exclusive or simply neutral, then the impoverishment and the divorce from reality (*desrealización*) of each of the two spheres are inevitable, and with that one loses the human but also debilitates the Reign of God.

Liberation and Freedom

It is important to confront the concept of liberation that only attends to one of the aspects, "liberation-from" or "freedom-from," without giving due attention to "liberation-for," or "freedom-for." It was known more or less that the human or society should be liberated, but not what they should be liberated for, or much less how they should be liberated. One could respond to this objection in a purely formal and abstract way that would claim that we have been liberated from sin, in all its dimensions, to reach the freedom of the children of God. This is accurate and already indicates what is fundamental for liberation: liberation from sin and liberation for the freedom of the children of God. Yet this needs to be made much more concrete, above all to clarify the discussion between those supporters of freedom and those of liberation. For some, freedom is, at best, the finest way to obtain liberation (justice); while for others, liberation is the only way to arrive at freedom for the whole human person and all humanity. The freedom of the first group is the freedom of liberals, of liberalism in all its forms. The liberation of the latter is not identified with any form of liberalism, but is closer to the different processes of historical liberation, although not identified with any of them.

For the moment, liberation is a process, a process that is fundamentally a process of conversion in the personal and a process of transformation, if not revolution, in the historical. Personal freedom, prescinding methodologically from its essential intersubjective and social component, is not given at once, but rather it must be achieved. This achievement presupposes, on the negative side, the liberation from all of those bonds, internal and external, that threaten and diminish the potential strength of freedom. On the creative side, it means the strengthening of one's autonomy and configuring auto-determination. This latter does not suppose the annulment of tendencies (concupiscence), or the end of dealing with the pressure of the exterior world in all its forms, but a certain control over them. This is a long process that never ends, but this does not mean that freedom is not given to men and women until they achieve full liberation. It does mean that one cannot speak of full, personal freedom without it being the result of a long process of liberation. If we define personal freedom by one of its essential characteristics, auto-determination, we can see how difficult it is to speak of freedom, even in those cases in which it is so highly extolled. Always, but in a very subtle form in the actual world, there are multiple ways to annul auto-determination or to reduce it to the response, apparently free, to demands and pressures that come from inside or outside. There is the danger of a perpetual personal servitude, however much one believes that one has freely chosen one's lord or other power to which one wishes to be slave. Although conversion does not say everything definitive about the process of personal liberation, from a Christian perspective, it signals one of its fundamental aspects.

If, in the personal, liberation is a process of conversion, in the historical, it is a process of transformation and/or revolution. One cannot speak of freedom in the personal or historical if material and objective conditions are not given for it. In fact, there is a grouping of material and objective conditions that limit (impede) freedom and, for its part, needs a set of conditions that will allow freedom to develop. So, it hardly makes sense to speak of the freedom of a child who is just a few months old because, among other things, it lacks a minimum of biological-cerebral conditions without which it is not possible to exercise freedom. In a similar manner, one cannot speak of freedom in the social sphere if there are not the socioeconomic and political conditions that make it possible—not just for some elites but for the majority part of a given social group. When these conditions oppress and repress human life, as a fundamental root of freedom, then it matters little that constitutional freedoms and individual and social rights are extolled. Despite all of the elections that are offered, it is difficult for individuals and peoples subjected to the oppression of ignorance, hunger, sickness, absolute vulnerability, etc., to reach a sufficient level of personal freedom and, much less, a minimum level of public freedom.

Democratic constitutions may propose all sorts of formal freedoms, but the only ones who may enjoy these are those who possess the real conditions to make them real. Thus, an authentic struggle for freedom demands transformation (revolutionary or not) of those real conditions that impede or make the maximal sociopolitical and economic freedom of the major part of a population difficult. Liberation from unjust structures and the creation of new structures that foster dignity and freedom are therefore constituted essentially on the way to freedom, freedom for individuals within their national context and for peoples in their international context.

Liberation is not just one process but a collective process, both because of its active subject as well as its passive subject. The liberal conception of freedom emphasizes that it has every individual as its proper subject—every person may be free and freedom may be formally spoken of individuals. Liberalism and individualism appear to call for each other mutually. On the other extreme of a totalitarian conception, it appears that only the state or specific collective authorities are the proper subject of freedom, because only in their hands would there be decision making without it being predetermined by other superior authorities. The ancient Aristotelian concept, in which the subject is exclusively one of whom everything is predicated and may not be predicated of another, would be functioning in these two concepts of freedom. Christian liberation would aim to avoid this double hurdle: not being individualistic, without diminishing or negating individual freedom, and not being collectivist, without diminishing or negating the corresponding freedom. The condition for Christian freedom is not the slavery of all others so that one may be free (Eastern despotism), or the slavery of many so that a few may be free (Greek democracy), but rather that all may be free so that each one may be so. Yet this scale, proposed by Hegel, does not permit one to speak of the third stage as the Christian one except to the degree in which the freedom of the whole is made concrete as the liberation of the majority populations that, in their collective liberation, free the elites from their oppressive freedom but because of this remain permanently threatened.

Christian liberation is announced with a priority on the poor (Isa. 61:1–2; Luke 4:14–21), for them preferentially it is an announcement of the good news. Not only are they the principal audience, but the poor are also the announcers par excellence of the new and paradoxical wisdom by which God wants to save human beings (1 Cor. 1:26–31; James 2:5–6), so that God's strength may be seen more clearly in human weakness, and God's love may be seen in God's preference for those who are most vulnerable. However, this communal collective that is the poor and that ecclesially constitutes the people of God is not an anonymous collective, since the spirit of freedom, which is the Spirit of Christ, is in the heart of each human being, and it is through that converted and changed heart that one unites with others in Christ. This occurs in such a way that the love, which is the bond of unity, does not come to be an objectified mass, neither in a social totalitarianism in which individual personality and freedom disappear, nor in an individualistic freedom, but rather a freedom of self-giving such that the self-giving makes freedom objective, and freedom qualifies the self-giving. It is not the freedom of base instincts, but the freedom of love that places the Christian at the service of others, because the entire will of God is fulfilled in the exact fulfillment of one commandment, to love your neighbor as you love yourself (Gal. 4:13–15). The Spirit of Christ that makes each one a unique and free being is the same one that accomplishes this in a communitarian process, and in its collective case, that liberation leads to true freedom. Jesus is historicized among many so that many might be saved, where many is not just an expression of a large number but of the unity of a multitude that does not annul the salvation, liberation, and freedom of each person. It should empower it, because the unity of those saved is itself one of the principal signs of salvation.

This connection of liberation-freedom with poverty and the poor is one of the essential points of the Christian idea. Bourgeois freedom, which underlies many of the announcements of freedom, is founded on private property, and more concretely, on wealth. Without the imbalance of a few possessing much and the majority having very little, one could hardly speak of freedom. Bourgeois freedom, which meant the liberation of the aristocracy and absolute monarchies, was founded upon the oppression of large social strata that without freedom sustained the development of the bourgeois class. This is not Christian liberation-freedom. The gospel message views in wealth a great obstacle to the Reign of God and for the development of the freedom of the children of God. This point has been made with great force by the majority of the great religious reformers. They have seen wealth as an enormous obstacle to holiness and seen poverty, chosen for the love of Christ, as a great impetus to perfection. One cannot deny, without rejecting essential elements of the gospel, that wealth is a great obstacle to Christian freedom and that poverty is a great support for that freedom. "Having-more" as the condition for "being-more" is a diabolical temptation rejected by Jesus at the commencement of his public mission.

Today, however, it is supposed that only in having-more, particularly in having-more-than-others, is it possible to be-more, to be truly free. Domination becomes a condition of freedom. From this, the chasm between the rich and poor, between rich peoples and poor peoples, keeps widening. Thus, liberation as a collective process, whose principal subject is the poor, is the Christian response to the problem of collective freedom that makes possible and strengthens personal freedom. There is no freedom without liberation. There is no Christian freedom without Christian liberation, and this latter makes essential reference to the poor and poverty. The Christian faith should be a scandal before a world configured historically by sin more than by grace. As long as there are poor, liberation will come from the poor. When there cease to be poor, because basic necessities have been satisfied globally and unjust inequality, which makes oppression and repression possible, overcome, then we would have arrived at a superior stage of the Reign of God. Until then, the desire for wealth and consumerist degradation, which is fueled by excessive abundance, continue being fundamental temptations that must be overcome by the strength of faith lived out in history.

The reference to the poor as definitive of liberation situates the concept in its proper perspective. The liberation narrated in the Exodus, in terms more strictly historical-political, is not annulled by the liberation to come in the final judgment. There is no rupture between passages such as Exodus 3:7–9 and Matthew 25:31–46. Both cases speak of the liberation of the most poor; though in the New Testament parable, the possibilities of doing so are less differentiated and precise than in the Old Testament account. However, both speak of a strict liberation and not just a liberalization. Without underestimating the virtues of liberalization for subjective and individual freedom, ideas forged from the time of the Renaissance and not without the profound influence of Christian faith, liberation makes a different proposal, more material and more integral; all in all, more real and more universal.

Liberation is, above all, liberation from the lack of basic necessities without whose satisfaction one cannot speak of human life, much less the dignified human life deserved by children of God to whom the creator gave, with a common and communicable world, sufficient for that satisfaction: what should be called liberation from material oppression. Secondly, liberation is liberation from those phantasms and realities that frighten and terrorize humanity. In this is included the overcoming of all those institutions, be they juridical, political, or ideological, that maintain individuals or peoples in a state of fear of punishment or terror of being crushed rather than offering human ideals and convictions: this is what should be called freedom from repression, which historically and socially can be presented in many different forms. Given these two liberations, but also simultaneous with them, there is both personal and collective liberation from all sorts of dependencies. The human being is conditioned in her freedom by multiple factors and may even come to be determined. However, to be able to speak of radical freedom, one must overcome dependencies, because potential freedom serves little purpose if one cannot break the ties from the object that univocally determines one and makes self-determination impossible. These dependencies take away freedom when they are interiorized, but those that originate from the interior do not lose their character as negating freedom either: these should be called liberation from dependencies (inclinations, passions, attractions, consumption, etc.). Finally, there is liberation from oneself, but of oneself as an absolutely absolute reality, which one is not, not liberation from the self as the relatively absolute reality, which one is. In the prior cases, one could arrive at a dependence on something that appears to be absolute and leads to idolatry. Yet in the case of oneself, where the proper centrism of all living things, and particularly of human beings can become a total auto-centrism not just in respect to other human beings but to God, it constitutes one of the most dangerous forms of idolatry. This liberation from oneself has been treated many time by ascetics and mystics of many different tendencies.

In different grades, all of these forms of liberation are at once individual and collective, social and personal. Obviously, they go beyond the notion of liberalization, which only takes a real meaning when what should be its foundation is assured: liberation. When this occurs, liberalization, as an exercise of personal initiative, public freedoms, and of civil, as well as economic freedoms, comes to have a full meaning without involving deception, or worse, freedom for a few with the real negation of that same for the rest.

Liberation is personal, social, and theologal. Liberation from sin, the law, and death occurs in each and every one of the described processes of liberation. Sin, the law, and death lead to liberation's negation, while the fullness of that liberation leads to the overcoming of sin, the law, and death. But it does so in a real way. So, even though liberalization appears to have freedom as its objective, it attempts to find it down a false way, moreover, down a way that few may pursue it. On the other hand, the primary objective of liberation is justice, a justice of all for all. Here, justice is understood as what everyone is, has, and is given, not what is thought to be already theirs, because they possess it, but rather what is due them by their condition as human person, member of a certain community, and, definitively, as member of the same species, in whose psycho-organic totality it corresponds to govern the correct relations within itself and with the natural world around it. One might say that there is no justice without freedom, but the reciprocal is even more certain: there is no freedom for all without justice for all. This interrelation must be conserved, because its two poles are the highest human values and gifts always offered by the Christian faith. However, their prioritizing, not so much as values but as steps in an integral process, must be defined with realism in each historical case.

The path to arrive at justice through freedom (liberalism) has had good results for the most powerful, as individuals and societies, in its specific moment, but it has left the majority of humanity without freedom (liberation). The path to arrive at freedom through justice has also historically left much to be desired in specific countries. Nevertheless, a liberation, as put forth integrally by the Christian faith, that does justice does not place definitive impediments to freedom; and demanding that freedom not place any impediments to justice, should be the path that the poor should undertake to go, realizing historically the project of salvation (liberation) that has been promised to them.

During this phase, in which justice and freedom are made possible by a process of liberation, it can be shown what participation in the divine life is for humanity. The creative freedom of humanity is a prolongation of the creative freedom of God, and it is more free and creative as long as it prolongs the action of God along the lines of love. In human beings, oppressed by sin, free creation by love is the result of a process of liberation. The possibility of and call for that creative freedom are already inscribed within human reality itself. This is so not just by the imperative will of God but in that reality itself is already the real potency placed by God in the community beyond its own personal life (Zubiri). However, that possibility and that reality are realized in a world of sin that also is rooted in human freedom and in the congenital limitation of human nature. In spite of the limited way of being God that humans possess as limited beings, they do have the possibility not just of overcoming sin but of becoming like God. This is by the very gift of Godself and not by any Promethean effort, which is certainly idolatry.

People of God and Liberation

Among the different partial descriptions of what the church is, the one that interprets it as the people of God originally (*Lumen gentium*), in light of the mystery of God, is the one most useful for asking (1) what the church should do and (2) who in the church should carry out the work of liberation. The instruction, *Libertatis conscientia*, confirms this by dedicating a special section to the church as people of God[12] and by insisting repeatedly that the poor are the preferential subject of liberation.[13] From this perspective of the people of God, which is the historical-salvific correlate to the Reign of God, the participation of Christians in the processes of liberation should be focused.

Liberation has, at once, a salvific and historical character. When the Christian speaks of integral liberation, he attempts to formulate, according to the demands of the majority populations of our time, the historicized version of salvation. He does not think that historical liberation goes by one way, and by another goes Christian salvation. Rather, Christian salvation has much to offer to historical liberation, which of its own although subordinately, is the necessary condition for the historicization of salvation. It is not easy to separate one aspect from the other, but neither can one confuse them as if they were the same thing. When the term "integral liberation" is understood as historical actualization of Christian salvation, it has that double aspect of worldly realization and transcendent realization, where the former is the objectification in each limited case of what claims to be, and the latter is the greater presence of God who is always greater.

Despite this unity, liberation, by its technical and material character, has certain demands that exceed the capacity of the church, at least until all humans constitute, objectively, freely, and consciously, to be a "people of God-church" as principal subject of the Reign of God. From this emerges the notion that liberation needs mediations. Theoretical mediations are needed to interpret the character of those things that negate liberation and to propose solutions leading to overcoming them. Practical mediations are needed to put that overcoming into motion. All human beings can and should contribute to that task, according to their theoretical and moral capacities, along with the intellectual and political autonomy that the very nature of things demands. Revelation and the tradition of that revelation may signal limits, in the sense that they demonstrate what cannot or should not be done, and even show by means of a utopia what can and should be done. Yet they cannot define, of themselves and without the needed mediations, the paths and models that should be followed to go realizing in each moment, in different persons and groups, societies and international communities, a process of integral liberation.

It does not make sense, then, to object that the social teaching of the church and liberation theology do not offer fully operative solutions to the problems of humanity. Because from that lack, it does not follow that their historical contribution is useless or could be substituted by that of others. Integral liberation cannot be achieved solely with the instruments that faith offers, but it cannot be achieved without them. The integrity of liberation demands the presence of faith, and this refers to historical liberation, and it is not just reduced to what could be considered the spiritual liberation from sin and the eschatological liberation from evil. It is historical liberation that affects humanity, here and now, in its concrete totality and that needs the Christian liberative contribution.

Yet that Christian contribution is not sufficient. Theoretical and practical mediations, which may be quite varied depending on the different stages of historical development, are necessary. However, one must choose among these mediations. Perhaps there are some mediations that might be considered strictly neutral, but even if there are elements that might be considered as such, the system in which they are inscribed gives them tendencies, if not makes them tendentious. At times, it has been thought that the indispensable condition for initiating assuredly the path to integral liberation for the majority population was the social appropriation of the means of production. Other times, it has been thought that only with private ownership of the means of production can one respect the fundamental freedom that leads to liberation. The examples could be multiplied: absolute monarchy in direct relation to God, constitutional monarchy, different forms of aristocracy or democracy, the primacy of the ethnic groups over states, sexual liberation or repression, etc. All of these mediations possess their own structure and dynamism, which cannot be substituted by circumstances foreign to them. This does not mean, however, that they cannot be subject just to moral judgment but also to a strictly theologal judgment according to liberation. That moral and theologal judgment should take into account, whenever possible, the criteria of praxis and historicization. For there may be a solution that, while it holds together theoretically, is not salvable.

The problem comes to the fore when a mediation is put into practice and its results are objectified in history, considered over a long period and, as much as possible, in its total spatial dimension. What good and evil has liberalism brought? To whom? For how long? What solution offers a more promising future? There are not always clear and univocal answers to these and other questions, but the Christian view of liberation can help find them, when it is situated faithfully in the proper place for theologal discernment, which is the poor, the majority populations. For the integral liberation of humanity, what is good is that which is good and multiplicatively so directly for the majority population.

The people of God, as the mediating and impelling subject of liberation, should understand itself preferentially as the people of the poor, as the church of the poor. That distinction comes before any division between hierarchy and faithful, between priests and laypeople, etc., as Vatican II clearly signals. The people of God are primary and original to the subsequent structuring and hierarchization of the church. It should already consider itself intrinsically configured by the preferential option for the poor. There have been popes who, to a greater or lesser extent, have configured the exercise of their primacy along the lines of the poor. There have also been bishops and other authorities who have exercised their ministry, hierarchical and priestly, along the same lines. Thus, in principle, there is no opposition between the institutional church and the church of the poor, because the very institutional nature of the church should be configured by the preferential option. However, there is room for distinctions. A fundamental distinction is that which pertains to the maternal character of the church, in contrast to its magisterial character. The maternal character of the church indicates how it is midwife to humanity and holiness, of new impulses and ideas in favor of liberation, and this character corresponds to whom God has given it through the Spirit of Christ, which does not necessarily correspond with the hierarchy, but rather frequently to the people who are most poor and not constituted within the hierarchy, those whom God has made holy and simply preferred. The magisterial character, that is, the authoritative determination of the meaning of various theoretical and practical pronouncements that affect the Christian life from revelation and at times in its historical concretions, corresponds better to those who hold ecclesiastical authority.

The church is mother and teacher, but it is so for different reasons. Moreover, there is a priority of its maternal character over its magisterial character. Its mission of giving life or transmitting life is more important than authoritatively sanctioning specific teachings. That the hierarchy of the church can and should realize maternal action before all else—and in this sense with other pastoral metaphors—does not signify that this action is exclusive to it, just as those who are not constituted with hierarchical authority (power) may develop a great magisterial labor, although that labor lacks the approval of authority desired by God for the superadded legitimization of a truth. Well then, it corresponds primarily to the maternal character of the people of God to give birth to liberative life within the church, and in favor of history and the magisterial character of the people of God, to discern authoritatively what conforms or does not conform to the truth of revelation, since this always enters in direct relation with liberative action. The interaction of these two functions may come into conflict, may be conflictive, but that conflict would always be healthy as long as it is dominated by the Spirit of Christ who gives birth to truth and life and, at the same time, sanctions the legitimacy and fullness of that truth and that life. The maternal and magisterial characters of the church are two complementary functions, but of the two of them, the maternal is the superior.

This being so, the principal contribution of the people of God to liberation would be its own configuration as a force of liberation. If the church as the people of God does not configure itself as a sign and force of liberation, only with great difficulty could it do anything important in the liberation of persons and historical structures. This has not always happened. If the conviction of the magisterium that liberation is an essential element of the Christian faith has been late, one must suppose that in the magisterium's internal praxis and its self-consciousness, the salvific power of this liberative configuration has not been seen. The church has configured itself more along the criteria of truth (orthodoxy) and authority (vertical) than along the criteria of life and liberation. They are not entirely exclusive because the hierarchical magisterium does not negate the maternal. However, the dominance of the former places the growth of the latter in jeopardy. According to this, the church constitutes itself more as a sign of the law and of order than of the Spirit and of change. The authoritarianism in the church, the fear of those "excesses" of the Spirit that blows where it will, the designation of revealed truth into very limited historical formulations, the predominance of legislation over inspiration, of the law over grace, of complacency over impetus, etc., these have not made the church a unique example of innovation and liberation.

This should change. The most glorious moments of the church, in the theoretical and practical, in mission and in the religious, in its credibility before its own daughters and sons and before the world, have come in epochs of growth, in epochs in which the maternal predominated over the magisterial. That is how it was in the primitive church; that is how it has been through its history—when creative prophecy has broken through the short-sightedness of habit; and that is how it is in modern times with John XXIII and Vatican II. There may enter the dangers of excess and dissociative dispersion, but for that there is the magisterial aspect. However, this aspect cannot be constituted as the dominant force because, when this occurs, not only does the liberative power inside the church close, but the church becomes a retarding force, as much against the freedom of the liberals as against the liberation of the popular movements.

The church configured as people of God more from the maternal powers within it than magisterial ones would be in better position to add its contribution to the liberation of human beings and history. It has done this on many occasions, notably in the sphere of culture, of the spiritual life, of the announcement of the Reign, of the denunciation of sin, etc. One cannot forget the fruits of holiness that the church, thanks to the Spirit, has brought about along the lines of liberation from personal sin, of conversion, and of commitment to others. Shadows have not always obscured the light, and secular worldliness has never completely choked the evangelical power of the faith. The persecution that has been suffered serves as proof of how it has resisted the powers of this world, above all when it has done so truly in the name of the gospel and not to defend its own interests or institutional prejudices. It is in receiving the Spirit of Christ and being moved by it that the church may contribute to liberation, creatively doing today what Jesus did in his own time and, as best as it can, to do so as Jesus did, preferentially from the poor, for the poor, and as the poor.

If the church fills its life with the Spirit of Christ and cultivates its prophetic potential, it can, from the gospel itself and from its specific means, be a radical force of liberation. It can do this not so much by adopting doctrinal forms but kerygmatic forms of announcement and denunciation. It is the kerygma, lived and proclaimed, that best leads to conversion and transformative action, to personal commitment and to historical action. The word, for example, and action that make the liberative power of the gospel and its call to conversion and transformation present in a life-giving way are the great contribution of the people of God to liberative tasks.

In the church as people of God, the ecclesial base communities are one of the optimal places of this transfusion of faith's power to the course of history. They are so through their special characteristics of reading the living word of God in scripture and tradition as a community, and allowing themselves to be challenged directly as much by that word as by the demands of reality, all from a preferential option for the poor. The base communities that are not determined by this option partially represent an element of liberative power, inasmuch as they put an actively personal life into play and not just a mere hearing and obeying of the magisterial and hierarchical structures of the church. However, it is the ecclesial base communities, intrinsically determined by the preferential option for the poor, that, by being situated in the very place of oppression and repression, best feel the liberative power of the faith in all its fullness, which is not reduced to their subjectivity, but rather applies to their social structures. Liberation is not just preferentially for the poor; it is that, moreover, it should come preferentially from them because they are the active and passive subjects par excellence of liberation according to the promise of God. This is what is particular about the ecclesial base communities, that they are qualified subjects to effectively announce Christian liberation in history.

Nevertheless, what is most proper for them is not historical action but the historical word such as was the case with Jesus. Or if one prefers, the historical action par excellence of the church, and in it the ecclesial base communities, is the efficacious word. Certainly, the word by itself is not enough, but the word in all its manifestations, in all of its expressive gestures is a power not only indispensable but profoundly effective. Definitively for human beings, only that which becomes conscious and intentional, that which becomes significant, brings liberation in history. If it is absurd to reduce the whole process of liberation to the word, it is also absurd to negate the decisive importance of the word in liberation. The prophetic word of the kerygma, made present in the course of history, is entirely indispensable. That word should have the same incarnational structure as Jesus, the word made flesh. That is, it should have the power of the divine Logos, but it should also have a full incorporation of flesh in history, as one that gives power to and animates history more than one that technically regulates it. That historical flesh is efficacious action that should be performed to realize liberation materially in terms of all that liberation has in a strict materiality.

Without identifying itself with, or even less subordinating itself to, any social or political organizations, the people of God or parts of it taking on the task of liberation need to enter in relation with them. Some should be positively fought against because their ultimate effect runs counter to the integral liberation of the majority or because their means are unacceptable to the Christian faith. Yet others can be positively supported, inasmuch as they present the most effective means for the liberation of the majority in a specific moment. It is not proper to the base communities to become such organizations, because the specificity of the ends and means advise against it, or to lose their Christian identity in their mission to other organizations, because when salt loses its own flavor it no longer serves as salt. It is proper to them, above all, to encourage the liberative spirit and power of the organizations that really are in favor of popular liberation and to see that that spirit and power, already liberative, conform to the ends, means, and the values and interpretations of fundamental points of the Christian message. The historicization and making operative of the faith demands this. Moreover, the intrinsic unity of salvation history may lead to very useful confluences between those mechanisms that more specifically guide or manage, as much history as salvation. It is a problem of discernment that brings with it its own dangers, none more so than the fundamental danger of not searching for that confluence or collaboration because of the possible dangers that the institutional limitations of the faith could encounter.

This does not mean that those called laypeople in the church cannot opt politically through organizational means that appear to them to be most apt for liberation, and to join them in a fully committed way. It could even be that those who are not laypeople in the church would occasionally have to do so as well, either because they must obey the call of their own consciences or the authority of those to whom they owe obedience. It seems obvious that laypeople, both as human beings and as Christians, should attempt to put the fullness of their Christian faith into so-called temporal tasks, and to do so explicitly and entailing dangerous risks in favor of the oppressed and the struggles for liberation. In a world of sin, truly liberative works historically entail a permanent sacrifice, which few people want to take on, to forgo that general temptation to make use of power for themselves. Politics as service and not as profession, in which one seeks not power but the betterment of the majority populations, could then become a place for living out Christian fullness. Of course, even in this case one must differentiate what is proper to the layperson within the people of God proper, in the base community, and what is proper to the layperson who remains always a member of the people of God in terms of political labor. The problem is one that is more functional and practical than it is properly theological, but in practice there are great consequences. Salvation (the Christianization) of history cannot be confused with its clericalization or even its religiosity. Neither can the historicization of salvation be confused with its political secularization. Here is where the distinction of charisms and ministries within the people of God is something fundamental when it comes time to find the proper path both for each person and the distinct ecclesial stations. The church can contribute a great deal on behalf of liberation both in a united and differentiated manner.

In some places, the church is still a great social force, and, as such, it should place its particular weight in favor of liberation. However, it should do so not as regards to being part of or in relation to political power, but as being part of and in relation to the social power of the people. The place where the church acts is at the base not at the cupola, and its particular mode of action is the prophetic word and not political negotiation. This is true even of the institutional church that should not understand itself as a political power alongside other political powers, but rather preferentially as a social power because of its insertion in the world. The church has carried out this task in favor of domination on many occasions within the structure of political power, but the church of the poor, as the most genuine expression of the church's holiness, should make it in favor of liberation and within what one can call a "popular" power, the power of a people who are prophets, priests, and kings. Because, although the liberation sought by the church is an integral liberation, one should not forget that in regard to that "integrality" liberation is historically a liberation from social and economic as well as political oppressions. These are sin and the fruit of sin, and they negate the primary condition of the children of God and heirs of the Reign—ones who correspond preferentially to the poor of this world.

Notes

[1] Congregation for the Doctrine of Faith (CDF), *Libertatis nuntius*, 3:4.
[2] Ibid., intro.
[3] CDF, *Libertatis conscientia*, intro, 1.
[4] Ibid., 2.
[5] Ibid.
[6] *Libertatis nuntius*, 1:1.
[7] *Libertatis conscientia*, intro, 2.
[8] Conférence des évêques de France, *Libération des hommes et salut en Jésus-Christ*, 1975.
[9] Second General Conference of Latin American Bishops, *The Church in the Present-Day Transformation of Latin America in the Light of the Council*, Introduction to Final Documents, no. 6. See *Liberation Theology: A Documentary History*, ed. Alfred T. Hennelly (Maryknoll: Orbis Books, 1990), 96.
[10] Second General Conference of Latin American Bishops, *The Church in the Present-Day Transformation of Latin America in the Light of the Council*, Document on the Pov-

erty of the Church, no. 2. See *Liberation Theology: A Documentary History*, ed. Alfred T. Hennelly (Maryknoll: Orbis Books, 1990), 114.

[11] Third General Conference of Latin American Bishops, *Evangelization in Latin America's Present and Future*, no. 281, in *Puebla and Beyond: Documentation and Commentary*, ed. John Eagleson and Philip Scharper (Maryknoll: Orbis Books, 1979), 161.

[12] *Libertatis conscientia*, III:58.

[13] Ibid., I:21–22; IV:62–69.

Bibliography

Boff, Clodovis. *Teología de lo político.* Salamanca: Ediciones Sígueme, 1981.

Boff, Leonardo. *Jesucristo y la liberación del hombre.* Madrid: Ediciones Cristiandad, 1981.

Congregation for the Doctrine of the Faith. *Libertatis nuntius,* 1984. In English, "Instruction on Certain Aspects of the 'Theology of Liberation.'" In *Liberation Theology: A Documentary History*, ed. Alfred T. Hennelly, 393–414. Maryknoll: Orbis Books, 1990.

Congregation for the Doctrine of the Faith. *Libertatis conscientia,* 1986. In English, "Instruction on Christian Freedom and Liberation," In *Liberation Theology: A Documentary History*, ed. Alfred T. Hennelly, 461–97. Maryknoll: Orbis Books, 1990.

Croatto, Severino. *Liberación y libertad.* Buenos Aires: Ediciones Mundo Nuevo, 1973. In English, *Exodus: A Hermeneutics of Freedom.* Maryknoll: Orbis Books, 1981.

Ellacuría, Ignacio. "Estudio teológico pastoral de la instrucción sobre algunos puntos de la teología de la liberación." *Revista Latinoamericana de Teología* 2 (1984): 145–78.

International Theological Commission. *Teología de la liberación.* Madrid, 1978.

Gutiérrez, Gustavo. *Teología de la liberación. Perspectivas.* Salamanca: Ediciones Sígueme, 1972. In English, *A Theology of Liberation.* Maryknoll: Orbis Books, 1973.

Ratzinger, Joseph. "Freiheit und Befreiung." *Internationale Katholische Zeitschrift Communio* 5 (1986): 409–24.

Segundo, Juan Luis. *Teología de la liberación. Respuesta al cardenal Ratzinger.* Madrid: Ediciones Cristiandad, 1985.

Segundo, Juan Luis. *Theology and the Church: A Letter to Cardinal Ratzinger and a Warning to the Whole Church.* San Francisco: Harper & Row, 1987.

Sobrino, Jon. *Liberación con espíritu.* Santander: Editorial Sal Terrae, 1985.

Sobrino, Jon. *Spirituality of Liberation.* Maryknoll, NY: Orbis, 1988.

—Translated by Michael E. Lee

3

Laying the Philosophical Foundations of Latin American Theological Method

(1975)

Ignacio Ellacuría wrote this essay as the text for his plenary address to the international Conference on Latin American Theology [Encuentro Latinoamericano de teología] held in Mexico City in 1975, ten years after the close of the Second Vatican Council. Liberation theology was a new theological trend that had exploded in popularity not only in Latin America but throughout much of Africa, Asia, North America, and Europe. The time was ripe for an in-depth examination of method in liberation theology, and the Mexico City Conference accordingly focused on "methods of theological reflection in Latin America and their pastoral implications for the present and the past." The conference gathered together a list of featured speakers that reads like a "Who's Who in Latin American Liberation Theology." Ellacuría's presentation was regarded as a high point of the conference and its subsequent publication brought him to the attention of the international theological community, establishing him as one of the leading theological voices in all of Latin America.

Although the argument of this essay is dense, it has a simple two-part structure. Ellacuría begins with an analysis of different approaches to theology as seen in two essays on Christology that appeared in a publication honoring Karl Rahner. He contrasts a theology that is self-consciously Latin American and thus "regional" (or, as we might say today, "contextual") and an approach to Christology "with certain pretensions to present a universal theology." On the basis of this analysis, he then sketches a systematic argument for a theological method that moves beyond the idealistic presuppositions of a so-called universal theology. He presents a method modeled on the "formal structure and differentiating function of intelligence" by means of which human beings are able to "engage real things in their reality." Of particular importance is his brilliant and succinct description of the threefold structure—noetic, ethical, and praxical—of the human encounter with reality, a description that has been cited by numerous other theologians and religious commentators. Ellacuría's profound understanding of liberation theology as a theology that engages historical reality introduces a dynamic and powerful way to link the universal and the concrete, the natural and the historical, and the divine and the human.

Pace Descartes and his followers, questions of method are not prior to the intellectual work that is already engaged in resolving specific problems. Method entails, even temporally, a certain posteriority: after having carried out an intellectually fruitful task one raises questions about how one went about it, by way of justifying it critically, correcting it, or launching it anew. Even more than doctrines and theories, methods have their own "hermeneutical circle." To fail to recognize this is to begin uncritically any attempt to be critical. Fundamental method is the very manner of thinking, and this very manner of thinking is only realized and verified when in fact it has produced a thought. In reality, it involves all of that thought as the ultimate foundation of what, from another point of view, appears as method. From this perspective, method is nothing but the critical and operative aspect of a system of thought, considered reflexively. It is no accident that it is so difficult to explain what transcendental method is, or dialectical method, or phenomenological method, without explaining Kantian thought, Hegelian or Marxian thought, and Husserlian or Heideggerian thought.

All of this is asserted, in the first place, so that Latin American theology, or Latin American theological reflection, does not fall into the temptation of losing itself in question of method, avoiding real questions of content and praxis because it is obsessed with being scientific and critical. Secondly, however, considered from the opposite extreme, the point is to keep Latin American theological work from being carried out uncritically, that is, without giving an explicit account of that which justifies it and is at the same time its norm and inspiration.

Understood in this way, the problem of method is one that, in our case, merges into the problem of Latin American theology itself, if not in the development of its content, then certainly in the characterization of what its fundamental orientation is. All of this makes us aware from the outset that the question of method cannot be confused with the question of what methods can and should be utilized in the concrete when we do theology. This distinction of method from methods is obvious, but if we do not take it into account, we run the risk of getting lost at the very outset of the journey. We can and should utilize methods that, in themselves, are more or less neutral and universal. Nor does this necessarily cause the Latin American character of fundamental method to suffer. This is how we might explain—although the explanation will not always prove convincing—the proliferation of outside references in the most representative and well-known writings of liberation theology. We can do this because, with all due critical caution, certain methods can be assimilated as instruments taking their orientation from the hand that utilizes them, without forgetting, of course, that not just any instrument can be used to accomplish any task whatever. We should do this because otherwise, under the guise of not being servants of alien methods, at times we convert the theoretical labor itself into the babbling of beginners or a sour grapes attitude toward that which we could not grasp.* Refusing a certain kind of intellectualism cannot lead to the renunciation of intelligence as a principle of liberation. It would be a radical mistake to surrender the full exercise of intelligence—the "let them invent" of Unamuno—to those who, in short, have grounded their power to dominate on intelligence.

So as not to commit this intellectual suicide, so as to be able to defend ourselves from those who stigmatize the theoretical works originating from the dominated periphery, out of a presumed monopoly on intellectual labor in general and theoretical labor in particular, and, above all, so as to positively advance the tasks we have undertaken, the moment appears to have arrived for laying some critical foundations for the method proper to Latin American theology. A series of recent writings has been undertaken with this intent,[1] and this has been the aim of the *Encuentro Latinoamericano de teología*.[2] After rapidly, intensely, and fruitfully creating its contents, Latin American theology is preparing to justify itself critically by reflecting on its own method, the method that it exercised from the beginning without raising critical questions about its foundation, although from the very start it was justified by its own way of starting off and by the results it obtained.

The point of the present work is to contribute to laying foundations critically for Latin American theological method from a predominantly philosophical point of view, knowing full well that this will not bring complete mastery of the problem. The latter because theological method, precisely because it is method, is inseparable from theological contents and attitudes. However, on the other hand, unless we look at our ultimate presuppositions, our justifications are always insufficient. What is worse, we leave theological thought at the mercy of people who control it from the vantage point of a particular theory of the "who, what, and why" of human knowing: who knows, what is knowing, and what is knowing for. The point here is not to produce an antecedent and all-inclusive theory of human intelligence independently of what theological work is today. These remarks are only trying to reflect on the fundamental presuppositions of theological work, from the vantage point of that work. They attempt to reflect on those presuppositions that, if they are not reflexively known, leave high and dry those people who, in short, do not know what they are doing. We have no dearth of profound explanations of different varieties as to why there is more of a Latin American theology than there is an explicit Latin American philosophy; but, looked at from the other end, there exists in Latin American theology a series of philosophical approaches that need to be brought to light and given some foundations, so that liberation can penetrate to the very roots of intellectual work.

The interests that we have just highlighted orient our way of proceeding. Since we are attempting to lay the philosophical foundations of Latin American theological method, we will start by presenting a theological model. Under the premise that the Latin American theological model has its own distinctiveness, we will set it in contrast to a theological model that is not Latin American. Under the premise that the difference between the two models implies a difference in their ultimate presuppositions, we will analyze these presuppositions in a similarly contrastive way. This avoids the dangers of proceeding in a purely theoretical and aprioristic manner, since the reflections will be built on quite specific examples. It is worth noting from the outset, however, that the non–Latin American model, both in the way it thinks theologically and as a way of laying philosophical foundations, is taken up only to provide a contrast. For this reason it most probably appears in a weak light. However, we are not seeking a critique of that model but a better grasp of those aspects that are proper to the Latin American theological method. Even less do we seek to reject what could be called European theology, relying on models that for many cannot seem at all representative of that theology. It is a matter of a purely methodological procedure. Its value and justification should be seen in the procedure itself and in its results. Likewise, its limits should be clear from the outset.

This essay is divided into two principal parts. In the first, the models are presented. In the second, I will reflect on their foundations *[fundamentos]*. In both the first and second parts, I will proceed by way of contrast, but a contrast that does not attempt to be a position *a contrariis*, but simply a position that is in itself in contrast with other modes of thinking and is best grasped and affirmed in its own distinctiveness in terms of this contrast.

Two Examples of Theological Method

The two models that I have chosen are taken from a recent publication in which different theological essays honoring Karl Rahner appeared. The essay representing Latin American thought, by Leonardo Boff, is entitled, "The Liberation of Jesus Christ as Seen from the Road of Oppression: A Latin American Reading." As the title itself indicates, it is an attempt at an explicitly Latin American reading. The non-Latin American essay—with certain pretensions to present a universal theology, that is to say, of not being a regional one, although it is, of course—an article by Olegario González de Cardedal, is entitled, "A Fundamental Theological Problem, the Preexistence of Christ: History and Hermeneutics."[3] Of these two essays, it could be said that one is indeed Latin American, and the other is not. Thus, the second serves as a contrast to the first. However, since some ways of doing theology in Latin America try to realize their objectives with mental and cultural schemes similar to the non-Latin American article, the comparison can have the subsidiary utility of highlighting some presuppositions of certain theological works produced in Latin America. This is not meant to imply that there is only one Latin American way of doing theology, much less that the unity of this way of doing theology— let us say, more precisely, of the fundamental method—implies that its analysis and answers will coincide. But it certainly does suggest that there is a new way of doing theology in Latin America and that this way has its own valid characteristics, which for some appear to offer a profound response to what faith needs in these peripheral and oppressed regions. What can be universally valid in this way of doing theology, compared with all the other ways one can do theology, is a question that we can bracket for the time being.

Olegario González

Olegario González examines the preexistence of Christ as something he considers to be a "fundamental theological problem." It is

> one that is of most interest and is most difficult for a Christology that seeks to be faithful to its origins and faithful to its ultimate nature: to be a significant word of salvation, spoken from the cutting edge of history and, because of this, spoken with intelligibility and the weight of the truth for some specific group of persons. (González 1975, 193)

He approaches this fundamental theme historically and hermeneutically. By history he understands a historical journey that starts with scripture and moves through the tradition until it arrives at contemporary theology; he takes hermeneutics to be the search for the meaning that different christological affirmations have in their dual aspect as something in itself and something for me. He thinks that both aspects, the historical and the hermeneutical, are essential to the work of theology if it is to be anything like a theology that corresponds to the demands of our cultural scene.

As far as history goes, he tells us that "any theological reflection on the theme of preexistence ought to start from a historical consideration of Jesus in his concrete destiny" (ibid., 179). Likewise,

> the history of Christ as preexistent is a function of the history of the existent Jesus. The content of the former is not exhausted in the latter, but we only discern and verify it by analyzing and contemplating the latter. Nothing is more alien to Christianity than a dehistorification of whatever type, be it ethical or gnostic, ideological or pietistic. (Ibid., 200)

As far as hermeneutics goes, the accent is placed on the theoretical comprehension of the meaning of specific affirmations. While these assertions no doubt are intended to refer to a reality, it is their experiential dimension that is sought first and foremost.

The way he works this method out in the concrete clarifies and confirms the fundamental direction of his theological approach. First, demonstrate the historical genesis of the concept that he is analyzing—in the present case, the preexistence of Christ—keeping in mind the literary genres in which it appears. Second, analyze the function that this concept fulfills in each of the cultural contexts in which it appears. "What does talking about preexistence aim to say or, if you will, what unknown quantity does it attempt to resolve, what difficulty does it wish to overcome?" (ibid., 193). Third, attend to the turn of modernity, which would consist in finding the meaningfulness of affirmations "to the extent that they are significant for the comprehension and realization of human existence" (ibid., 193). He thinks that these three steps are fundamental because what he judges essential to his investigation is determining the presuppositions that carry with them

> this conception of Christ as preexistent, and the degree to which they are overcome by the contemporary conception of reality. . . .

> This is where the great question emerges, no longer a historical
> kind of question (the sources of the idea, its crystallization, and
> application to Christ), nor even a phenomenological one (the sig-
> nification and intentionality that it has in each context in which
> it was applied to Christ) but rather the hermeneutical question.
> (Ibid., 200–01)

Moreover, this hermeneutical kind is ultimately a question about the
meaning and function of the biblical and dogmatic affirmations of preexistence—whether they say something about the very reality of Christ or
only something about our existence to the extent that we are redeemed
by Jesus.

The place for verifying this meaning and function is religious experience. "Any theoretical discourse about the preexistence of Christ from all
eternity only makes sense from the perspective of a religious encounter
with him in our human time" (ibid., 207). The place "where this category
is originally born and permanently verified is religious experience: the
encounter with Jesus as encounter with God and therefore the salvific-
eschatological encounter" (ibid., 207).

The conclusion that this essay reaches is, naturally, consistent with the
steps that precede it and the method followed.

> The world is a function of Jesus. History, both cosmic and hu-
> man, is derivative with respect to his personal history, and thus it
> divides into a creating prehistory and a consummating post-history.
> If Christ were only a function of God for history, which would
> be to say that his meaning is fixed within the boundaries of the
> God-history relation, without being at the same time a function of
> the very mystery of God, then history would still be open and we
> would not have the certainty of a positive end. All the messianisms
> . . . all the programs for restoring a heaven on earth . . . would still
> make sense. If we do not have in Christ the only-begotten Son,
> with whom God is God as Father, then we could not say that we
> know God anymore. (Ibid., 210)

Leonardo Boff

Leonardo Boff does not treat the preexistence of Christ but the liberation that Christ brings to an oppressed people, a theme that he thinks is
absolutely fundamental to Christology. On an initial, superficial reading, his

methodological starting point might appear similar to the one we just reviewed. "Our concern is the question: How do we announce the liberation borne by Jesus Christ in a way that is meaningful for the people of today?" (Boff 1975, 241). But the question probes the meaning that liberation carries not for people in general and not just for some putative person of today, but for the marginalized and oppressed person who is counting on specific historical incitements and whose fundamental need is not a matter of theoretical comprehension but of a work for liberation that will do something. This is the person who finds himself or herself having not to opt for one or another system of interpreting the universe, but rather for one or another system of transforming his or her historical reality.

Consequently, history and hermeneutics take on a different meaning from that presented above. "We do not want to be hermeneutically naive" (ibid., 242) when we confront the question of the liberation that Jesus Christ provides, or the meaning proper to it.

> This question takes its orientation from an interest that is quite clear. It attempts to detect and establish the concrete mediations that the liberation of Jesus incarnates in history. Universal discourses are not sufficient. These have to be verified in the warp and woof of human life. Without this mediation they are unreal and ideological, and end up fortifying the dominant interests. (Ibid., 242).

Every reading, every interpretation is oriented by interests, be they existential or social. The important thing is realizing what this interest is and how this interest conditions our way of approaching and comprehending reality.

The liberation of Jesus Christ is not so much a doctrine to be announced as it is a praxis to be realized. In order to discover this doctrine and this praxis today, we have to turn our eyes to the deeds and words of Jesus with the aim of discovering in them what they contain of permanent significance—but in a hermeneutically precise sense that breaks through the historical pictures of Jesus and sees in them a transcendent meaning. The point is not to get lost in this transcendent meaning but to incarnate it in new historical contexts. The universality and transcendence of Jesus Christ are total, but they need to be mediated and made visible in concrete liberative steps. "Christ himself brought his universal liberation through a liberative process within his own situation. Similarly, in our praxis we should translate universal liberation into liberative situations within the situation in which God calls us to live. Only in this way does the liberation of Jesus Christ become meaningful in our lives" (ibid., 244).

Consequently, the methodological task that Boff proposes is twofold.

> On the one hand, to show how the liberation of Jesus Christ was a concrete liberation for the world that he encountered. . . . On the other hand, to find within this concrete liberation a dimension that transcends this historical concretion of liberation and, by virtue of that, is of interest and concern to those of us who are living now in another situation. (Ibid., 263)

However, we can only speak of liberation and redemption starting from their opposites, starting from oppression and perdition. That is why the fundamental questions are these: "How are oppression and perdition present themselves today in our experience? How should the redemption and liberation of Jesus Christ be articulated as a consequence, so that they might really be faith's response to this situation?" (ibid., 263). And this is where the social scientific and historical mediations come in directly: "In the first place, a pertinent social-analytical reading of the context becomes necessary in order to disclose the structural and systematic character of cultural, political, and economic dependence. In the second place, it is an urgent task to articulate a theological reading of this same situation which for faith does not correspond to the designs of God" (ibid., 264). This involves not only a denunciation that unmasks the alleged progress of our time but an annunciation that anticipates a new meaning for human society and utilizes the instruments of today's civilization not for domination but for freedom and solidarity. Nevertheless, it is not necessary to make of Christian liberation something that is identified with and exhausted by any of the historical steps of liberation; nor is it necessary to reduce faith and theological reflection to an intramundane ideology.

Boff's theological way of proceeding is to turn as critically as possible—using historical criticism, ideological criticism, hermeneutical criticism—to the deeds and words of the historical Jesus as they can be derived from the gospel accounts. Thus, he recovers for Christology the historical reality of the life of Jesus. Interpreting this reality accurately and translating it correctly into our own historical reality, with an essential and primary reference to praxis, make up not only a way of proceeding in theological reflection but a clear and emphatic position concerning what the task of theology should be here and now.

Comparing the Models

Merely juxtaposing the models places striking differences in relief. The choice of theme is already one of these differences, and one of the most significant ones. This does not only or principally have to do with one of the themes being more "contemporary" than the other but with the very possibility of their verification. Neither of the authors is a stranger to this concept of verification. However, where in the first case verification has a primarily contemplative and experiential character, in the second it is real and praxis-based, something that can be substantiated to some degree in historical reality itself. Obviously, the preexistence of Christ and the liberation of Christ have different significances and different verifications, since in one case we are talking about a static attribute and in the other about a dynamic intervention. It could well turn out to be the case that only a preexistent one could liberate, but then preexistence would be seen and verified in liberation, which would mean that it would take on a new and more significant character. It is not, then, that this dynamic consideration cannot but collapse without escape into functionalism, but that to get off the ground it turns to the fundamental theological place of faith and of theological reflection.

Both authors are looking for meaningfulness and for a meaningfulness for contemporary men and women. But in the first case meaningfulness primarily concerns an intellectual order and in the second case a real, historical order. What is, in the first case a meaningfulness of assertions, the weight of truth, is in the other a meaningfulness for real interests. What is in one case a meaningfulness primarily for intellectual elites who need formulations that can be appropriated for scientific and intellectual uses, is in the other case meaningfulness for the people of God who need to believe and to survive. It might seem in the latter case that by confusing preaching the faith and intellectual reflection, intellectual work ends up being cut back, which can certainly be a danger these days. But in principle there is no reason it has to turn out this way, since it is one thing to ask about the theological place where theological reflection begins, and in reference to which it continues; it is another thing to ask about the qualities that belong to this theoretical reflection as a labor of human intelligence so that faith shows its proper fullness.

Furthermore, a different conception of history is at play in each of these cases. History can be the critical attempt to keep in mind events of the past and to interpret them correctly, or it can be understood as reality itself in all of its dynamic fullness, which no one can get out of. From this second point of view, the historical method cannot be reduced to traversing historically something for which one is seeking its meaningfulness. Rather, historical method ought to be adequate to what history is: a real process encompassing all of human reality, personally and structurally considered. History is not primarily critical authenticity but a process of realization and, all things considered, a process of liberation. When one speaks of the turn to history, this turn could be understood as an appeal to the historical data, and then we are dealing with a merely methodological process, however necessary it be—and however necessary it ought thus to be considered. It would be to keep us from getting lost in fantasies or speculations. But it can also be understood as a turn to the structural totality of the real in its unitary process as the primary place of verification. That is why, in the case of Christological questions, the greatest dehistorification would arise from a historicization reduced to the reality of the historical Jesus itself, which would not be understood from the perspective of his concrete historical, personal and social action, and/or from a historicization, just as truncated, of contemporary Christian experience itself, understood outside of the conditioning factors that are proper to it.

Consequently, hermeneutics also takes on quite a distinct meaning and methodological reality. Faced with a problem of personal biography, which is not eliminated but subsumed into a concrete, social-historical framework, it proposes the problem of social interest as determining modes of thinking and living. This is why a historical hermeneutics comes to the fore, in contrast to a theoretical hermeneutics. Confronted with the concept of history as historical chronicle with its own hermeneutics, there is a concept of history as historical action, a real historical process with the historical and social hermeneutics that correspond to it. Without doubt, references to the historical Jesus involve hermeneutics. But we should not utilize a hermeneutics that is only or primarily an idealist hermeneutics of meaning, however experiential this meaning is. Rather, we should utilize a realist hermeneutics that takes into account what every action and interpretation owes to the actual conditions of a society and the social interests that sustain them. We should do this with regard to both the interpreted and the interpreter. This is not to exclude technical, methodological hermeneutics but to subordinate them to an approach to the hermeneutical labor that is more general and more profound.

The reference to the social sciences as an integral element of the theological labor is quite explicit in one model and is practically absent in the other. What mediation there is in the latter, philosophical in one way or another, is in the latter fundamentally a sociological mediation. The reason is clear. The one is mainly interested in meaning and the comprehension of meaning, while the other is mainly interested in the transformation of reality and, in this, the transformation of the person. The efforts for conversion and personal conversion that would be common to the two would be made in one primarily from an intellectualist position that believes in the profound change that can come from changing ideas or changing how the ideas are formulated. From the other, it would happen mainly from a realist position that believes that real changes in men and women, and of their ideas too, cannot happen unless the real conditions of their existence change.

As was mentioned at the beginning, we are not judging these models, but rather we are illuminating their different directional possibilities that present us with a specific issue: different models of theological reflection exist. Now, we have not studied the non-Latin American model in order to highlight its positive aspects, but to show how, as a counterexample, it functions as a call to attention. It is not simply accidental that some theologies cultivated in Latin America, along with their corresponding pastoral plans, end up in initiatives that should be abandoned and resumed, in their positive aspects, within a new way of doing theology whose presuppositions we now turn to examine.

The Problem of the Philosophical
Foundations of Latin American Theological Method

In this essay, we understand by method the fundamental, all-encompassing orientation with which and from which theological activity should be exercised. As we have already said, it can and should include a series of partial or instrumental methods—not only the methods proper to the study of scripture, the tradition, the magisterium, the history of theological thought, etc., but also all the rich array of instruments capable of furnishing specific scientific insights. We are not here inquiring into the concrete ways of proceeding in theological intellectual labor, whether the method should be transcendental, deductive, structuralist, dialectical, linguistic-analytical, etc. All of these methods can have their proper validity, provided they remain suitably free of ideology and placed at the service of fundamental method, whose suppositions we will try to describe and critically ground. We are interested here in the prior characterization of this fundamental method, understanding by "prior characterization" the analysis of those fundamental philosophical presuppositions on which theological activity should be based, which should serve to inspire this activity and to give it its criteria.

The principle for determining this fundamental method should be sought in the historical determination of what we should understand today by theology in Latin America. How should we understand theology in Latin America today is a theme that we have already addressed, at least schematically elsewhere.[4] If we were to try to treat theological method itself, we would have to engage a series of problems that were sketched out there and that we cannot even list here. Here we seek only to discuss the thematic of presuppositions philosophically. Using the model we have just exhibited, we have enough of a sense of the contents and theological attitudes of the Latin American model to allow us to go immediately to the problem of the philosophical presuppositions, which are not always sufficiently explicated and justified.

We do not take up here the general problem of method. We will only allude to those questions that directly affect the problem set by this essay. Theological activity has an essential moment of knowing, and this obliges us to be precise about what this cognitive moment is. It is certainly true that this cognitive moment cannot be separated absolutely from other moments that are not formally cognitive, but it does have its own autonomy. It is not simply a passive reflection; nor is it the mere reproduction of a reality already given to it or a response unmediated by the particular interests of certain fixedly defining structures. And it is this cognitive moment of theological method, with its own relative autonomy, that we will be attending to explicitly.

Here, too, we will proceed by way of contrast. We do so for the same reasons and with the same intention and measure with which we proceeded in the earlier part. Over and against a given model, which could well serve to give theoretical foundations to what was presented earlier as a non-Latin American scheme for doing theology, we will propose another model as a beginning from which to lay some philosophical foundations for Latin American theological method.

Some Philosophical Presuppositions of Theological Method that Should Be Superseded

We select as a contrast a recent book of Emerich Coreth's, which can represent the way that theoretical foundations are laid for a certain non-Latin American way of doing theology.[5] The book continues to circulate among Spanish-speaking readers and, together with other books by the same author, can be considered influential among us. We insist once again that our aim is not to attempt a global discussion of the ideas expressed in the book that we are reviewing. Rather, these ideas are taken only as a contrast in order to understand better certain theological positions that are not Latin American and in order to get closer to the way a Latin American theological method should be grounded. A general and global discussion regarding method would have to take into account other more explicit strategies.[6]

Coreth's book is dedicated to questions of hermeneutics, and among these, the question of the "hermeneutical circle" appears basic. Following Heidegger, all intellection reveals a "circular structure," "since it is only within a previously projected totality of meaning that 'something' be disclosed as 'something,' and all interpretation—as a recapitulation of intellection—moves in the field of prior intellection, and consequently, presupposes it as a condition of its possibility" (Coreth 1972, 37). Gadamer, for his part, insists on the historical character of all knowing and on the circularity proper to all historical knowing: knowing is conditioned by what was in its time historical comprehension and what, by so being, participates in our own history and in our comprehension of it. Humboldt had already insisted on this point of unity, relying on language as the bond of comprehension:

> Language *[lenguaje]* is the unity in opposition to the individual and subjective spirit, because while it is certainly true that each speaks his or her particular language *[idioma]*, he or she is, however, at the same time introduced by the particular language *[idioma]* into a linguistic *[idiomática]* community, and with this into the 'objective spirit' of an historical and cultural configuration of humanity. (Ibid., 43)

Finally, with respect to hermeneutical problems, he has a very specific position regarding issues that belong to so-called analytic philosophy that seeks "to determine the meaning of synthetic propositions" by means of their verification: "the meaning of a phrase is determined by the way it is verified, which ought to be done in experience. Further combination of meaningful phrases can only happen with logical relations that do not bring about any amplification of meaning" (ibid., 46–47).

Coreth confronts this entire problematic from his own position on the problem of knowledge. For him, intellection is a comprehension of meaning starting from what he takes to be the original form of understanding, which is human understanding—above all in dialogue (ibid.,

73)—although there are other forms of understanding, such as practical understanding, which consists in a well-informed doing and which opens up to the world of good deeds and obligations.

This intellection, understood as comprehension of meaning, has, in effect, a circular structure because it always presupposes a "world," "the totality of this world . . . in the sense of previous experience . . . forms the *a priori* that confronts each further experience. The horizon of this background and this continuity of meaning is the condition for our understanding in its meaning something which leaves us each time we encounter it" (ibid., 91). Horizon here signifies "a totality that is co-comprehended unthematically, or rather, is pre-understood, a totality which, conditioning it and determining it, enters into the knowledge (perception or intellection) of a singular content, which is disclosed from within this totality in a specific way" (ibid., 104). And so every singular content, whether it be a word, a thing, or an event, "is comprehended in the totality of the horizon of meaningfulness previously opened up" (ibid., 101). But it is not just a world that is empirically determined and transcendentally conditioned, "but rather . . . it is also a world that is historically molded and linguistically interpreted, a world, consequently, that is 'mediated' in multiple ways" (ibid., 134).

If we relate this problem to what theological knowledge is, then we will come face to face with the fact that

> in the conditioned what comes forth to encounter us is the unconditioned, in the relative the absolute is revealed. The human is open for the infinitude of being, but at the same time is tied to the full reality of his or her world and history. One element is not possible without the other. They are mutually conditioning and penetrating. This essential constitution of the human is integral to the event of salvation that God works in the world and history. (Ibid., 244)

Hence, by what is related to theological method, the hermeneutical task will entail all the following phases together: the search for the original meaning of the scriptural affirmation, its historical interpretation and the development of its meaning in the tradition of the Church's life and doctrine, and the way its significance for salvation is open to being understood by today's man or woman. These are distinct tasks, but they cannot be totally separated from one another.

The book develops these ideas further and expounds on others besides, but for our purposes, this summary is sufficient. These few lines sketch out the guiding philosophical presuppositions for all knowing, including theological knowing. The following can be indicated.

1. Intellection has a circular structure and it demands, therefore, a circular hermeneutics. We always understand from something and this "from something" is presupposed and implied, however much it is not totally independent with respect to that which is understood.
2. Intellection is primarily comprehension of meaning. It is, above all, comprehension and, moreover, that which is comprehended is the meaning of something, which means that intellection turns out to be reduplicatively theoretical and speculative.
3. That which yields both the "world" and its "horizon" is the background and continuity of meaning, even though it is not simply a meaning that is purely a priori, but one mediated in multiple ways.
4. That which is being sought in knowing, even in theological knowledge, is always a search for meaning, that is, something predominantly interpretative.

Against this conceptualization of the intellective task we must propose another that does justice to what the reality of human knowing is and to what theological labor tries to be. This is what we will attempt to do in the following section. We think that our conceptualization responds better to what the reality of human knowing is. It responds better to what in fact the theological thought of Latin America is trying to be.

Some Philosophical Presuppositions for a Correct Conceptualization of What Human Intellection Is with a View to Determining Latin American Theological Method

We will not attempt here to create and, even less, to ground a theory of intelligence. We will simply make a series of affirmations that appear to us to respond to what the reality of our intellective production is and should be, in such a way that if one fails to bear these affirmations in mind as one's fundamental hermeneutical criteria, all one's intellective labor ends up mystified from the very outset.

Human intelligence is not only essentially and permanently sensitive but is initially and fundamentally a biological activity. This affirmation does not try to say that intellective knowing is not differentiated from a purely sensorial exercise but only that it is always sentient and, above all, that it always performs a biological function.[7]

Human intelligence can only act from the senses and in reference to the senses, which are, above all, biological functions that primarily serve the subsistence of the living being. Even more, human intelligence is, in itself and formally, a biological activity, to the extent that its initial function, by virtue of which it arose, as well as its permanent exercise, is oriented toward giving biological viability to the human being, considered individually and as a species. Zubiri used to say that a species of idiots is not biologically viable, even though a species of superior animals without intelligence is perfectly viable. In the fundamental biological activity that is life, intelligence is a special instance of this activity, even though human life would never be reduced to a purely biological activity. Human intelligence has, without doubt, a structure proper to it by which the other notes of the human reality are differentiated. This "structure proper to it" permits a precise specialization, irreducible to what is proper to the human reality's other notes, in such a way that only intelligence apprehends intelligently *[la inteligencia inteligente],* and what the other notes do is something formally distinct from this intelligent apprehension. But what intelligence does, however formally irreducible it be, it does in primary unity with all the other notes of the human reality. Therefore, recognizing this "structure proper to it" does not mean attributing to it a complete substantiality and autonomy, for it is always conditioned and determined by the primary unity that the human constitutes as a living being. This total physical reality of the human is the primary reality whence the human apprehends intelligently *[inteligente],* knows *[conoce]* and understands *[entiende].* The first human utilized intelligence to keep on living, and this essential reference to life, from the perspective of the primary unity that the human constitutes as a living being, is the primary "what for" of intelligence and, correctly understood, also the primary purpose of all intelligent apprehension: in order that they might have life and have it more abundantly, we might say, if allowed to use a secularized version of the formula so essential to the Christian faith.

It would appear that this sensorial character of human knowing is recognized by many philosophies, among them the so-called realist philosophies. But a prior recognition is not enough. It is necessary to be consistent with this recognition. For in none of the exercises of the intelligence, not even in those pretentiously called "the highest," does there cease being present and operative this sensorial character and biological orientation toward the active maintenance of human life and its improvement. Never toward its negation. The realist philosophies are not always able to be consistent with the essential material dimension of human knowing, or with its necessary praxical character, precisely because they disregard the vital roots of all human activity.

The formal structure and differentiating function of intelligence, within the structural context of human notes and of the permanently biological character of the human unity, is not a structure of comprehending being or capturing meaning, but rather the structure of apprehending reality and engaging it [en-frentarse con ella— *"confronting oneself with it"].* The comprehension of meaning is one of intelligence's activities, one without which it does not give of itself *[da de sí]* all that it is and all that the human needs from it. But it [comprehension of meaning] does not happen *[no se da]* in every act of intelligent apprehension, and when it does happen, it can serve to evade contemplatively and to negate in practice that which is the formal condition of human intelligence. In relation to its primary reference to life, the specific and formal aspect of intelligence is to bring the human being to confront his or her very self and to confront all other things insofar as they are real things that can have this or that meaning for a person only by virtue of their essential respectivity *[respectividad]* with the human.

Engaging real things in their reality has a three-fold dimension: *becoming aware of the weight of reality [el hacerse cargo de la realidad]*, which entails being present in the reality of things (and not merely being present before the idea of things or being in touch with their meaning), being "real" in the reality of things, which in its active character of being is exactly the opposite of being thing-like and inert and implies being among them through their material and active mediations; *shouldering the weight of reality [el cargar con la realidad]*, an expression that points to the fundamentally ethical character of intelligence, which has not been given to us so that we could evade our real commitments, but rather to take upon ourselves what things really are and what they really demand; *taking charge of the weight of reality [el encargarse de la realidad]*, an expression that points to the praxical character of intelligence, which only fulfills its function, including its character of knowing reality and comprehending its meaning, when it assumes as its burden doing something real.

Precisely because of this priority of reality over meaning, no real change of meaning occurs without a real change of reality. To intend to do the former without attempting the latter falsifies intelligence and its primary function, even in the purely cognitive order. To believe that by changing one's interpretations of things, one has changed the things themselves or at least one's depth consciousness of his or her embeddedness in the world, represents a grave epistemological error and a profound ethical breakdown. Interpretative changes of meaning and even the purely objective analyses of a reality in its social-historical features do not constitute real changes. They are not even real changes of their proper meaning but most of the time changes in their formulations. This does not prevent intelligence from having an irreplaceable function as the theoretical potency for the changes that ought to occur in historical reality in the technical order and in the ethical order.

The question of meaning only has real relevance from the perspective offered by engaging reality and confining oneself *[atenimiento]* to reality. What matters is the meaning of reality, but it matters because humans also really need to raise the question of the meaning of things. But this real need for meaning together with this need for real meaning are inscribed in the dimension of reality. Consequently, when the interpretation of intellection as the comprehension of meaning is being debated, the debate is not about whether the human being and human intelligence should raise the question of meaning. It is only about the radicality of the way this is being posed.

Human intelligence not only is always historical, but this historicity pertains to the essential structure of intelligence itself. The historical character of knowing *qua* activity involves a precise historical character of the cognitive contents themselves. This fundamentally historical character of the intelligence and of knowing is increasingly recognized, at least verbally, but what is understood by history is in many cases something substantially different. Here we will only point to three aspects of this historicity because they are especially important for determining the characteristics of theological method.

1. The activity of human intelligence, even in its purely interpretative dimension—even more in its character of projection and praxis—is conditioned by the historical world in which it finds itself. Intelligence, in effect, depends in each case upon specific theoretical possibilities[8] that are constituted as a result of a historical journey and represent the substratum from which it thinks. It was not possible, for example, to lay the foundations of

the theory of relativity except from certain specific theoretical possibilities proportionate to the real history of mathematics and physics. Likewise, particular readings of the faith are not really possible except from very precise historical determinations that make possible, really possible, concrete situations and diverse historical mediations. Even more importantly, intelligence has— even in the most theoretical cases—a moment of option conditioned by a multitude of elements that are not purely theoretical but that depend very precisely on biographical and historical conditions. Consequently, hermeneutics, even as a search for meaning, cannot be reduced to a search for what has been objectified in theoretical formulations, as if these, by themselves, give rise to the final and complete meaning of the formulations. Rather, there has to be an ongoing and thematically focused investigation into the social world to which these formulations respond, since not even a purely theoretical formulation is fully explained only from itself. Turning to an example of a classical model of theoretical and aprioristic formulation, it is interesting to note what Max Scheler wrote about Kantian ethics:

> It can be demonstrated by historical and psychological routes that what Kant believed authorized him to inquire into pure reason itself, with a general validity for all persons, was simply the rooting of the *ethos*, rigidly delimited both ethnically and historically, of the People and the State in one specific epoch in the history of Prussia (which does not take anything away from the greatness and excellence of that *ethos*).[9]

2. Human knowing, as an objective and social function—above all in disciplines such as theology, which make explicit reference to human realities—performs, together with its contemplative and interpretative function, a praxical function that comes from and returns to the configuring of a specific social structure. This does not mean denying a proper rule and a certain autonomy to knowing, not even to the particular ways of knowing such as intellectual activity. It only entails affirming that this rule and autonomy respond to something that is a structural moment of a historical totality, socially conditioned by specific interests and, more generally, by specific social forces. The configuration of these social forces demands and

re-creates a specific intellectual production, as a function of the predominant interests, of whatever kind, and not exclusively socio-economic ones, although it ought not to be understood necessarily as their automatic reflection.

Human knowing thus has a strictly social dimension not only by virtue of its origin but also of its destination. What this requires, therefore, in order that it not fall into obscurantist ideologizations, is that it hermeneutics be extended into critical analysis and, when necessary, the unmasking of the social origins and social destinations of every act of knowing. That this has to be done in terms of individual persons, both in its creative phase and its phase of being received, so that they not be reduced to being numerical instances of a presumed macro-I, does not deny the social character of knowing, the social dimension that accompanies every other human activity.

3. Human knowing also has an immediate reference to praxis, even as a condition of its own scientific nature. On the one hand, it is itself a praxis and one of the essential moments of every possible praxis. If praxis is not to end up being a pure reaction, that is, in order that it be precisely a human praxis, it needs an active moment of intelligence as an essential element of its own. But, on the other hand, human knowing, according to its type and with this or that object, needs praxis not only for its scientific verification but also so as to put itself in touch with the source of many of its contents. If we attend to the necessarily dynamic character of the known reality itself and of the reality that we are in, then the necessary reference to reality as a principle and foundation of every realistic activity takes on a special character. But this dynamic character is not, to put it thus, purely intentional and idealistic. Neither is it purely passive and receptive. It is necessary to be in reality actively, and the knowing achieved therein should be measured and verified by a presence in reality that is just as active. What is valid for the general problem of theory and technique, is also, with its own characteristics, a problem for all knowing and, of course, for disciplines like theology that are related to a faith that seeks to be life itself for human beings. This active dimension of knowledge is not purely praxic, as Aristotle wanted, but has to be strictly *poesis*-based, in the sense that it has to objectify itself in exterior realities beyond the active immanence of one's own interiority and subjective intentionality.

Critical Determinants of Latin American Theological Method

Drawing upon the previous sections, in this section I succinctly outline certain determinants without which Latin American theological activity would not be critical and would not respond to what it is fair to demand of it.

Every human activity and every sphere of reality has its proper scientific nature and critically requires its own method, which should comply with the structure of that activity and that sphere. The activity itself should be accommodated to the demands of the sphere of reality toward which it is directed. By "sphere of reality" we do not understand here an object or a series of objects, but the concrete, historical totality that a particular activity engages *[enfrentrarse con]*. There is a mutual determining between activity and sphere of reality. Only from specific modes of activity do we reach certain spheres of reality, and only facing specific spheres of reality is it possible to exercise certain modes of activity. The things of God, for example, just as they are given in the human and are presented to the human, presuppose a precise attitude and activity without which it is impossible to grasp them. On the other hand, certain dimensions of the human are not actualized, much less realized in their fullness, if they are not exercised facing the presence and incarnation of the divine.

As far as its own activity goes, and the sphere of reality to which it is directed, Latin American theological method should keep this specificity of its own activity very much in mind.

With regard to what concerns its sphere of reality, it should be noted that the sphere itself is not simply God, but God just as God makes God-self present in the historical situation itself. Here and now the problem for faith and consequently for theology is one that has clearly marked features. It does not depend principally on the will of the ecclesiastical hierarchy, or on the pretensions of theologians, but on what the concrete reality of the people of God is. God's salvation and the salvific mission of the church and of faith concretize their universality here and now in very precise forms. The theologian will have to investigate this, reflecting in a first moment on the signs in which are revealed and concealed the salvific presence of God in a Jesus who continues becoming flesh throughout history.

As far as its activity goes, it is important to emphasize that when we are talking about theology, we are not dealing with a pure science. We cannot begin as if we already had a univocal definition of science to count on in order then to accommodate theological activity to that definition and theological discourse to what previously and generally had been established to be scientific. We should start by determining the sphere of reality, determining what theological activity should pursue, and determining the critical conditions necessary for theological activity to achieve its concrete ends. In our case, it is necessary to decide what we mean by Latin American theology, for herein lies the fundamental presupposition for what Latin American theological method ought to be. It is also necessary to determine what, for Latin Americans in their present situation, is the historical way of living the faith and perceiving their own reality. Finally, it is necessary to determine what is expected or what could be expected of theology in Latin America so that the continent lives its own style of faith in relation to its own historical situation, and so that it works for this historical situation from an adequate way of living its faith.

In the case of both the sphere and the activity, it is necessary to stick closely to the reality of that faith by means of acute and critical attention to popular religiosity. Popular religiosity is not simply the faith of the people. Even less is it a certain popularized form of theology. But this does not mean that we should ignore it as a theological place of inspiration and verification. Political approaches, and theological ones too, are not always free of elitism, even though there is always all this talk about the people. As Latin American theologians and believers, we will have to ask ourselves, as contrasted with an academic cult of meaning that looks to be recognized by academic elites, whether we are championing a political cult of meaning that looks to be recognized by revolutionary elites. Faith and faith reflection need to be alert so as not to fall into the same false worldliness by a different path.

Theological activity has a strictly social nature. If it is not assimilated critically, this nature can lead to grave theological deviations. We spoke earlier of the social nature of all knowing, but this social nature is augmented in the case of theological activity and, consequently, in the case of theological knowing.

There are at least three reasons for reflecting upon the social nature of theological activity and for taking note of what it would mean not to bear that social nature in mind.

1. Theological activity is conditioned by, and at the service of, not just "faith" but also of an ecclesial institution that, as institution, is deeply configured by the sociohistorical structure in which it is found. With respect to this ecclesial institution, theological

activity takes on a specific social character in configuring the institution at the same time as it is configured by that institution. Moreover, through the institution that it serves, it ends up either favoring or resisting certain social forces.

2. Besides being subject to multiple pressures in the social order that, if they are not unmasked will end up mystifying its results, theological activity has no choice but to make use of theoretical resources that may be the result of more or less overt ideological process. This is true both in the theoretical order and in the praxical order where theological thought gets utilized.

3. Theological activity is especially historical, not only because of the very nature that belongs to it, but because of the sphere of reality to which it responds: hence it has a reduplicated optive character. This comes not just from a set of individual options but also from something formally social.

The question then of the "what for" and the "for whom" of theology, which is summarized in the question of whom what we do is serving and what purpose what we do in fact serves, has to be front and center in order to determine what theological activity ought to be in its themes, in the way it considers them, and in the way it presents them. This question should not be confused with or mitigated by the question of who in fact receives theology or to whom theology has to reach out so that they can receive it. The reason is that this would presuppose that theology is of itself an elitist endeavor and that the only thing that could be required of it would be to put itself broadly within everyone's reach. The question is more radical: Be it this or that person who receives what theology has to offer, the important thing is to determine who in fact is being served by the transmission and the contents of this transmission. And determining this ought to happen from the perspective of faith and of the critique of theology itself. To approach the problem this way is not to ask that theological activity cease to have intellectual standing, as if it would not need an immense exertion of purely intellectual activity. The only thing that is being required is that we ask what type of intelligence and what manner of intellectual work is proper to a theological activity that is truly Christian and truly Latin American. We also have to be absolutely clear—and this is in itself a serious theological problem—about who the people of God is here and now, and why it is, and to be clear about how to read in it the revelatory presence of God.[10]

The circularity to which Latin American theological method ought to attend primarily is a circularity that is real, historical, and social. In accordance with what was noted earlier about the character proper to intelligence and about the reduplicative social character of theological activity, it is necessary to talk about a primary circularity. The fundamental circularity, which happens even in human knowing—not to mention other dimensions of human activity—is not the circularity of a theoretical horizon and some theoretical contents that are understood against that horizon and partly reconfigure that horizon. Rather, if there is real transformation of concrete realities, we are talking about the circularity of a historical-practical horizon and some structural, sociohistorical realities that flow from that horizon and also reconfigure it.

There is no pure circularity between a theoretical horizon and the comprehension of the meaning of some specific thing. The circularity is physical: it is physical in the point at which all comprehension and all activity starts, and it is physical in the movement by which the concrete determining factors are constituted. Therefore, before one asks about the theoretical horizon—however experiential it be—of one's comprehension and one's choosing, the important thing is to ask about the real horizon against which any type of human function whatsoever is exercised. This might appear to ignore the character of horizon itself. But it really points out the fact that "horizon," in its technical sense, is not explained simply in its own terms as the result of some purely transcendental openness, but that it, in turn, is preconditioned by a series of elements, running from properly biological structures to the ultimate sociopolitical determinants, with a large range of other kinds of determinants in between.

As a consequence, hermeneutics ought to be a hermeneutics that is real and that is historical because what it is trying to get some critical grasp on is not *what* a specific theoretical meaning is, but rather *how* a specific meaning has been able to come to the fore from a particular physical *whence*. This is what really matters when it comes to a fundamental method, although after that more theoretical and technical steps are necessary in the process of breaking down the total horizon into more partial horizons.

Among the other issues to which a Latin American theological method ought to attend is the analysis of its own language. Once again, this should not be purely a research in linguistic analysis, as if we were dealing exclusively or fundamentally with a problem in theoretical meaning or of intentional signification. Rather, it should be an investigation of what the terms utilized discover or cover over. It is not for nothing that Aristotelian language has brought faith's intellection down roads that today seem partial and debatable; for the same reason, it is worth asking today whether Marxist language cannot lead us into similar equivocations if it is not used critically. That theological reflection always has to make use of a specific recognized and operative language seems to be a necessity. The important thing, then, is to interrogate this necessity and this from two perspectives: taking care that the language we use does not distort the fullness and purity of the faith, and taking care that theology does not turn into a sacralized version of some secular discourse.

To transform the world in a Christian way, we need mediations that are both theoretical and praxic. Theology is not a pure reflection on faith itself—something that cannot be maintained without forgetting that faith itself is no longer pure faith. Neither can Christian activity be carried out in this world without operative helps. But these mediations cannot end up being absolute guides, either in faith as a whole or in Christian praxis. If the mediation is absolutized, it becomes an idol and as a consequence turns into the negation of that for which it had intended to be a relatively adequate mediation. This use of mediations is something that cannot be brought off without tensions both in the realm of theory as well as in the realm of praxis: those who accuse Latin American theology and specific Latin American movements of being "Marxicized" take as their starting point the false supposition that their theology and its praxis have not been co-opted. But those who do not grasp the degree to which the Marxist theoretical-praxical framework can be a mediation—and an ambiguous mediation, at least insofar as it is a partializing mediation—are co-opting in turn the faith and praxis of the people of God. And co-opting (*mediatizar*) is not the same thing as mediating (*mediar*).

It is not possible to do theology today ignoring Marxist theory. And this is the case not only for Marxism as a critical principle but as an illuminating principle. The whole campaign, within and outside the church, to theologize and act on the fringes of Marxism's core insights is a myopic campaign and most of the time a partisan one, consciously or no. But the exaggerated actions of a few cannot lead to exaggerations on the part of others. A critical reading of the Christian fact from a Marxist perspective ought to go hand in hand with a critical reading of Marxist interpretation and action carried out from the perspective offered by the most authentic Christian faith. Faith and theological reflection cannot be cast purely in a Marxist mold, however much they ought to respond to the challenge posed by Marxism when it comes to interpreting and transforming humanity and society.

We have insisted on this point not because Marxism is the only or the most serious way that the strength and the integrity of faith can be endangered. But when it comes to Latin American theological method, Marxism can help a people who are on the way take their bearings on reality; it can help a great deal in orienting that work in which salvation has to be historicized. This notwithstanding, there is no need to be naive about the consequences for faith that can follow from its indiscriminate use and, above all, from the absolutization of its use. Precisely because of the service it can render, precisely because it has to be taken very seriously, it ought to be subject to an ongoing critique that shows its limitations. And this is true for its method, since methods are not divorced from contents or from the fundamental dynamism of thought and of action, whose epistemological canons it is the task of a fundamental method to express.

To conclude, there are four conditioning factors which Latin American theological method ignores at its peril: the specificity proper to theological method, the social character of theological activity, the primordial circularity of theological reflection, and the critical analysis of its own language. With them the philosophical foundations for theological method will be adequately laid. What a fundamental theology whose foundations have been laid in this way ought to look like in operation can be left an open question here. Indeed, laying philosophical foundations represents nothing more than a first step, however indispensable, in the search for an adequate theological method. The examples adduced in the first part show how important different philosophical bases can be; the difference is not due so much to the philosophical bases, dealt with more or less explicitly. It is due more to a specific way of living the faith and of living out the charge of being a theologian. But revising philosophical assumptions means revising the foundations of this specific way of living out the faith and the office of theologian. And I think that if we start from the foundations that have been analyzed here, then we can structure a method that is faithful to the demands of theology and to the needs of a large part of the people of God who are setting off in search of their full salvation.

Notes

* The original reads, *el rechazo de las uvas que estaban verdes porque no eran alcanzables.*—Ed.

[1] For a representative sample of the many works dedicated to the problem of Latin American theological method, see the bibliography in this essay.

[2] Held in Mexico, August 11–15, 1975, the *Encuentro* was dedicated to the theme: "methods of theological reflection in Latin America and their pastoral implications for in the present and the past." This essay was prepared for that *Encuentro*. The publication of the

proceedings and communiques will give evidence of continued interest in determining what Latin American theological method is.

³ Leonardo Boff, "Libertação de Jesus Cristo pelo caminho da opressão. Uma leitura latino-americana," and Olegario González de Cardedal, "Un problema teológico fundamental: la preexistencia de Cristo. Historia y Hermenéutica," in *Teología y mundo contemporáneo: Homenaje a Karl Rahner en su 70 cumpleaños* (Madrid: Ediciones Cristiandad, 1975), 241–68, 179–211. [Citations to both articles will appear in the text.—Ed.]

⁴ Ignacio Ellacuría, "Tesis sobre posibilidad, necesidad y sentido de una teología latinoamericana," in *Teología y mundo contemporáneo,* 325–50.

⁵ Emile Coreth, *Cuestiones fundamentales de hermenéutica* (Barcelona: Ed. Herder, 1972). [Citations to Coreth's work will appear in the text—Ed.]

⁶ For example, those of Bernard Lonergan.

⁷ All of these moves owe much to the thought of Zubiri, although they entail a reelaboration in order to resolve problems posed in the reality of Latin America. For this reason, my development here does not attempt to repeat exactly the explicit thought of Zubiri, although his inspiration is very much present in this development, as well as, I would like to think, many of his better potentialities.

⁸ Here we understand the concept of "possibility" in a strictly Zubirian sense. It has nothing to do with classical philosophy. See Xavier Zubiri, "La dimensión histórica del ser humano," *Realitas* 1 (1974): 11–69. I treat at length the concept of history, of historical reality, in a book soon to be published.

⁹ See Max Scheler, *Etica,* vol. 1 (Madrid: Revista de Occidente, 1941), 10.

¹⁰ On this theme, see Juan Luís Segundo, *Liberación de la teología* (Buenos Aires: Carlos Lohle, 1975), 207–66.

Bibliography

Alonso, Juan. "La teología de la praxis y la praxis de la teología." *Christus* 444 (1972): 228–41.

———. "Una nueva forma de hacer teología." In *Iglesia y praxis de liberación.* Salamanca, Spain: Ediciones Sígueme,1974.

Assmann, Hugo. "Teología política." *Perspectivas de diálogo* 50 (1970): 306–12.

———. *Teología desde la praxis de la liberación.* Salamanca, Spain: Sigueme 1973.

———. *Theology for a Nomad Church.* Maryknoll, NY: Orbis Books, 1976.

Bravo, Carlos. "Notas marginales a la teología de la liberación." *Ecclesiastica Xareriana* 24 (1974): 3–60.

Comblin José. "El tema de la liberación." "El pensamiento Cristiano Latinoamericano." *Pastoral Popular* 1134 (1973): 46–63.

———. *Théologie de la pratique révolutionnaire.* París: Éditions Universitaires, 1974.

Dussel, Enrique. *Caminos de la liberación Latinoamericana.* Buenos Aires: Latinoamérica Libros, 1972.

———. *Método para una filosofía de la liberación. Superación analéctica de la dialéctica hegeliana.* Salamanca, Spain: Ediciones Sígueme, 1974.

———. *Para una ética de la liberación Latinoamericana.* Buenos Aires: Siglo Veintiuno Argentina Editores, 1973–74, vols. 1–2.

Ellacuría, Ignacio. "Tesis sobre posibilidad, necesidad y sentido de una teología latinoamericana." In *Teología y mundo contemporáneo: Homenaje a Karl Rahner,*325–50. Madrid: Cristiandad, 1975.

Facelina, Raul. *Liberation and Salvation*; also published as *Libération et Salut*. Strasbourg: Bibliographie Internationale, 1973.

Gera, L. "Cultura y dependencia a la luz de la reflexión teológica." *Stromata* 30 (1974): 169–227.

Gutiérrez, Gustavo. *Teología de la liberación*. Salamanca, Spain: Ediciones Sígueme, 1972.

———. *A Theology of Liberation*. Maryknoll, NY: Orbis Books. 1973.

Malley, F. *Libération, Mouvements, analyses, recherches, théologies: Essai bibliographique*. París: Centre L.-J. Lebret, 1974.

Richard, Pablo. "Racionalidad socialista y verificación histórica del cristianismo." *Cuadernos de la realidad nacional* 12 (April 1972): 144–53.

Scannone, Juan Carlos. "El lenguaje teológico de la liberación." *Víspera* 7 (1973): 41–47.

———. "Teología y Política. El actual desafío planteado por el lenguaje teológico de la liberación." In *Fe cristiana y cambio social en América Latina*, ed. María Agudelo, 247–64. Salamanca: Ediciones Sígueme, 1973.

———. "Transcendencia, praxis liberadora y lenguaje. Hacia una filosofía de la religión postmoderna y Latinoamericana situada." *Nuevo Mundo* 1 (1973): 221–45.

Schooyans, M. "Théologie et libération: Quelle liberation?" *Revue Theologique de Louvain*, 6 (1975): 165–73.

Segundo, Juan Luís. *Liberación de la teología*. Buenos Aires: Ediciones Carlos Lohlé, 1975.

———. *The Liberation of Theology*. Maryknoll, NY: Orbis Books, 1976.

Van Nieuwenhove, Jacques. "Les théologies de la libération Latina Américaines." In *Le Point théologique, no. 10 : Théologies de la Libération en Amérique Latine*, 67–104. Paris: Editions Beauchesne, 1974.

Varios. *Pueblo oprimido, senor de la historia*. Montevideo: Tierra Nueva, 1972.

Varios. *Hacia una filosofía de la liberación Latinoamericana*. Buenos Aires: Editorial Bonum, 1973.

Varios. *Fe cristiana y cambio social en América Latina*. Salamanca, Spain: Ediciones Sígueme, 1973.

Varios. *Liberación: diálogos en el CELAM*, Bogotá: Secretariado General del Celam, 1974.

Vekemans, R. "Antecedentes para el estudio de la 'teología de la liberación': Comentario bibliográfico." *Tierra Nueva* 1 (1972): 5–23.

Vidales, Raul. "Cuestiones en torno al método de la teología de la liberación." In *Servicio de Documentación MIEC-JECI*. Lima: MIEC-JECI, Secretariado Latinoamericano, 1974.

—Translated by J. Matthew Ashley and Kevin F. Burke, SJ

4

The Liberating Function
of Philosophy
(1985)

Ignacio Ellacuría wrote "The Liberating Function of Philosophy" in 1985, the year the UCA celebrated the twentieth anniversary of its existence and granted a posthumous honorary doctorate to Archbishop Oscar Romero to memorialize the fifth anniversary of his martyrdom. He devoted the majority of his publications that year to the political and economic situation of El Salvador five years into the disastrous civil war. Yet, ever cognizant of the university's unique role in the midst of the national crisis, he took time to develop his philosophy of liberation, knowing that such intellectual labor was crucial to the mission of a university committed to engaging reality and promoting peace with justice. Additionally, Ellacuría's aim in writing this essay appears related to his role in the Latin America academy. Instrumental in founding a colloquium of Jesuit philosophers, he felt acutely the need to complement the society's commitment to liberating praxis with the development of a distinctly Latin American philosophy capable of limning the critical and creative dimensions of that praxis.

Ellacuría introduces this essay with two observations that further explain his motivation for writing it. Against the backdrop of the philosophical importance of the themes of liberation and freedom, he notes that (1) the majority of the people living in Latin America live in conditions of extreme poverty and repression; and (2) Latin America has never produced a philosophy of its own, one that grows out of its own reality and exercises a liberating function on its reality. He seeks to make a theoretical contribution to redressing the first point by producing a philosophy that is "really effective in liberating, not just a small enlightened elite, but the whole culture and all the social structures within which people must attain self-realization freely." Written one year after the Vatican Congregation for the Doctrine of the Faith issued its highly critical "Instruction on Certain Aspects of the 'Theology of Liberation,'" this essay represents one of several that Ellacuría penned in the mid-1980s that, taken together, form a carefully considered response to the "Instruction." (See "Estudio teológico-pastoral de la 'Instrucción sobre algunos aspectos de la teología de la liberación,'" Revista Latinoamericana de Teología 2 (1984): 145–78; see also chapters 2 and 6 of the present volume.) Mindful of the importance of establishing the "metaphysical substance" of the theme of liberation and, at the same time, of developing an approach to "Catholic philosophy" rooted in historical realism, Ellacuría concludes this essay with attention to these two points.

We can say that philosophy has always had to do with freedom, though in different ways. It has been assumed that philosophy is the task of free individuals and free peoples, free at least of the basic needs that can suppress the kind of thinking we call philosophy. We also acknowledge that it has a liberating function for those who philosophize and that as the supreme exercise of reason, it has liberated peoples from obscurantism, ignorance, and falsehood. Throughout the centuries, from the pre-Socratics to the Enlightenment, through all methods of *critical* thinking, we have ascribed a great superiority to reason, and to philosophical reason in particular, as a result of its liberating function.

Reason has also been used in pseudo-philosophical ways to suppress differing opinions or to maintain a specific established order; that is, philosophy has also played—especially, but not exclusively by its mediocre practitioners—a dogmatic and even tyrannical role that has blocked the free exchange of ideas and, even worse, the free self-determination of individuals and peoples. There are those that claim that philosophy only mirrors the institutional order and economic infrastructure, having only a relative autonomy and a minor reactive capacity with respect to that order. However that may be, this matter of *philosophy* and *freedom* gets to the fundamental purpose of philosophical knowledge, which even if it is understood as a search for truth, cannot be reduced to being a search for truth for its own sake. Such classical ideas as the relationship between truth and freedom (John 8:32), or between interpretation and the transformation of reality (Marx, Thesis 11 on Feuerbach), are an eloquent refutation of that reductionism.

But this essay does not approach the contribution of philosophy to freedom out of a purely speculative concern; it has a practical purpose. It is a double purpose, or rather a single purpose with two aspects, one subordinate to the other. This practical purpose in turn begins with a double observation: the Latin American continent—and other regions—live in conditions of structural oppression and even repression, especially where the popular majorities are concerned. This is partly due, perhaps not to specific philosophies as such, but to ideological presentations or manifestations of those philosophies, and/or of the socioeconomic and political realities from which they grow and which are their principal concerns. Naturally, that oppression-repression is not fundamentally ideological but real, but it has diverse ideological elements as one of its justifications and even active causes. The second observation is that the Latin American continent has not produced a philosophy of its own, growing out of its own reality and exercising a liberating function on that reality. That is all the more surprising because Latin America can be said to have produced a theology, a certain socioeconomic system, and of course a powerful artistic expression of its own, especially in the realms of poetry, novels, and the plastic arts. We should also note that these fields have achieved a recognized universality, which cannot be said of Latin American philosophies, even when they have tried to be nationalistic, indigenous, autochthonous, etc.

This double observation gives shape to the double tasks of this essay. Why not produce a Latin American philosophy, which, if it is truly both Latin American and philosophy, would become a universal theoretical-practical contribution and would also exercise a liberating function, together with other theoretical and practical efforts, on behalf of the popular majorities who are living in a secular state of oppression-repression? The principal feature of this task would certainly be the liberation of those majorities, because that should be the main goal and to some extent the fundamental horizon of philosophy. However, also closely linked to this would be the constitution of a new philosophy—there have been and continue to be so many attempts—that could really be called Latin American, if it were thought out from and for the Latin American reality and at the service of the popular majorities who define that reality, because they are so numerous and they possess the capacity to qualify that reality.

In this essay, therefore, I shall try to define the liberating function that corresponds to philosophy here and now, if without ceasing to be philosophy—but rather, renewing itself as philosophy—it is to be really effective in liberating, not just a small enlightened elite, but the whole culture and all the social structures within which people must attain self-realization freely. I am not thinking of a popularized philosophy, which the masses could accept directly as their own liberating ideology. This can and should happen in some way, but in order for it to avoid being mimetic and dogmatic, that ideology requires a strict and demanding intellectual collaboration in which the popular majorities and their historical praxes are its subjects and objects without participating in the particular and technical task of philosophizing. This does not mean leaving the popular majorities out, even in the philosophical task, but it does shape the way they participate in it.

The Critical and Creative Function of Philosophy

The best philosophy has never been, and given its specific purpose never could be, merely a more or less autonomous reflection of the existing socioeconomic structure and the ideology that expresses it. Philosophy can criticize and it can create; it has a critical and creative capacity. Obviously these are two powerful factors of liberation, not only internally or subjectively, but also objectively and structurally, though in a lesser and complementary way.

The Critical Function of Philosophy

The critical function of philosophy is directed primarily toward the dominant ideology, as a structural element of a social system, but also toward other elements of the same social structure (e.g., economic, political, and social arrangements, etc.). However, this critical function directly confronts ideological aspects of the social structure, acknowledging that the ideological can be driven not only by all sorts of theoretical mechanisms but also by a series of objectifications and social relationships. Thus, the critical function of philosophy is largely defined in relationship to the phenomenon of ideology.

Here we shall not establish a philosophical definition and evaluation of ideologies—which is itself an important theme for philosophy, and especially for a Latin American philosophy—but a few words on this topic are needed in order to focus more clearly on the critical function of philosophy.

We can say first that although ideology is an ambiguous phenomenon, it is both necessary and important in determining social, community, and personal life. It is ambiguous because it carries with it positive, negative, and neutral elements. There is clearly a pejorative meaning of ideology, understood as concealing the social reality, but even in that pejorative sense we can see the importance and inherent character of the ideological to a social reality. It is not enough to say that ideology exists because a particular social class or ruling estate must impose or maintain whatever social power it has. We must ask why that imposition is carried out on the ideological plane. Again, it is not enough to answer that ideology takes the place of other, more crudely repressive activities, which can elicit both a more violent response from the repressed and oppressed, and a guilty conscience in the repressors and oppressors. We must explore the question more deeply, in order to explain why people need theoretical explanations and justifications, and why those explanations and justifications have to carry the appearance of truth and goodness. We can say that this very appeal to truth and goodness is the result of a cultural process that is itself ideologized. But that explanation has not been proven, and it would only explain the ways in which truth and goodness are presented, rather than explain the historical tendency (that is considered correct, at least when made theoretically explicit) to choose good over evil, truth over falsehood or error. The stubborn persistence of ideological elements not only requires explanation; it demonstrates a certain historical necessity of the ideological element itself, whether in more elaborate intellectual forms or in the less sophisticated forms of preaching and propaganda. Certainly people would not turn to ideology, including its negative aspects, if it did not serve a useful and even necessary purpose. They would not turn to ideology, if it did not have at least the appearance—and in that sense some reality as well—of something positive, behind which so much deformed and deforming reality is often concealed. There will always be ideology in its negative sense; that is why theoretical work is needed to combat it by unmasking and shedding light on it.

But there is also a nonpejorative meaning to ideology, especially in areas where strictly logical-scientific thinking is impossible; this happens with respect to some areas of reality, some totalizing and globalizing interpretations, and some extremely important human attitudes and behaviors. Even if we concede—and we do so here for practical reasons—that non-ideological, scientific knowledge is possible in some areas, those areas do not exhaust the whole of the reality with which people must wrestle in a human way. Those areas may even be less important than others where strictly scientific thinking does not and cannot reach. If we set aside, because of their specific epistemological situation, the so-called natural sciences and related fields, or the purely formal sciences, and focus on the sciences of humanity, society and history, we find something very interesting. The so-called positivists try to avoid what they call "value judgments" in their explanations. This may not be possible in a strict sense because they must still explain why it is better to avoid value judgments, but without carrying the paradox too far, in that very affirmation they are claiming to leave out everything that has to do with value. This leads to the conclusion that anything related to value is not an object of science, although hardly anyone will dare to say that anything related to value has no being or seriousness, and that we can think whatever we want about it without need for a rational basis. If that is so, we will need to draw on processes of reason, or at least in the scope of the rational, even though they do not meet the strict conditions to be called scientific.

Is it appropriate or useful to describe these rational processes as ideological? Is there enough difference between science and ideology, so that any exercise of reason fits entirely into one or the other category? Some people may think so, and in some sense the question involves something of a terminological dispute. In the end, we can establish three types of rational explanation: (1) one that has to do with common sense, with good sense, with life experience, with natural logic, with popular wisdom, etc.; (2) one that has to do with a critical exercise of reason that makes explicit its presuppositions, method, proofs, degree of certainty, consequences, systematization, etc.; and (3) one that fits the mold of the natural sciences with their standards of observation and even of mathematization. In relation to these three, we can say that each allows for the ideological factor (analyze Zubiri's last work on intelligence to confirm the number and importance of the moments of freedom that appear in the very structure of human understanding), but we can also say that this ideological factor, when it is used reasonably and to differing degrees in each case, can act as a principle of complementarity and even progress rather than a principle of distortion.

Ideologies can have a nonpejorative, necessary meaning if we understand ideologies as a coherent, comprehensive and evaluative explanation through concepts, symbols, images, references, etc., which goes beyond simple, fragmented observation, both in narrow areas and especially in more general and even all-embracing areas. This means that ideology plays, not only a substitutive and/or merely preparatory role vis-à-vis what might be a nonideological and/or scientific way of thinking, but that in some way it is always present and effective, not only for those who have not reached a scientific level (which of course means most of humanity, at least in a wide range of profoundly human aspects), but also for those who are considered scientists with respect to their own scientific field. While this may be evident in the first case, it is also clear in the second because even when more or less verifiable scientific theories lead to some certainty—we never know the one or complete reason for anything, because the reason we discover can be replaced by or subsumed under some other reason (Zubiri)—there is still the problem of value and of the meaning about which purely scientific thinking has little to say but that still remains as a substantive problem.

Nevertheless, we cannot deny that there is a factor of ideologization in ideologies and especially in those that can be considered scientific thinking. Of course, in some extreme cases it is no longer ideology but simple, premeditated deception, a social and not purely individual phenomenon, which attempts to persuade public opinion that something is true and just, which is really false and unjust. When this is done with the appearance of truth, it is usually done by appealing to great abstract principles in order to conceal and deform what is really the result of unthematized interests. At this point, philosophy has a critical function to perform, first by measuring the general or universal validity of those principles, but above all by revealing the falseness of their application. This intervention is legitimated precisely by the abuse of principles and terms that by their generality and abstractness fall into the domain of philosophy: for example, freedom, self-determination, natural law, personal development, the common good, etc. But this legitimacy is even greater when ideology is turned into strict ideologization.

What distinguishes ideologization from ideology is that it unconsciously and unintentionally expresses visions of reality that, rather than manifesting the reality, hide and deform it with the appearance of truth because of interests shaped by classes or social, ethnic, political, and/or religious groups. The following elements are present in these cases: (1) a totalizing, interpretive and justifying vision of a specific reality, in which important elements of falsehood and/or injustice are hidden or disguised; (2) the deformation has a certain collective and social character which works publicly and impersonally; (3) the deformation unconsciously responds to collective interests, which determine the ideologized representation in what it says, what it does not say, what it distorts and deforms; (4) it is presented as true, both by those who produce it and by those who receive it; (5) it is usually presented as universal and necessary, as an abstraction, although the reference is always to concrete realities that are subsumed and justified in broad, general formulations.

This phenomenon of ideologization is the truly dangerous one, for it is closely linked to social realities deeply rooted in both collective and individual awareness. Thus, it is that every social system or subsystem seeks ideological legitimation as a necessary element of its survival and/or effective functioning. Clearly when that system is unjust, or simply inert, its ideological mechanism goes beyond ideology to ideologization. It seeks to maintain the status quo to protect its social survival or inertia, and the system itself generates ideologized products that reflect their origin and therefore appear as innate. It seeks unconsciously to hide its own evil, and consciously to highlight the good, confusing reality and replacing it with ideal expressions that are contradicted by the reality of the facts and by the methods it uses to put in practice the ideals it claims. This is true in the social system as a whole, for example, in constitutional frameworks that do not at all reflect reality or in highly restricted social institutions like the army or the church, not to mention the political parties, whose conceptual discourse bears no relation to their everyday practice—although we assume that the discourse is honorably maintained except in cases of obvious hypocrisy. The people themselves sometimes produce and sometimes receive this kind of ideologization through many different channels, so that either there are parallel understandings with no connection between what is said and what is done, or there are connections, and while in fact it is the reality that determines the understanding, it is only allowed expression in beautiful words that justify what is really dirty and deforming.

In this context, which is important because it is so general and frequent, philosophy can be a powerful weapon if it is careful not to become a weapon of ideologization. Of course it is neither the only nor a sufficient form of ideological struggle, because ideologization is broader and deeper than anything philosophy can reach. But it is necessary because it is fundamental and critical.

Indeed philosophy has been distinguished historically by its critical character. All new philosophies have arisen from the philosopher's, or the philosophical school's, dissatisfaction with previous philosophies. The great philosophers have always dissented from received thinking, and they are not only mentally prepared for true gigantomachies, but they are critical by nature and able to distinguish between truth and appearances, between proven fact and unproven assumption, etc. Marx rightly accused the leftist Hegelians of wasting time criticizing other critiques in a purely ideological discussion without looking directly at reality. He, too, was primarily devoted to criticism, although he was criticizing aspects of reality in the political economy. On the other hand, the constant Marxist practice of attacking religion as an ideologizing function shows the clear need for criticism, either from a scientific viewpoint (historical materialism) or that of philosophy (dialectical materialism). However, philosophical criticism deals better with ideological formulations than with objective realities, and such criticism is not merely an ideological discourse at the same level with that which it criticizes. Certainly there can be philosophical or apparently philosophical thinking that is ideologized; this, however, would be a practical matter of philosophical critique toward other unsatisfactory philosophies. As long as the ideologization is not disguised as philosophy, philosophical criticism can easily deal at a rational level with important theoretical contradictions, thus permitting a strictly ideological struggle—more effectively when demagogic forms of expression are set aside in favor of a fully rational critique.

Philosophy must also be distinctively fundamental, that is, searching for the foundations. In the search for foundations we can expect to reveal better the unfoundedness of ideologized positions. A position that seeks ultimate and totalizing foundations risks slipping into ideologization, but it also has great possibilities of identifying and combating an imaginary foundation presented as a real foundation. Epistemological and metaphysical debate over foundations prepares the way for philosophical thinking to play a timely and effective role vis-à-vis different ideologized positions. When this is turned into a fundamental question, it can and should become a metaphysical question.

The critical and fundamental nature of philosophical thinking permits it to play a de-ideologizing role. Heidegger (*Was ist Metaphysik?*) considered nothingness the foundation of the possibility of the "no," and of negativity in general. Thus perhaps, instead of asking why there is something rather than nothing, he should have asked why there is nothing—no being, no reality, no truth, etc.—instead of something. Ideologization presents us with nothingness that appears as reality, with falsehood that appears as truth, with nonbeing that appears as being. Clearly this is not absolute nothingness, but nothingness is present in a way that inexorably entails the need for a negating action; this is not unique to thought or even to purely theoretical effort, but in philosophical thinking it holds a preferred place and offers an irreplaceable opportunity. This critical negativity can bring us in touch with founded reality, beyond the *unfounded* reality with which ideologization is exclusively concerned. The nothingness of ideologization leads us to negation, and this negation allows us to sweep away what is nebulous in ideologization.

By sweeping away the nebulous we see reality more clearly, which permits us both to affirm the foundations of reality and to deny, indeed wipe away—at least at the theoretical level—the false foundation of the false reality that the different forms of ideologization would impose on us. Our attitude in this situation would be not so much anguish as protest, in conformity not with something evanescent but something omnipresent, even though its presence is hidden by the pervasive phenomenon of ideologization. Thus, the question about why we have the nothingness of ideologization rather than the reality of truth, becomes a fundamental question whose response cannot be found in merely sociological or psychological explanations but must be philosophical and even, ultimately, metaphysical. The liberating function of philosophy is required then by its own critical and fundamental nature, and in turn it requires those who do philosophy to think fundamentally and critically.

The Creative Function of Philosophy

The contribution of philosophy to liberation is not limited to what it can do as a liberating critique of the ideologizations that conceal reality, both human reality and that of the world we live in and the world we see ahead. The critical task is not merely negative. It begins from somewhere and for something; critique and negation also include positive expressions and, perhaps surprisingly, unanticipated aspects of reality. Of course criticism need not be a purely destructive movement and/or one that hardens the opposing position. The negation of a negation, when it is not limited to a purely judgmental function that sets nonbeing against being, an "is not" against an "is," gradually opens into an affirmative process—but one that is both conditioned and made possible by its negative point of departure. Yet, we do not describe a point of departure, in this case an ideologized and ideologizing discourse, as negative in contrast with something we have already judged as positive, at least as concretely positive; rather it is described as something that contains elements of nothingness, which inspire what we have previously called protest and nonconformity.

That said, we should still move toward more creative forms that not only identify what is ideologized in a particular discourse but establish a new theoretical discourse, which, instead of concealing and/or deforming reality, discovers both negative and positive elements within it.

The very confrontation with the problem of ideology as a metaphysical problem places the latter on a different level. This is not because it introduces the problem of knowing into the problem of reality—which is a traditional part of classical philosophy—but because it brings to reality a specific way of knowing, a knowledge that by its situated nature makes it easy to ideologize. The important part of this question is that it becomes a new spur to rethink the serious problem of expanding the framework of the ultimate concept of metaphysics (being, reality, objectiveness, the absolute, etc.) in order to make room for something that apparently has not yet been fully present.

Indeed it is often said simplistically, but not entirely incorrectly, that the ultimate concept of first philosophy (being as being, etc.) was based on the meaning of natural being. It was simplistic because it paid inadequate attention to the place of pure act or *noesis noeseos* in being, but the accusation was not really arbitrary because, at least at the intramundane level, primary weight was given to categories like matter-form, potency-act, substance-accident, etc., whose origin was, above all, in the *natural* world and that are best applied in the natural world. With the discovery of subjectivity, ultimate reality came to be perceived in more subjective terms. This is especially clear in the radical change in meaning of the word "subject," from the Greek *hypokeimenon* to the German *Subjekt* like *Ich* or *Bewusstsein*, which is wrongly interpreted as a movement from realism to idealism, when it began as a movement from the physicalism to the subjectivism of reality. That change certainly broadened and refined the concept, but with a duality that leads to permanent dichotomies such as subject-object, spirit-nature, etc. After the nineteenth century it seemed necessary to broaden this concept even more, so as to give full recognition to historical reality, which as such appeared to have been left out of the meaning of a full reality that was finally reserved to what is always so.

Thus, the complexity and richness of the historical requires us to reformulate not only the exact dimension of the ultimate and the appropriate categories for developing it but also the "relation" of "thinking and being" in new terms, which require us to insert the problem of ideology and ideologization into the very heart of metaphysical discourse, beyond purely sociological or psychological considerations; the latter are not to be left out, but they must be rethought as strictly philosophical considerations.

From this metaphysical perspective we must arrive at not only critical, but positive expressions, in which there is a permanent interaction between the new metaphysical understanding of ultimacy and the different social, political, and especially historical realities that have now achieved full standing in philosophical thinking. These realities enrich the complexity of what we call ultimate and as such are a primary object of philosophy. But by expressing them in terms of the ultimate, we place them in a different light—as happened in the case of natural or subjective realities when they were considered not only as such but in terms of being, reality, existence, absolute, etc. This new light would bring out new theoretical expressions, not fixed but processual ones, that would attempt to serve as a theoretical-justificative backing for a historical praxis and provide an orientation to the ultimate for that praxis and the subjects who drive it.

It would be naive to think that great social achievements and even personal behaviors ultimately depend on philosophical expressions. This illusion may have been more widely held in the past, when social relations and the economic structure were much weaker and there was more space for effective action by a hero, a genius, an individual. Today, that is less and less true, although free and conscious subjects have more space in the area of personal self-determination than in the determination of socioeconomic processes; they may also have some appreciable space in the cultural area. So we cannot say that Marxist analysis, let alone Marxist-Leninist praxis, depends in any substantial way on dialectical materialism understood as a philosophical expression. The great mass movements, revolutionary processes, and the establishment of vanguards depend even less on theoretical materialism, even in the form of historical materialism. Clearly in analysis, and especially in practice, there are necessary ideological presuppositions that are really operative, especially in inducing the many to follow the dictates of the few, as a way of strengthening the action through the understanding of its meaning. But philosophical thinking is not directly involved in this process, although it may be the ultimate source of motivating ideas or emotional images. Let this be a call to modesty for philosophers who, in trying to interpret the world, suppose that they are managing or transforming it.

But that said, we must add that theoretical formulations, including philosophical ones, have an indispensable and necessary role in analysis and interpretation, in evaluation and justification, and in action and transformation. There is no such thing as pure praxis, and when we try to make it the only source of light, it will become not only blind praxis but also obsessive. Certainly the principal source of light is reality, and not some a priori condition of the human subject. The classical *tabula rasa*, despite its simplicity, can serve as a warning for immodest idealists. But that reality is only a source of light in the context of intelligence, and clearly intelligence must be directed at reality. Reality does its part, but so does intelligence, and their respectivity functions in different ways. This does not deny or annul the priority of reality, but that priority does not annul the dynamism and even the activity proper to the human mind, in its zeal to extract all the light it can from reality by looking at it in the different ways that intelligence itself is able to generate. This perspective opens up a whole field for strictly philosophical effort, as a theoretical way to encounter reality in order to shed light on it, interpret it and transform it.

Here we shall not dwell on how philosophical effort should provide theoretical accompaniment for a specific praxis, in order to become the reflective and critical theory of that praxis. We shall return to that point immediately, but we must say first that this is not enough. The philosophical effort in general at the moment of its creation must do more than accompany praxis; it must at least bring forward the waters from the past and move the stream further ahead. In other words the correct theory-praxis correlation, where philosophy is concerned, cannot be established unless there is a certain theory about some essential points, to which philosophy must return again and again, even in order to adequately accompany a specific praxis. I shall briefly outline here the themes that, unless philosophy deals with them, are not fully philosophical and do not adequately contribute philosophically to the human person's and humanity's need to discover themselves and to better carry out their tasks in history.

Above all, it seems necessary to have a theory of intelligence and of human knowledge, which accounts for the possibilities and limitations of human understanding. Whether we call it a theory of intelligence or of understanding, criticism, epistemology, etc., it seems to be a necessity, one that philosophy has always helped to fulfill and for which no other discipline can take its place, although many can be helpful. Human beings have a peculiar way of confronting reality, an intellectual capacity that, whatever its structural origin, nature and conditioning, must be studied, not only in order to understand what the human being is, but, prior to that, in order to make critical use of that intelligence. The liberating function of philosophy has much to say and to learn about this theme, because intelligence can liberate but also oppress and constrain human beings. It is not enough to criticize; we must build a theory of intelligence in order to use it responsibly, for purposes of science as well as wisdom and practice.

In the second place, we need a general theory of reality—not of each and every reality, but of reality as such. The fact that achieving it is a problem, that perhaps the goal is unattainable, should not keep us from trying, at least with the reality that in one way or another is given and made present to us. Such a theory of reality should take into account the natural and the historical, the objective and the subjective, the social and the personal. Only by achieving it to some degree can we avoid either misappropriating what is real in reality or reading into the domain of reality certain categories that belong to another domain. Both the misappropriation and the uniformization of reality are enormous obstacles to understanding the world and living in it. But even this is not enough to establish a metaphysical system. We must rethink the appropriate categories with which to explore reality without leaving out any of its complexity and richness. Just by way of example, if we think of reality as systematic, dynamic, and in some way dialectical, we will need a full analysis of the categories that explain its systematic, dynamic and dialectical nature. Finding, developing, and building on them is an enormous creative task.

In the third place, we also need an open and critical theory of the human being, society, and history. Humanity, society, and history are three closely interrelated realities, but each has its own peculiarity. Here I am not thinking of history as the "historical reality" that I have elsewhere proposed as an appropriate object of philosophy as such, but rather as that which distinguishes history from the person and society. Many sciences are concerned with these three realities, but only philosophy has something to say about the "type" of reality that pertains to each one, about its focus as reality. If what philosophy has to say is meaningful, it should not be said a priori but after carrying out its task and comparing it with what other forms of knowledge say or do not say on the same themes. To say that philosophy only speaks "until" the sciences begin to say their word, is a regression to a Comtian formula that has not been able to establish its future truth and effectiveness. After a century in which the sciences have said so much about humanity, society, and history, philosophy has more information and problems to confront, but the philosophical domain has not been eliminated.

In the fourth place, we need a theory to provide a rational foundation for an adequate evaluation of human beings and their world—or that says rationally that such a rational or reasonable foundation is not possible. The value and meaning of things apparently need to be clarified, and many people, even thinking people, are still concerned with them. It is not that philosophy has an exclusive claim to the value and meaning of things, but it has addressed them in depth, and other theoretical domains have not adequately taken its place. The broad problem of ethics has not disappeared or become irrelevant; rather it continues to be of concern to philosophers who have left other tasks behind.

In the fifth place, we need a philosophical reflection on what is ultimate and transcendent. Philosophy as a search for ultimacy is always transcendental, but this does not mean that we must arbitrarily affirm some transcendent reality, either relatively or absolutely transcendent. Yet, the question is there and must be answered to the fullest extent possible. Whether or not there are transcendent realities may be hard to determine or prove, but it is not a pseudo-question—despite the fact that it is hard to answer and that the answer itself has special characteristics that are inherently unsatisfying to positivistic minds that would rather circumvent the limits of information by other methods, less reasonable than philosophical methods.

In fulfilling a liberating function, it is not enough for philosophy to criticize the constraining, concealing, or simply distracting elements in these five areas, which include many others. We must also create, give positive answers, or if necessary, say why we must remain silent. The Latin American historical reality, and the people who comprise it, need these questions. Indeed, in their very questioning they may already possess the beginning of answers, which may require more conceptual development but which are surely laden with reality and truth. Perhaps that reality and that truth have already been expressed to some degree by poets, painters, and novelists, and also by theologians. It remains for philosophy to express it and reformulate it in the specific manner of philosophy, which has not yet been done in even a minimally satisfactory way.

Conditions That Make the Liberating Function of Philosophy Possible

Philosophy does not carry out its liberating function in the same way in distinct locations and times. The liberating function is always a concrete labor, as much as it refers to that which one wants to be liberated from to the mode by which one will bring that liberation to pass and the goal of historical freedom that one can propose in each situation. Philosophy should always carry out a liberating function, but the mode by which it carries it out is distinct, and this will mean that there will be distinct philosophies with their own proper universality. Philosophy has no abstract and ahistorical liberating function. One must determine beforehand the "what" of liberation, the mode of liberation, the "where to" of liberation, the shift from the preliminary to the definitive, and the shift from antici-pation to con-firmation (*com-probación*) that results in an original and liberating philosophy, if it has really been placed in an adequate space of the liberating process. The fundamental dynamism of history is a dynamism toward freedom and personhood, a point that may be debated, although it is in itself plausible and it responds to philosophical judgments of a wide range. What is less debatable is that Latin American peoples urgently need a process of liberation, which at least in its origin *a quo* does not require much discussion.

Liberating Philosophy and Liberating Praxis

In their attempt to be liberating, philosophers have often made the mis-take of considering themselves capable of contributing to liberation by themselves. Some believed there could be a fully liberating philosophy apart from any liberating praxis, and indeed that philosophy could liberate without being rooted in a liberating social praxis. Their mistake is both in attributing special liberating conditions to that kind of thinking and in focusing more on individual persons than on persons in their social context. The present reality in Latin America, however, leads us to the hypothesis that philosophy can only carry out its critical and creative function in favor of an effective praxis of liberation, if it is adequately situated within that liberating praxis, which in principle is independent of philosophy.

It is true that philosophy, like any authentic way of knowing, by its own theoretical nature and its relative autonomy has possibilities and needs that are independent of any specific social praxis within certain limits that may change. Among other reasons, this is because it is absurd to think that the logical correctness of thinking and the formulation of theoretical instruments for approaching reality will necessarily arise as a mechanical reflection of a specific praxis. In fact, there is a whole series of intellectual resources that have more to do with the rightness or correctness of method than with the truth of content; and since these resources are less related to concrete reality, they can and should be cultivated in conformity with their own dynamic and their own laws. This separate interaction has its own liberating function, especially at the merely intellectual level, which is important in itself. There are in fact some social processes and groups that are pregnant with truth but are tangled in a series of intellectual nets, which distort their own real knowledge both in expression and in the resulting practice. In these cases and others like them, a correct intellectual approach to the formality of their operations may be useful in different degrees. Therefore, philosophy does have a certain autonomy that allows it even to correct other kinds of discourse.

Nevertheless, we must insist that philosophy depends in a special way, especially in its orienting foci, on the social and historical reality within which it is done, on the dominant interests in that reality, and on the horizon that frames it. Of course philosophy is also dependent on other things. We must remember its enormous dependence on whatever scientific knowledge is available in its time and on the accumulated cultural experience. We cannot imagine how differently Aristotle might have thought if he had lived in our time, with the theoretical knowledge we have today, with our different forms of social reality and ethics, etc. In many strictly philosophical aspects, it may be more dependent on the knowledge it starts with than on the social reality in which it is rooted. But that does not diminish its dependence on social reality. We must recognize that the horizon of interests, concerns, aspirations, etc., and especially social pressure, both limits and enables philosophy's questions and the type of answers it finds—regardless of whether it responds positively and favorably, or negatively and critically, to those conditions. This is not only the problem of mentality that Zubiri identified so well: reason always has a concrete character because intelligence takes on a concrete shape in its formal way of approaching reality, in the method of approach as such. "This is not primarily a psychological, social or ethnic concept but a structural concept" (*Inteligencia y razón*, 1983, p. 152.) It is that a mentality, understood as such, is qualified by a series of conditionings, including social conditionings, which enable us to speak for example of a Semite mentality (an ethnic concept) or a feudal mentality (a sociohistorical concept).

Therefore, one of the things that most determines the different mentalities, including theoretical ones, is praxis, and it is with great difficulty that philosophy could contribute to a liberative praxis if the philosopher and her strictly philosophical task are not immersed in a praxis that is properly liberative. This does not negate the division of labor or the specificity of areas, but if one holds that there is no identity or uniformity between philosophy and praxis, neither is there a strict separation. Even when, in a social confrontation that carries with it a historical praxis, one does not claim that one type of philosophical thought is more useful and utilized more by some than by others; it is evident that, for example, philosophies of a liberal type tend to support the dominant capitalism while philosophies of a social type contradict it. Yet, when one seeks a total separation intentionally, one fears the critical presence of philosophy, because a determined ideological domination had been assumed to succeed. Neither does this negate that truth creates freedom, although one should accept as well that without freedom it is difficult to reach for the truth (if not embrace it). Truth makes freedom, but the truth is not given to us gratuitously; rather it should be sought diligently. On the other hand, when there is not freedom, the possibilities of creation and discovery are significantly reduced. All of this is to demonstrate, without a doubt, the relative autonomy of philosophy, an autonomy that is greater when the theme that is treated philosophically has less directly to do with social praxis. Nevertheless, it is curious to note how social regimes put up so much resistance to themes that appear so distant from social praxis, such as whether the material is eternal or whether God does not exist. Yet this is not proof of the necessity to engage oneself in a liberative praxis, if philosophy wishes to constitute itself as liberative and if it wants to collaborate in a real liberation.

By praxis, we mean here the totality of the social processes that transform natural reality as much as the historical. In these processes, the subject-object relations are not always uni-directional. For that reason, it is preferable to speak of a codeterminative respectivity in which, nevertheless, the social grouping adopts more characteristics of an object that not only reacts but also positively acts and determines as well. The social subject though (that does not exclude personal subjects, but presupposes them beforehand) has a certain primacy in the direction of the process. Without going in depth into the problem of the totality of praxis, it appears that we can say without exaggeration that the phenomena of oppression have a structural-social character and that because of this, the processes of liberation should also have a structural-social character. Ideas alone do not change social structures; there have to be social forces that counteract, in a process of liberation, the other social forces that established the process of oppression. This claim does not intend to divide the world in a Manichean way, but it does valorize the fundamental direction of a process that gives meaning to its totality as a process and also as the collective of subjects that are affected by it. If a real praxis of liberation is given, even if in an incipient manner, it is in relation to that praxis of liberation that philosophy can carry out its liberative function, first in respect to the liberative praxis itself as a whole, and later as an integral part of it, as much critically as positively, in favor of a liberative process and in search of a new social structure in which persons can reach the proper realization of freedom and communion.

In fact, theory is not opposed to praxis. For instance, it was not true of Aristotle, where the opposition is between praxis and poiesis and not between praxis and theory. The Aristotelian meaning of praxis as immanence can be recovered, if we understand social and historical reality as a whole, because then the immanence of sociohistorical praxis would be maintained and would take on the full meaning of self-realization. For that reason I do not think it appropriate to speak of theoretical praxis, scientific praxis, etc. Praxis is the unity of everything the social system does to transform itself, and dynamically includes the subject-object respectivity as we understood it earlier. That praxis has theoretical moments of different degrees, from the consciousness that accompanies all human action, to the reflexive consciousness, and to reflection on what is, what is happening, and what is being done. That reflection may take different forms, whether prescientific or strictly scientific, according to the particular characteristics of each of the sciences. All theory is transformative from its minimal level of observation, as Heisenberg demonstrated in what would seem to be an unlikely area for proving it. Every theory transforms something, although not necessarily the object of the theory, at least not directly. This does not mean that pure theory is the greatest force of transformation. Therefore, it is better to speak of the theoretical moment of praxis, which can attain different degrees of autonomy—but only by seeking a proper relationship with praxis as a whole, which in part it can guide, though perhaps not directly, and from which in turn it receives direction and guidance.

So if philosophy, as a theoretical moment, is to carry out its full liberating capacity and also fulfill itself as philosophy, it must consciously and reflectively recover its role as the appropriate theoretical moment of the appropriate historical praxis. Indeed praxis is complex and in our case contradictory. The unity of praxis is not a uniformity or a static identity, but rather the unity of diverse, and even contrary, praxes. What is crucial about these praxes is that they are moments of a single praxis, and thus do not allow for Robinsonian isolationism; for things come into play by presence but also by absence. For example, the fact that philosophy or theology does not speak about the violation of human rights diminishes the importance of that question and thus facilitates the violations. The same holds true when the church as an institution ignores the violation of human rights. On the other hand, if philosophy and theology take human rights as a relevant point of social praxis (a redundant expression), they give that historical reality a relevance that would otherwise remain disguised for the convenience of the dominant classes or groups.

Not only must philosophy enter critically into the liberating moments of historical praxis (another redundant expression) in order to contribute ex officio to liberation; it also gains enormous benefit from a deliberate incarnation in that praxis *as philosophy*, as the way of knowing that philosophy represents. Liberating praxis is not only a principle of ethical correctness, but also of creativity, as long as we enter into it with a theoretical quality and intensity and maintain a critical distance. Here I shall say two words about the enabling moment of presence and about the corrective moment of distance.

Historical praxis is itself, to a supreme degree, a principle of reality and a principle of truth. It is a principle of reality in that praxis, understood as a whole, presents a *summum* of reality; it is a principle of truth, both as a principle of reality and because the historicization of any theoretical formulation definitively shows its degree of truth and reality. But historical praxis also constantly raises new, live questions, which lend creativity to thinking as long as the latter is fully alert and willing to be incited by a reality that must be known and transformed. More concretely, a liberating praxis as an ethical commitment gives fuller meaning to philosophical thinking. Certainly philosophy has what we might call its own internal ethic, when it is zealous about clarifying and grounding the questions it sees as most pertinent at a given time, and by extension, the questions that directly or indirectly seek its help; but in addition to that ethic it must think about what it is representing as part of the overall social praxis in order to contribute to it appropriately. Thus, the search for truth is one of the principal dimensions of philosophical ethics; it is not the only one; nor is it sufficient to characterize the philosophical task as fully ethical, independent from the philosopher's own ethics. Philosophically it is not enough to seek the truth but also to try and realize it philosophically in order to do justice and establish freedom.

Nevertheless, philosophy remains a predominantly theoretical task, requiring a special kind of ability and preparation that cannot be replaced either by a willing commitment or by even the most enlightened exercise of social praxis at moments most pregnant with reality. Therefore, along with presence and participation, there must also be critical distance from the dominant praxis, even when the latter is fundamentally correct. The philosopher cannot be a dutiful bureaucrat or a dazzled admirer of the social praxis; no intellectual, not even an organic intellectual, can be that, but especially not a philosopher with a fundamental attitude and a critical capability that frees her from bureaucracy and rapturous wonder, not to mention uncritical fanaticism. Critical distance does not mean remoteness or separation or is it a lack of commitment; it is just a sign that not even the best actions fulfill their *telos* all at once, but rather they will probably get bogged down or detoured long before. Vanguards do not meet all the people's needs; nor do political projects meet the fullness of reality, and even less does the need to maintain power exempt them from practicing evil. The philosopher can understand the need to tolerate some evils and that the presence of some evil does not make a project, or a vanguard, or a state power evil; the *bonum ex integra causa, malum ex quocumque defectu* is almost never applicable in historical matters. But we cannot deceive ourselves by describing a necessary evil as a good justified by its intended but unattained goal. Contrary to what Plato sought, philosophers should not rule, but they should be allowed to lead a Socratic existence, always pointing out deficiencies of knowledge and action. And if they are not allowed to live the philosophical life of Socrates, they should undertake it themselves even if it leads to condemnation or ostracism from their society.

Liberating Philosophy and the Subject of Liberation

Philosophy cannot develop all its liberating potential, unless it is taken on by the real subject of liberation, whoever that subject may be in a given case, which of course cannot be determined dogmatically.

Certainly in the human domain there is a preponderant role for ide-ology, which is an essential element of authentic *metanoia*, of authentic conversion. Philosophy can contribute to this change of mind, at least indirectly. There is also a clear need for ideology in social change, but that should not lead to the illusion that a change of ideas is a change of real-ity, or that a change of intention—the purity of intention—is enough to change reality. We should not dismiss, even as a moment of praxis, the role that philosophy can play in the mental processes of people and even of the social sectors that are important for social change. Nor should we dismiss what philosophy can contribute to the ideological struggle, which is an essential element of historical praxis. But neither ideological refutation nor the establishment of a new ideology is sufficient by itself to change a social order, and ideological change can become a pretext for the avoidance of real social change. No matter how necessary and even primary ideological work, including philosophical work, may be considered, it is not sufficient. We see most clearly how necessary it is in a situation like scientific and technical research, which leads later to effective action; but even there, little can be done without a decision to make use of the research and technol-ogy and without actually putting them to work, fleshing them out. This is even more true in matters of important values, great ideas, and even changes of mentality.

The liberation of peoples, like their antecedent oppression, is brought about by social forces. An individual can oppress and repress an individual or a group of them. But when it is a matter of whole peoples, there are social forces that really drive the processes of oppression and liberation. In principle, the social forces that can contribute most to liberation are the ones that constitute the principal contradiction between the forces responsible for domination and for oppression. This affirmation may be debatable at a strictly political level; however, I am not posing it here in strictly political terms but in ideal-real terms. This means that although at the level of political action, the main contradictor—and patient—may not be the person best able to overcome domination. At the level of theoreti-cal description that seeks ultimate reality, to situate oneself in the place of principal contradiction is a very reasonable judgment. In order to be not only effective in the liberative task, but to be true to it and even to the philosophical task, it is necessary to situate oneself in the place of historical truth and in the place true liberation. Thus, in order to be liberating, it is necessary that the philosophical task can be done (the problem of its basis) and, in fact, is done (the problem of presentation) by the social forces that are really engaged in an integrally liberating effort.

In each case, determining that place-that-offers-truth involves a moment of theoretical discernment, even though it also involves a moment of enlightened opting. The theoretical movement implies focusing critically on the present history, to identify both liberating and dominating forces and actions. We choose the perspective of freedom, not only because of what it offers the ethical task as a privileged place of reality and the realization of human persons and humanity at large, but also because of its theoretical potential, in both the creative and the critical, de-ideologizing phases. History understood in this sense is not the master of life, but it is the master of truth. The moment of option, which seeks that place-that-offers-truth and does the truth, should not be blind but enlightened. It is enlightened first by its ethical assessment of justice and freedom, or better, of "no-justice" and "no-freedom" that are primary facts in our situation, an essential point of reference; and secondly, it is enlightened by the theoretical assessment that sees in injustice and the absence of freedom one of the fundamental sources of repression against the truth, "the injustice that suppresses the truth" (Rom. 1:18).

This choice to situate oneself in one location or another when doing philosophy is one of the most important distinguishing characteristics among philosophies, not only from an ethical viewpoint, but a theoretical one as well. Those who are situated in the place of science will do one kind of philosophy; those who situate themselves primarily in the place of interior experience will do another; those situated in the place of the larger historical praxis, yet another. It is by option that we are situated in one place or another, whether or not we are aware of the option, and the option is conditioned not only by personal characteristics but social ones as well. The location is exclusive because it is the "from where" that philosophy is done, which is not to say that in the exercise of philosophy one may not draw on resources from other places. However, the utilization of those resources remains situated and incorporated by the primary location where one's philosophy is being done: a location that determines the principal questions, appropriate categories, and, certainly, the horizon of the whole philosophical task.

From this perspective we can speak of a "Christian" philosophy in a new sense. It would be that philosophy that places its autonomous philosophizing in the privileged location of historical truth, which is the cross as hope and liberation. To seek what is Christian of philosophy by means of dogmatic agreement or submission to the ecclesiastical hierarchy goes against the very nature of philosophy and has led it to sterility. Christian philosophy in that sense, just as its structural equivalent in Marxist philosophy, is proof not only of the intellectual sterility of that way of describing a philosophy but often of the reversion of the essentially liberating function of philosophy into an essentially controlling and dominating function "at the service of" what is considered immutable truth or an unassailable institutional structure. It would be a different matter, from the starting point of Christian inspiration, to seek the place most pregnant with truth, from which, with the greatest possible philosophical potentiality and autonomy, to carry out a philosophical work of clarification and liberation.

From the Christian viewpoint, in general that location is the cross as a general category, and historically it is the crucifixion of the people under all forms of domination and exploitation. This is a radical theoretical affirmation that is disputed not only by those who uphold the "utopian" character of philosophical thinking but also by those who in theory or practice have chosen another "place where" they philosophize. This choice of the cross is paradoxical, but the paradox is viewed, on the one hand, as typically Christian and, on the other, as a dialectical theoretical principle of primary importance. The foolishness of the cross over against Greek and occidental wisdom is a quintessentially dialectical place, not because it denies wisdom in general, but because it denies precisely the kind of wisdom formulated by the active crucifiers, that is, by those who are not concerned by the massive phenomenon of the historical crucifixion of humanity. The foolishness of the cross is also a radical basis for the dialectical method, which is not a method of logic initially or a universal method, equally applicable to nature and to history, to any individual and to the person, but rather a method that follows history and that history imposes on whoever wants to perform it. From Christian inspiration we can affirm, moreover, that the cross is situated in the privileged location of the revelation of God and the resurrection of humanity, uniting and reconciling the absolute and the relative, the infinite and the finite, death and life, solitude and companionship, abandonment and encounter, the political and the religious, etc.

The historical characteristics of the cross may vary from case to case, depending on the situation of the peoples, the condition of the persons, the development of the social forces, etc. In a third world perspective, there can be no doubt that the cross has a very clear profile, immediately recognizable in the shape of the crucified ones here and now, the immense majorities of humanity, stripped of all human visage, not by abundance and dominance but by the deprivation and oppression to which they are subjected. To insist on this from the perspective of love would seem to be an adequate form of doing something like a new Christian philosophy, much more fruitful than others have been—other philosophies whose real and even bibliographic location is far more unChristian or anti-Christian than Christian.

To speak of a philosophy of Christian inspiration, it is not enough to put oneself in the place occupied by the oppressed of the earth; but we cannot speak properly of Christian philosophy without placing our philosophical thinking in that privileged place of wisdom, which according to the Christian perspective belongs to those who are dispossessed, who are unjustly treated, and who suffer. Here again is the problem mentioned earlier of the nothingness that discovers being (*ser*), the nothingness from which all things are creatively made, not because nothingness becomes creative, not because *ex nihilo omne ens qua ens fit* (Heidegger), but because there is one who is able to make being (*ser*) out of nothingness. Being (*ente*) cannot "be made" from nothingness; one must make it, even if from nothingness, from that nothingness that appears to us as negation and even as crucifixion. Although it is true that in order to speak of a philosophy of Christian inspiration, or of a liberating philosophy, it is not enough to put oneself in the place of the oppressed, there has been much wandering around in other directions when that really is the place to philosophize, because that is where there is an originality that is fundamentally Christian.

When philosophy is authentic philosophy, as a specific exercise of human thinking, and when it is authentic because it seeks a truth that really liberates people from what really oppresses and represses them, from that place—which is inherently privileged for this task and in the service of the social forces that drive it—philosophy will have converted fully to what it should be. It will have recovered its own being and will again be what it is called to be, a privileged moment of true praxis.

This is possible especially in the specific case of Latin America. If we wonder why there is a Latin American theology, a Latin American socioeconomic theory, a Latin American literature, etc., one of the main reasons is that all those different discourses are inserted in a liberating praxis, from the place represented by the popular majorities as a universal and basic fact of our historical reality. That alone is not enough; it has also required talent and preparation in theology, socioeconomics, literature, etc., but there can be no doubt about the creative spirit conferred by a reality to which one has become present and committed oneself. It is not clear that this has happened in philosophy. Perhaps the philosophical moment has not yet arrived, perhaps it is inherently slow in coming and is inappropriate to young nations; but one also suspects that the community of philosophers has not been able to do what other creative communities have done. The diverse expressions of Latin American philosophy or nationalistic philosophy have not inserted themselves properly in the right praxis and have not sufficiently understood the liberating role that philosophy can play. Those of us who have tried to draw on Marxism, as a philosophy committed to processes of liberation, have found it to be a fully formed philosophy, not helpful in the dawning moment of new realities. In some cases, because they devoted themselves to philosophy in less than radical and technical ways, in some cases, because they were in the wrong place, because they did not understand in depth the possibility of philosophy's liberating function, today we do not have a Latin American philosophy capable of speaking to the world a valid and original philosophical word. Perhaps if philosophy and the philosophers find their rightful place and become committed to the appropriate praxis, if in addition there is talent and preparation, we can hope to begin to build a philosophy that is at once Latin American, regional, and universal, but with a historical universality. What is essential is to dedicate oneself philosophically to a liberation as integral and well rooted as possible in our peoples and our persons; the constitution of a philosophy will then be added unto it. Here too the cross can be transformed into life.

Conclusions

By way of conclusion, we can propose some theses, not because they have been "proved" in the previous paragraphs, but because they offer landmarks for the road we have followed. They do, however, show that the theme has metaphysical substance and is not simply an animating introduction to the philosophical task.

All of historical reality comprises a whole, unfolding in time, which is so complex that sometimes we can speak of objectifications of the spirit, and other times of the spiritualization of the objective, of the naturalization of history or the historicization of nature, etc., depending on the categories we use in our minds to unify the complex unity of reality. The ultimate concept of philosophy must include all the qualitative differences in an articulated and structural way, just as they are in historical reality itself. Historical reality is radical reality, seen from an intramundane viewpoint, in which all other realities reside, although the latter, if not completely absolutized, can be viewed as relatively absolute.

This reality is intrinsically dynamic. It is the whole dynamism of historical reality that should be understood as praxis. This praxis is an immanent, active totality, because its activity and the results of that activity lie within the same totality, a totality in process, which is being shaped and directed in the process. Praxis, understood as such, takes multiple forms, both as a whole, which in each case is its most appropriate subject, and by its mode of action and the results of that action. But, in particular, the activity of historical reality is praxis, understood as a dynamic totality.

Praxis as a whole, and many of the moments of that praxis, are accompanied by a theoretical moment. Theory is not the opposite of praxis, but rather one of the moments within it, the moment that initially has to do with awareness of praxis, with the conscious character of praxis. Not all moments of praxis are conscious, and not all moments of praxis have the same degree of consciousness. When that degree of consciousness is reflexively separated from praxis and becomes a point of discernment toward it, of judgment and crisis, we can begin to speak of theory, which can begin to develop in relatively autonomous moments, apart from its existence as an accompanying reflection of a praxis. Thus, there is not really such a thing as a theoretical praxis; rather there are different theoretical moments of praxis, which brings them together and gives them meaning. To the extent that they are moments of a total praxis to which they relate, and remain autonomous, active, and effective in that relationship, we can speak of them derivatively as a theoretical praxis. That term does in fact overcome the usual opposition between theory and praxis, as it should; on the other hand, it overly broadens the meaning of praxis and thus risks confusing formal praxis with the theoretical moment, which may include praxis as a whole and some specific forms of praxis.

The theoretical moment of praxis acquires, provisionally, the form of ideology, in the nonpejorative sense of that term. Praxis in fact is accompanied by a series of representations, evaluations, and justifications that give it meaning and drive it, and that in turn, in some way, produce a specific whole or a system that totalizes them. This aspect of ideology is necessary and inevitable, and entails an ambiguity that can lead either toward critical and systematic reflection or toward a simple reflection of the praxis itself. In the latter case, it becomes ideologization because although intelligence appears to be exercising critical initiative toward what is happening in reality, it is a falsified reality that justifies itself through the exercise of intelligence.

Philosophy can deteriorate into ideologization, but by its very nature it can also move in the other direction, turning pure ideology into critical, systematic, and creative reflection. It would do this especially if, while remaining true to its own epistemological order, it intentionally carries out a liberating function in both the critical and creative aspects. The critical aspect is made possible by an ethical attitude of protest against the nothingness that becomes present in the defective (especially unjust and oppressive) reality. The creative aspect is possible as a way of overcoming nothingness in the context of a reality, which is conceived ideally as a negation of that which is nothing "by privation," and as following a praxis that in some of its moments moves toward the negation of specific aspects of historical reality.

The liberating function of philosophy, which implies the liberation of philosophy itself from all ideologizing participation, and at the same time the liberation of those who are subjected to domination, can only be fully developed by keeping in mind and participating in the historical praxes of liberation. It is difficult for philosophy to constitute itself as philosophy separated from these praxes; but it is even more difficult for it to be liberating or much less as contributing in a real way to liberation.

In order to be immersed in the praxis of liberation, philosophy should be properly related to the subject of liberation. Ideally, the subject of liberation is the one who is inherently the greatest victim of domination, the one who bears the cross of history, because that cross is not the mockery of the one who suffers but the one who imposes it; and it brings with it a process of death that can and must lead to a different life. The cross is the verification of the reign of nothingness, of evil, which (defined negatively as nonreality) is what annihilates all things and makes them evil, but for the negated victim can lead to a new life that bears the marks of creation.

If it makes sense to speak of a Christian philosophy, or a philosophy of Christian inspiration, it is because a philosophy done from among the poor and oppressed, in favor of their integral liberation and of a universal liberation, can—in its autonomy—walk along the same path followed by those who work on behalf of the Reign of God, as prefigured in the historical Jesus.

If we in Latin America are able to do authentic philosophy at the formal level, in relation to the historical praxis of liberation and from among the oppressed who make up its universal substance, it may yet be possible to build a Latin American philosophy, in the same way that others have built a Latin American theology and a Latin American literature, which by being Latin American are also universal.

—Translated by Margaret D. Wilde and Michael E. Lee.

Part II

Liberation:
The Christian and the Historical

5

The Christian Challenge of
Liberation Theology
(1987)

Ignacio Ellacuría wrote these reflections for a conference held in Madrid in 1987 on the theme "The Temporal and the Religious in the World Today." His lecture was published posthumously in the popular UCA newsletter, Carta a las Iglesias [Letter to the churches] in 1992. Unlike most of the chapters in this collection which were originally published in various academic journals, this insightful and bold reflection was intended for a more general audience, even though the argument it makes involves a "debate" of sorts between Ellacuría and Cardinal Joseph Ratzinger (then prefect of the Vatican Congregation of the Doctrine of the Faith and later named Pope Benedict XVI).

Several of the chapters in this book demonstrate how Ellacuría responded to the criticism lodged by Cardinal Ratzinger in the first Vatican Congregation for the Doctrine of the Faith "Instruction on Certain Aspects of the 'Theology of Liberation'" (1984). This chapter responds, not to the formal Instruction issued by the Congregation in 1984, but to an interview of Cardinal Ratzinger published the following year in a book entitled, "Informe sobre la Fe" (The Ratzinger Report). As becomes clear, Ellacuría regards this second criticism as no less problematic than the first. Notwithstanding his explicit embrace of the theme of liberation, Ellacuría points out that Ratzinger's interpretation of liberation theology—above all, his claim that liberation theology reduces the Christian faith to history and reduces history to politics—is both narrow and fundamentally mistaken. In the course of this reflection, Ellacuría seeks to develop a clear and positive interpretation of the theology of liberation, beginning with his central thesis that history is the "place" where humans most fully encounter reality and also, therefore, divine salvation. On the basis of the structural unity that obtains between a history of liberation and a history of salvation, he then argues for the necessity that theology and the church

*become "incarnated" in historical reality, above all, in concrete "places" like Latin
America, a point that runs directly counter to the ecclesiastical temptations to over-
centralization and the "Romanization" of the church. In all of this, Ellacuría never
loses track of his primary aim, which is to show that the root inspiration and point
of liberation theology is to provide a Christian reading of the historical from the
perspective of those most in need of historical liberation:* the poor.

I have been asked to treat the problem of the religious and temporal from
the perspective of liberation theology. Cardinal Ratzinger has accused the
theology of liberation of reducing the Christian faith to history, and history to politics.

In order to show from the beginning that this reductionism does not
exist, I would like to demonstrate that the proposal of liberation theology is not simply between the religious and political. Liberation theology
considers the problem essential, but it does not speak of the religious in
general but of what is Christian. Moreover, it does not speak simply of
politics but of history. The approach of liberation theology toward the
problem of the religious and temporal is that of "the Christian and the
historical," Christian faith and history. Politics is an important dimension
of history, but in no way do we attempt to reduce history to politics, above
all if politics is understood as the structuring of society by power and,
concretely, from the power of the state. Historical liberation is an integral
liberation and not just political. In addition, there is no lack of religiosity
or of the sacred in Latin America. What liberation theology searches for is,
in the first place, to make this religiosity Christian and secondly, to make
it efficacious.

What is certain, and Ratzinger has realized this clearly, is that the concept of history has an enormous importance in the theology of liberation.
According to Ratzinger, "one can say that the concept of history, in the
theology of liberation, absorbs the concept of God and revelation. . . .
History has assumed the role of God."[1] I accept that history is a crucial
and fundamental concept in liberation theology, but I do not accept that
it absorbs the concepts of God and revelation in such a way that the latter are annulled and history assumes the role of God. Something of this
may be true, but we will have to see in what sense. For Ratzinger, the
only thing that remains after the dismantling accomplished by dualisms
would be "the possibility to work for a Reign that is realized in history
and its political-economic reality."[2] In this, he has a point: liberation theology struggles against dualisms, but Ratzinger claims that we work only in
and by history, in its political-economic reality. For this reason, we in the

theology of liberation are accused of politicizing everything: the Reign of God, the people of God, faith, hope, love, the sacraments, morality, salvation, and the Bible.

Ratzinger continues, "Here the fusion of God and history is produced that offers the possibility of conserving the Chalcedonic formula for Jesus but with an entirely distinct meaning."[3] That is to say, he recognizes that we accept the formula of Chalcedon that confesses that Jesus is truly God and truly human but claims that we give it a totally different meaning and—according to him—a heterodox one. Thus, he claims, all of this lends itself to a great confusion: "What results as theologically unacceptable and socially dangerous is this mixture of the Bible, Christology, politics, sociology and economics."[4] This statement may be read positively or negatively. That is to say, undoubtedly liberation theology is socially dangerous. Rockefeller saw this perfectly before liberation theology even breathed that deeply. What needs to be asked then is why is it dangerous and to whom.

Ratzinger says that liberation theology is a massive jumble in which everything is confused. We will see up to what point this may be true. Obviously, when someone accuses you of these things you must recognize that there may be something in what he claims. However, in spite of the fact that we have not yet arrived at an adequate theoretical elaboration, because perhaps the talent, preparation, or circumstances have not permitted it, I believe that we have made some efforts to confront this problem seriously: that the Christian faith is related to history and how it is related, what it has to do with history; and within history, how it relates to its political and economic dimensions, but also with the scientific and cultural dimensions. That is, all that has to do with history. Thus, this would be the primary point, which I would formulate in this way: history as the fullest location of reality and salvation.

History as the Fullest Location of Reality and Salvation

One might think that the place where reality manifests most is in the material universe. One might also think that the place where there is most reality is in human subjectivity, in the I, in the person. We Latin American theologians, in one way or another—some more philosophically, others more theologically—think that where reality is given most fully is in history.

But, how is "history" to be understood? In my view, historical reality is the differentiated and structured totality of reality. Naturally, a restricted concept of history is a possibility, for example, Zubiri's "history as the realization of possibilities and creation of capacities." But another possibility is a full concept of history. This would be history as the encompassing dimension of all reality. History would be not only the tip of the spear that has arrived and advances but that which envelops all forms of reality. In reality, there is not history without nature. And the historical subject is not other than the human species but differentiated in persons and social groups. This totality is differentiated and structured. On one hand, it includes all material and biological nature, the social in all its complexity, but it also includes the personal. These differences are structured or form a complex structure that, without annulling their differences, make of them "one" historical reality.

If history is the fullest location of reality, and if one allows history some ruptures, it can become the fullest location of salvation. We do not deny that the person may be a great reality and that in the person there is given both a special form of the fullness of reality and the possibility of salvation. What we say, for both theological as well as philosophical reasons, is that God has self-revealed in history. Christian revelation and salvation not only have appeared in history, but they constitute a salvation history. Because of that there is no possibility of revelation except in the historical and for those who are a part of history. Revelation itself can only continue by passing through history and cannot be completely concluded. One can say, on the one hand, that revelation has concluded. However, on the other hand, it has not concluded. In this latter sense, one has to wait for history to continue for humanity to be revealed in all that is, and in that way, we have a better perception of God.

Thus, we try to conclude that salvation history implies a progressive salvation of history. And, undoubtedly, liberation theology will put all of its energy into saving history, but history understood as the fullness of reality, in which persons and individuals are not excluded. Without excluding metahistorical dimensions, the Reign of God should be realized in history. What do we understand by "Reign of God"? The Reign of God involves a maximal presence of God, as that God is revealed in Jesus, and of God's will in human history. Simply put, one can say that it is when God reigns. This may recall formulas such as "the Sacred Heart will reign in all places" that had a meaning quite different from the one we wish to give here. It does not deal with the church. The church is not the Reign of God, but rather a part of it, subordinate to it. The reign deals with the divine ever becoming more historical among human beings.

We want the Reign of God to be realized in history. We are not excluding metahistorical dimensions, in the sense that with the end of history comes the end of reality. When I say that the fullness of reality is in history, fundamentally I mean the fullness of reality we call intramundane. But in this intramundane reality, and precisely in its historical aspects, is perhaps where, in some manner, without confusing them, the reality of God is present. But not every historical realization is the presence of God in the same mode. The fact that God is all in all has its own history of sin and grace.

We say that we do not know God, except in Jesus, taking into account immediately that the true God is only the one who revealed Godself historically and scandalously in Jesus, and in the poor who continue Jesus' presence. This is not obvious. Some accept as a given that, having studied Aristotle and other authors, they know perfectly well who God is, and then they preach that Jesus is God. But we say that God is the one whom Jesus reveals. Certainly, this is a strange God. It appears that he resembles very little of God. Obviously, if Jesus is seen in his mortal flesh, in his historical journey, in what he realized on earth—according to what we read in the gospels—it was very difficult to accept that he was God, if by God we understand that concept mentioned beforehand, whatever that might be.

The History of Salvation as a History of Liberation

There is only one history that, without excluding differences, does not permit the existence of two histories, that of humanity and that of God. Liberation theologians do not accept—nor do many European theologians—two distinct histories, in the sense that there is a profane history and a Christian or sacred history. We cannot accept that history possesses two distinct lines of development. It is a history of salvation and a history of condemnation. It is a history of sin and grace. What history possesses is profane and sacred. Perhaps there is need to make this more precise. In history, there are sinful things and graced things. We imagine the coming together of these things is a history of grace and salvation, but we can also imagine that other times they come together as a history of sin and condemnation.

There is but one history. Without excluding differences, we are not monists, we speak about structures, which is an entirely different thing. We admit a strict unity to history, not because there is only one thing in history, but because all things in history form a structural unity, which is different. It does not imply monism or dualism. Nor are there two separate things that later relate to each other, but rather a structural unity. A structural unity, by definition, exhibits a qualitative plurality of elements, and that qualitative plurality of elements enriches the unity, but in a way in which all of those distinct things are of the whole and constitute a primary unity. Moreover, this structural unity in history is *sui generis*.

Within that unique history, the exercise of Christian faith maintains its relative autonomy. I do not wish to limit the autonomy of other spheres, but rather wish to safeguard the relative autonomy of faith. There is nothing that cannot be influenced in some way by faith; of course, there is the personal sphere in its different dimensions but also the structural. In respect to salvation (sin and grace), there is not a substantial difference between the individual and the social. There is original sin and historical sin that affect social life in a real way and that should be overcome. There is also a personal sin that, in its subjective repercussion, should also be treated. We are speaking then, of a transformation and conversion. It is here that, in different historical conditions, Christian faith favors ways of life and action, but structures as well, that have the most affinity to the Reign of God.

The historicity of Christian salvation, in its necessity to accommodate itself and incarnate itself, or, as we say, to historicize itself in reality, presents itself in Latin America as liberation. Christian salvation, and consequently Christian liberation, is understood as a historical process with historical visibility, for the reasons expressed earlier, though perhaps not with a full visibility. I do not deny that there may be mysterious elements or those that cannot be grasped, but what we are speaking of here is a historical process that actively brings about integral liberation. Obviously, this does not overlook liberation from personal sin, but it places special importance on historical sin, which is understood as injustice and domination. One can confirm the presence of social and historical sin as the negating and blocking of the Reign of God.

The theology of liberation seeks more just and free structures and behaviors. Although Christian faith itself is not sufficient for liberation—and, in that sense, we cannot fall back into autocracies, Christendoms, or anything resembling them—we understand that faith can make a fundamental contribution to the integral liberation of persons without any dualisms. It is obvious that for as much as we preach, as much as we process, as much as we celebrate, we will not be able to make history right by faith alone. Technical skills are needed; politics are needed; many things are needed. Integral liberation cannot be made outside of processes of development and political change that are, more or less, revolutionary. However, the contribution of faith—and this we have not taken from other theories, but from our experience in Latin America—offers values, directions, attitudes, etc., that, in each case, must be translated. In this way, history takes on the character of salvation. We understand salvation as liberation—as integral liberation in our situation.

The theology of liberation insists that the fullness of historical salvation understood as liberation, which includes all salvation, cannot be obtained except from a preferential option for the poor. The church cannot be what it should be unless it is configured as a church of the poor. Without delving into its historical reasons, we can say it is evident the church is not a church of the poor in its totality. It is not. It is not in developed countries where one could say that it need not be so. It is not in most places in the world. The church in Africa, I understand, is not a church of the poor. The church in Latin America—understood in its totality, with the hierarchy and all the rest—is not a church of the poor. And so, successively, the church is not a church of the poor. Therefore, the theology of liberation claims that the church cannot do what it should do, as sacrament of salvation, as efficacious instrument of salvation, unless it is configured as a church of the poor.

Now, this being so, the preferential option for the poor is ordered to efficacious action for their liberation. It means a liberation of the poor, and not just the poor in an economic sense, but also in a theological and political sense, an analogical sense. In respect to this point, we have been accused on occasion of confusing the poor with the proletariat. How are we going to do this if, in large part, there is no proletariat in Latin America? There are majority populations who are oppressed. There are majorities, peasants and indigenous, who are exploited and, sometimes, not even exploited, but rather completely marginalized from history.

So the poor, without identifying themselves as the proletariat, not only are the poor in an economic sense, but they are also the dispossessed who struggle to overcome the state of injustice. Although one cannot reduce the poor to being the subject of social struggle, they tend to support those social struggles that oppose domination in favor of justice and liberation. Liberation theology attempts to situate itself, really and intentionally, in the situation and perspective of the majority populations in order to understand, interpret, and transform reality so as to live out the fullness of the gospel, as much personally as in community.

Liberation theology does not propose a new form of Christianity, but neither does it shut itself away to the sphere of opinions or interpretations. Contrary to what it has been accused of, liberation theology does not have a defined political project; nor does it claim that the church, as a whole or some of its parts, shapes the direction of history out of its own power. Liberation theology has no political project, but rather a utopian "ideal," and it lets others "realize" the ideal and put it into action using their power. Thus, liberation theology does not have to have power for itself, much less be aligned with power. It does not accept participation in power but seeks always to be with the opposition, that is to say, with the oppressed.

What is important is that, from the perspective of liberation theology, we are not proposing any new form of Christianity, but rather we are proposing that history should be transformed by the poor as the true subjects of history. However, while we do not wish to fall into the temptation of Christendom, neither do we want to fall into that of interiority. There is a Jesus-project that neither reduces Jesus to a project nor concretizes into a single particular project, but has definite and operative norms: that which favors, and integrally favors, the poor, the poor as a people. It seeks to struggle and overcome all forms of domination and injustice, according to the spirit and letter of the beatitudes—all of this from personal and efficacious love. It proposes the civilization of poverty as an alternative. To liberation theologians it appears obvious that the human person, as a being in the world, cannot realize herself without realizing a world—a world that, as a dwelling, both welcomes in and gives an outward impulse. Although they are not unconnected, the personal and the social are two distinct dynamisms, and it is not enough to dedicate oneself exclusively to one of them.

The theology of liberation proposes a spirituality that, far from spiritualizing the human person, historicizes her evangelically. It is a matter of developing a new spirituality that accompanies all of these historical struggles that are unfolding. In reference to this, Gustavo Gutiérrez, drawing upon the formulation of Ignatius of Loyola, claims that what a person of the church should be, in conformity with the theology of liberation, is a contemplative in action, not just any action, but liberative action. Spirituality must be from and for integral, liberative action. This spirituality is not an evasion, or even a parallel concomitance, but a reflection of and animation for action and for works to which it contributes spirit, but from which it also receives nourishment. That is to say, the Christian should ask herself, "What liberative action should I follow now?" It is an active spirituality: "What action does reality require of me in this process of integral liberation?" And, then, from this place, be a contemplative. That is to say, there, in that action, see what there is of God, how God makes Godself present there, and how one perceives God in that place.

Neither liberative action nor the materiality of poverty, however necessary, is sufficient. The gift of God must be received, and a place for this must be made explicitly. One must remain open to mystery and must live it in all of its manifestations. It is not enough simply to do; one must take care of one's being: doing good and being good.

The configuration of the human person as a follower of Jesus is a very important aspect, so that praxis and morality are a following of Jesus. Liberation theology accepts the divinity of Jesus without ambiguity, while maintaining mystery and the historicity of the path Jesus walked. It does not direct itself so much to the cultic spirituality of the resurrected Christ but that of the Jesus of history. It values the historical character of Jesus' life as that which explains the persecution he suffered from the powerful. It believes that the Jesus of history leads to the metahistorical Jesus, but one cannot arrive at the latter without going through the former.

Liberation theology places a special emphasis on poverty as that which generates spirit. It highlights this notion in the life of Jesus without making it banal. It retrieves the great Christian tradition that has made this point an essential element of conversion and reform.

Another essential factor of liberation theology is the giving of one's life for others but especially the most poor in the correlative forms of martyrdom and persecution. It is the offering of one's life out of love, in an incarnational way, to those most needy and oppressed. The world of sin responds with persecution and martyrdom.

For liberation theology, hope, without losing its transcendent and meta-historical value, is historicized in order to continue living and struggling. We have this experience with our people; a people that has been bombed and massacred—I come from a country in which the ruling powers and international powers have murdered more than sixty thousand Salvadorans in these past five or six years. In the face of this, we will not begin to wonder if it is a sin that they have killed sixty thousand or not. Are the regime and the international relations that lead to the murder of sixty thousand people good? This is ridiculous. It is obviously a monstrous sin! It is so because in order to be able to kill sixty thousand people in a country of five million inhabitants, the entire structure must be so perverted, so corrupt that it explodes in sixty thousand murders. The history of these countries is filled with sin, and thus, one must struggle against this sinfulness.

We see clearly that God does not will that things be like this and that God wills a struggle to change things. The security of the resurrection does not take away the desire to struggle but strengthens it. As a follower of Jesus, one tries to do this out of hope. It is a struggle taken on through the Christian vocation and not because of class hatred, and those who are really enduring this, these are the ones who give us the most hope. "And you, you really aren't losing hope?" (They could have had five siblings or children killed.) "No, no, no. This will serve to bring about the Reign of God," will say the most humble ones. "We will continue, we will continue."

Of course, they say it in a different way. They say, "If they are going to kill us anyways, it is better this way. . . . We struggle so that our children will have a better life, and at least we die in a different manner." Everything has its remedy. Because after five years of murder after murder, even the most Christian hope suffers a bit. In these circumstances, liberation theologians are aware of the dangers of messianism and politicization.

Here is where one must contemplate the problem of popular religiosity as well. "The people that lives out the faith" is the ultimate point of reference for any consideration. It is the font of its spiritual life. Despite some symbolic distortions, there is an inherent evangelical sense in the people, for example, in the communal retrieval of the Bible as the gift of God and a guide for history. They become privileged depositories of the spirit of Jesus because of material historical conditions and the divine promise. Popular religiosity then is put at the service of the historical project.

The Decentralization and De-Westernization of the Christian Faith

The greatness of this aspiration, not attempted but fecund, has been recognized by the authorities of the church. Fortunately, Rome and especially Ratzinger recognize that what liberation theology claims is enormously important. They have recently said that liberation and freedom are essential elements of Christian faith and that liberation theology has brought attention to this point. Ratzinger recognizes the importance of this engagement, but he says that although liberation theology deals with a universal phenomenon, it is also a fundamental danger to the faith of the church.[5] It is "a totally new orientation of theological thought."[6] Because "liberation theology claims to give a new, comprehensive interpretation of Christianity; it understands Christianity as a praxis of liberation; it claims to present itself as a guide for praxis."[7] He then offers to restore it from "Rome."

On the other hand, some Latin American bishops, base communities, and theologians see this movement as necessary in their churches, and non-Christians, especially Marxists, see it as either necessary for the revolution or for the humanization of the revolution and/or historical project of poor nations. Although it is seen as a phenomenon born from and for Latin America and other similar situations, there is a certain claim to universal, not uniform but historical, validity.

The Christian faith standardized by the exigencies and opportunities of the Western world and the present Western Christian civilization entails a grave reduction of itself and in its capacity for inculturation. For liberation theology, the form that Christianity has taken in Europe after so many centuries, the ancient and the modern is, in the best case, if it had been done well, one of the possible forms of living out Christianity—one. But by no means is it the best way to live out Christianity. This form of living out Christianity, across the board, I will say briefly, is that which esteems itself *the* most profound Christian form of living out the gospel.

We accept that the faith must be historicized and that historicization always brings with it mistakes, weaknesses, specificities, etc. Obviously, Christianity, the Christian faith, was born in a thoroughly third world nation, in material conditions of poverty and domination, such as Palestine is in this moment, and then adopted in Rome. Later, Rome falls into Constantinianisms and configures itself in a different manner. It historicizes the faith. Now, I will not judge whether that historicization is good or not. It was historicized, and it attempted to accommodate itself to that situation that there was in that moment. The great problem here is not taking notice of the manner in which the faith was historicized by categories, needs, and problems that are typical of this world. Today, the major preoccupation concerns what happens to Christian faith fundamentally in this small part of the world: the North Atlantic part of Europe.

The historicization of the faith as it has come to the world through Western civilization, even with its universal ideas, is a limitation of the Christian faith. One can accept the necessity of the historicization of faith but not the fundamental identification of the faith with historical forms of interpreting and living it. One can verify the fact that the Christian faith has been reduced, if not deformed, by historical incarnations that present themselves as official.

We believe that this historicization has brought great deviations, and fundamentally, we understand that this is because it has occurred in a historical context in which the phenomena of domination-dependence and wealth-poverty are essential. Faith is not reduced to simply responding to these phenomena, but the phenomena historicize the faith first in a basic way. The post-Constantinian Western historicization takes the faith through the path of power, wealth, and worldliness. The faith has been shaped more by the needs and interests of those countries of worldly wealth and societies of worldly domination. A church that is preferentially for the poor and weak becomes a church preferentially for the wealthy and powerful, for the maintenance of an order that benefits it, and not for transformation.

What has happened is tremendous: that the Christian faith in these worlds has become a conservative element, an element of support for the established order, a defense of the situation of the most powerful and most dominant. Obviously, for the one who reads the gospel with clear eyes, these have transformed not water into wine but wine into water. It cannot be the other way.

Later, the faith has been translated into very interesting Greco-European intellectual categories and into a Roman-European institutionality that, undoubtedly, have offered very valuable possibilities for the interpretation of Christianity. However, there is no reason to consider these the best possibilities because they do not take into account all of the faith, and they are not those that best respond to mentalities of a different kind.

In this mind-set, it is thought that one has arrived at formulations, dogmatic and nondogmatic, theoretical and practical, that are not only correct but cannot be surpassed. It does not understand what this means for the universal catholicity that Christian faith claims. This includes the problem of postmodernity that, while it is not completely alien to the underdeveloped world, cannot be the fundamental driving element.

Liberation theology recovers historical universalism in order to break the Western limitation and actualize unprecedented possibilities of the faith. We say, in order for Christianity to offer all that it can of itself to history, it must be situated where it must be situated. Therefore, liberation theology situates Christianity in the material-historical place where it is most suited, and with that, recovers the subversive potential of the faith. In other words, the material-historical place of Christianity is rooted in situations of poverty and in poor countries.

Liberation theology subjects Christianity to a severe criticism with regard to its assimilation to power and identifying itself or subordinating itself to dominant powers. The church has supposed that to be able to proclaim the gospel, it has had to possess papal states and be a state and be a perfect society. The historical and Christian universe, which is the poor, is retrieved so that it might be really catholic and universal. In what sense? In the sense that has been stated earlier: the immense majority of the people of this world are truly poor, and thus, that is a historical universal. One must read "the people of God" from the church of the poor, and the latter from the former. Then it can configure itself in a language and along a direction that really can serve the majority of humankind. This would strengthen the church to commit itself to sacrifice, loss, and death with those who suffer most in their historical struggles.

Well, those would be some points that—only intimated and that one would have to develop—could indicate how the theology of liberation could confront the problem of the relation of Christian faith with history and not only with politics. The fruits—for some, bad fruit—are there. The Latin American church possesses a great vitality, a great strength, even though much effort has been taken to subjugate it so that all of its historical-evangelical potential not come to light. However, it is still there, and we hope it will be for many years.

Notes

[1] Joseph Ratzinger and Vittorio Messori, *Informe sobre la fe* (Madrid: La Editorial Católica, 1985), 202. In English, Joseph Ratzinger and Vittorio Messori, *The Ratzinger Report* (San Francisco: Ignatius Press, 1985). The citations refer to the Spanish edition.

[2] Ibid, 204.

[3] Ibid., 202–03.

[4] Ibid., 211.

[5] Cf. ibid., 193.

[6] Ibid., 196.

[7] Ibid.,195.

—Translated by Michael E. Lee

6

The Historicity of
Christian Salvation
(1984)

"Historicidad de la salvación Cristiana" served as the lead article in Volume 1, Number 1 of Revista Latinoamericana de Teología, the journal launched in 1984 by the UCA, which quickly took its place among professional theological journals not only in Latin America but worldwide. Ellacuría's essay engages the conclusions of the 1976 Vatican International Theological Commission, and takes into account the concerns about liberation theology published by then Cardinal Joseph Ratzinger in the journal Thirty Days, a harbinger of the more formal critique issued several months later by the Vatican Congregation for the Doctrine of the Faith that Cardinal Ratzinger headed. While the dramatic struggle between the Vatican and proponents of liberation theology stands in the background of this essay, no less important is the larger philosophical-theological question of the relationship between the divine and the human that Ellacuría probes here in dialogue with two of the greatest theologians of the twentieth century: Karl Rahner and Wolfhart Pannenberg.

This abridged version of "Historicidad de la salvación Cristiana" focuses on the way Ellacuría poses key questions about the historicity of salvation (Part I) and on his constructive response to those questions (Part IV). "What do human efforts toward historical, even sociopolitical, liberation have to do with the establishment of the Reign of God that Jesus preached? What do the proclamation and realization of the Reign of God have to do with the historical liberation of the oppressed majorities?" The direction he proposes to address these questions presupposes the unity of historical reality in which "God's participation does not occur without some form of human participation, and human participation does not occur without God's presence in some form." The brilliance of this essay emerges in the "how." Probing God's history taken as a whole and the need to distinguish grace and sin in this unified human history, he moves into a breathtaking consideration, rooted in his

Zubirian understanding of reality, on the one history of God in light of the doctrine of creation and the presence of the Trinitarian life to creation. Against this discussion he engages anew the ancient problem of theodicy, not as an intellectual puzzle, but a heart-wrenching encounter with unjust poverty. He probes different models of religious power in view of their approaches to transcendence and sketches the liberating spirituality by which Christians live fully the presence of historical transcendence.

Setting Out the Problem

The historicity of Christian salvation continues to be one of the most serious problems for understanding and practicing faith. It is a problem in the North Atlantic countries, in the oppressed countries, and, finally, in the preoccupation of the magisterium and discipline of the institutional church.[1]

There are different understandings of the phrase "historicity of Christian salvation." A first distinction might be made between those who question the historical character of salvific acts and those with questions about the salvific character of historical acts. Those in the first group are mainly concerned with historically grounding and objectively proving fundamental acts of faith, from the resurrection of Jesus as the most important act, to the miracles or the series of salvific events in the Hebrew scriptures. Those in the second group are especially concerned with which historical acts bring salvation and which bring condemnation, which acts make God more present, and how that presence is actualized and made effective in them. These are not mutually exclusive perspectives; rather, the second presupposes the first and accepts without serious reservations that the great salvific, revealing, and communicating acts of God have taken place in history, even though their critical justification cannot achieve or be reduced to proofs from historical science.

The present essay locates itself within the second of these perspectives and seeks to rethink the classical problem of the relationship between Christian salvation, which would seem to be that which formally defines the mission of the church and of Christians as Christians, and historical liberation, which would seem to be that which formally defines states, social classes, citizens, human persons as human persons. Taking up this problem once again does not mean simply attempting to solve a purely intellectual preoccupation, the calming of an anxiety born from a theoretical paradox. Rather, the intent is, first, to clarify a fundamental point for the understanding of faith and the effectiveness of Christian praxis, especially in the context of the third world and Latin America, in particular, and second, to respond to those who would declare invalid the efforts that liberation theologians have made: to rethink the whole of revelation and the life of the church in the search for the salvation-liberation of the poor but to seek as well for a profound renewal of the thinking, the spirituality, the pastoral practice, and even the institutionality of the universal church.

Liberation theologians are increasingly accepted as representing a new way of doing theology, which has great importance for the life of the church and for the understanding and explanation of the Christian faith. After a first stage in which their importance was discounted on the grounds that their work was more sociological than theological, and that at best they were dealing with issues of social ethics, it was later recognized that their issues are fundamental to theology and, moreover, that it is a comprehensive theology, capable of replacing other forms of theology that were considered uniquely classical and universal. Thus, the International Theological Commission, meeting in 1976, assumed that the principal object of the theology of liberation was the connection between Christian salvation and human promotion, and that "this unity of connection, as well as the difference indicated by the relationship between human promotion and Christian salvation, in its concrete form, should be sought for and re-analyzed; that is, without any doubt, one of the principal tasks of theology today."[2] At that same meeting, Hans Urs von Balthasar concluded his critical observations with these words: "The theology of liberation has its specific place in a theology of the Reign of God; it is one aspect of theology among others, and it demands practical action from the church to shape the world around Christ."[3]

But more recently, Cardinal Ratzinger has given special emphasis to the universal character of the theology of liberation by recognizing (1) that it seeks to be "a new hermeneutic of the Christian faith," that is, a new way of understanding and realizing Christianity in its totality; (2) that it brings together several currents of thought, and in turn it influences regions far beyond the geography and culture of Latin America; (3) that it acquires an ecumenical character: "a new universality for which the classical separation of the churches should lose importance."[4]

This question of the historicity of Christian salvation, as we have said, is not exclusive to the theology of liberation, but the theology of liberation gives it singular importance and special characteristics.

Its singular importance is not due to the supposed nature of the theology of liberation as a formal political theology. The book of Clodovis Boff, so many chapters of which are excellent, might cause a distorted image of the theology of liberation or might lead it into theological regionalizations that are neither necessary nor desirable.[5] Although secondary considerations

may occasionally suggest methodical separations, the theology of liberation
should not be understood as a political theology, but as a theology of the
Reign of God, so that [Boff's] material distinction between a T 1 that deals
with the classical themes of God, Christ, the church, and a T 2 that deals
with more specifically human and/or political themes, is not acceptable.[6]
In fact, liberation theology primarily deals with everything that has to do
with the Reign of God; but it focuses on this and all of its subtopics, even
the most elevated and apparently metahistorical, in the context of and
often with special attention to their liberating dimension.

The special characteristics of liberation theology do not come from its
supposed primary emphasis on politics or even on liberation understood
in an integral way. They flow from the "locus," Christian and epistemological, in which theologians situate themselves, from their preferential option
for the poor and from their desire to place the potentialities of the Reign
of God at the service of the historical salvation of humanity, keeping this
historical salvation in the closest possible relationship with the Christian
salvation of humanity and the world.

The permanent problem of the relationship between the divine and
the human thus takes on new importance and, above all, is seen from a
new perspective. What do human efforts toward historical, even sociopolitical, liberation have to do with the establishment of the Reign of God that
Jesus preached? What do the proclamation and realization of the Reign
of God have to do with the historical liberation of the oppressed majorities? Such questions represent a fundamental problem for the praxis of the
church of the poor as well as an essential problem for the present history
of Latin America. It is not primarily a conceptual issue but a real issue; it
requires the use of concepts to resolve it in theory, but it is not primarily
or ultimately a purely theoretical question. It is not primarily a problem
of bringing two abstract concepts together in theory, one referring to
the work of God and the other to human work. It causes unnecessary
difficulties to start with concepts and with the more or less explicit assumption that adequately distinct concepts represent different realities. The
assumption is that there are two clearly different concepts to which are
attributed two clearly different realities as correlates. In other words, a long,
intellectual elaboration, realized over centuries, has led to the conceptual
separation between what appears in biographical and historical experience
to be united. Not only has that conceptual separation been increasingly
taken for granted, it has become the point of departure from which to return to a reality no longer seen primarily in itself, but through the "truth"
attributed to the concept. The problem not only is not resolved but is

concealed by separating the concept from real historical praxis and placing it ideologically and uncritically at the service of institutionalized interests. The problem is concealed, not mainly because the concept is abstract, but rather because it is not historical. There is an ahistorical conceptual universality, and there is a historical, or historicized, conceptual universality. The former may seem more theoretical and more universal, which is not so much because it conceals a historicity that by its concealment serves to deform it, but rather because it ignores the properly universal dimension of historical reality that appears when correctly conceptualized. If one does not reflect critically on what specific historical praxis conceptualizations come from and what praxis they lead to, one places oneself at the service of a history that the concept may be trying to negate.

This epistemological suspicion, repeatedly confirmed in the historical praxis of the church in Latin America, leads us to liberation theology's position on the problem of the "relationship" between the different moments of a single praxis of salvation. It is not primarily a problem of conceptualization or a theoretical problem that must be resolved in order to protect orthodoxy. It is, at least primarily, a problem of praxis, the praxis of certain Christians who have sought to participate in a Christian way in the struggles that the people have undertaken for their own liberation. These Christians, compelled by their faith and as an objective realization of that faith, seek to make human action correspond as much as possible to God's will. They have heard the cries of the people—of my people, as the bishops of northeastern Brazil have written[7]—an exploited people who deserve something better, who often know that they are children of God. These believers have seen that those who call themselves Christians are responsible for many of the evils that befall the poorest people, while those who call themselves nonbelievers have committed themselves truly and sacrificially to the liberation of the poorest and most oppressed. Faced with this terrible paradox, they wonder how it can be this way, and what they should do with their faith and their works to put an end to this scandal, which can put an end to the faith that today remains so vigorous among the popular majorities.

To approach this problem, which is so fundamental to ecclesial praxis and to the confession and understanding of the faith, we shall make use of a traditional concept: transcendence. Without getting into previous arguments on the concept of transcendence, we can see in it something that allows one to note a moment of structural difference without accepting a duality—something that allows one to speak of an intrinsic unity without implying a strict identity. Although in the last part of this essay we will offer some reflections on this unity without separation or confusion, from the outset we will assume that there are not two histories, a history of God and a human history, a sacred and a profane history. Rather, there is a single historical reality in which both God and human beings take part, so that God's participation does not occur without some form of human participation, and human participation does not occur without God's presence in some form. What we need to discern is the different ways in which God and human beings intervene, and the distinct mode of "relation" in those interventions. God's intervention and God's presence in human interventions are of different types when the human intervention occurs in the context of sin and when it occurs in the context of anti-sin or grace. God's omnipresence in history is always divine, by definition, although that presence takes different forms not easily classified in the simplistic division between natural and supernatural.

Christian thinking on this point suffers from pernicious philosophical influences, which do not respond to the problem as it is presented in the history of revelation. Transcendence is identified with separateness, and it is thus assumed that historical transcendence is separate from history. The transcendent must be outside or beyond what is immediately apprehended as real, so that the transcendent must always be other, different, and separated, whether in time, in space, or in its essence. But there is a radically different way of understanding transcendence, more in line with the way reality and God's action are presented in biblical thinking. This is to see transcendence as something that transcends *in* and not as something that transcends *away from*; as something that physically impels to *more* but not by taking *out of*; something that pushes forward, but at the same time retains. In this conception, when one reaches God historically—which is the same as reaching God personally—one does not abandon the human, does not abandon real history, but rather deepens one's roots, making more present and effective what was already effectively present. God can be separated from history, but history cannot be separated from God. And in history, transcendence must be seen more in the relation necessity-freedom then that of absence-presence. God is transcendent, among other reasons, not by being absent, but by being freely present—sometimes in one way and sometimes in another, choosing the ways freely as the Lord, with different levels of intensity, in God's own self-giving will. As we shall see later, even in the case of sin, we are fully in the history of salvation; sin does not make God disappear, but rather crucifies God, which seems like the same thing but in fact is profoundly different. It may be possible to divide history into a history of sin and another of grace; but that division presupposes the real unity of history, and the real and indissoluble unity of God and of the human being in history. It also presupposes a very close relationship between sin and grace, so that sin is defined by grace and grace by sin.[8]

Here we do not propose a philosophical discussion on the problem of transcendence, although we will use the concept in order to give it a precise meaning from some examples from the Old and New Testament. Rather, what we propose here is to show the primordial unity of the divine and the human in history, a unity so primordial that only by long reflection has humanity been able to make separations and distinctions, some of them justified and some not. The transcendence of which we speak presents itself as historical, and history in turn presents itself as transcendent, despite the great difficulty of finding adequate concepts to maintain that indivisible unity without confusion.

Several essential points of the Christian faith could be used to illustrate this point; above all, the transcendent mystery of Jesus' humanity. It is in Jesus—true human and true God, as the Christian faith maintains—that the unity is best realized and can best be studied. We will not do that here, because the limited scope of this essay could not even begin to outline that study. The same problem could also be studied using the church, with its obvious and palpable history, on the one hand, and, on the other, its character as a mystery that is confessed by faith. Such a study could offer important theoretical clues, since the historicization of the mystery of the church, subjected to the appropriate criticism, would undermine many of the arguments used to attack the historicization of the faith proposed by the theology of liberation. We could also study the singular case of the sacred books, in which, on the one hand, human action is so evident as a vehicle of revelation, and, on the other, God's authorship has to be acknowledged by faith.

For practical reasons, we shall take two more modest cases as the object of study, in order to show what historical transcendence might be in the Old and New Testament. We do not assume that we are dealing with two different forms of divine transcendence in history, with the second surpassing or invalidating the first. When von Balthasar affirms with respect to the theology of liberation that "in Israel the religious is always political, and the political religious, down to the very core of the people's eschatological hope," and adds that "this monism of religion and politics, which constitutes the essence of Israel, has been and remains entirely detrimental for the church, always and in all its forms (caesaropapism, *cuius region*)," his affirmation distorts the problem.[9] Liberation theology has often been accused of being more like the Hebrew scriptures than the Christian in its fundamental historical-political concern. Citations have been offered to that effect, and we will not overcome that objection by abandoning the inspiration of the historico-salvific events of the Hebrew scriptures but by shedding on them the light of the Christian scriptures, without putting the problem in terms of the age of grace that leaves behind the age of the law. It would be a mutilation of the Hebrew scriptures to try to take from them only their religious spirit while abandoning all that there is in the way of historical flesh. Likewise, it would be a mutilation of the Christian New Testament to desire to take what is spiritual and not take notice of its historicity, or to limit the meaning of that historicity only to support a religious spirit. In both cases, there is spirit and flesh, God and history, so inseparably united that the disappearance of one would disfigure, if not destroy, the other.

Clearly we are not going to study historical transcendence in depth in either the Old or the New Testament, or the relationship between them, in this essay. It is enough to point out some of their significant aspects, in order to reach a greater clarity on the problem at hand; Christian histori-cal transcendence includes both perspectives, but it also includes what the Spirit has been creating and making manifest, which must be discerned as "signs of the times."[10]

The Search for Christian Historical Transcendence[11]

Keeping in mind the perspectives of historical transcendence in the Old and New Testaments, we can now return to the question of what Christian historical transcendence should be. The problem has two currents: on the one hand, it concerns the "relation" between so-called profane history and salvation history; on the other hand, it deals with attempting to see the specifically Christian contribution to that moment of historical transcen-dence in which the transcendent becomes historical in some way and the historical becomes transcendent in some way.

To present the problem in a general theoretical way before entering into a more concentrated analysis of the perspective of liberation theology, let us briefly outline two European viewpoints, one Catholic and the other evangelical, in which the problem is meaningfully expressed.

In a brief essay titled "*Weltgeschichte und Heilsgeschichte*" (History of the World and Salvation History), Karl Rahner has formulated certain theses that, although they come from a time when he was less interested in the political projection of the religious, taken together express viewpoints that are fundamental to his thinking.[12]

1. The history of salvation occurs in and is interwoven with the history of the world, for salvation occurs now; it is freely accepted by the human being; and it remains hidden within profane history in its dual possibilities of salvation and condemnation.
2. Salvation history is different from profane history, since profane history does not permit a univocal interpretation with respect to salvation and condemnation. Although one must speak of a constant interaction and coexistence between profane history and the history of salvation and revelation, nevertheless, God through God's word, which is a constitutive element of salvation history, has set apart one part of history to establish it expressly, officially, and properly as the history of salvation.
3. Salvation history clarifies profane history by demythologizing and denoumenizing[13] it, by viewing it as conflictive and shrouded in darkness, by interpreting it as existentially powerless, and by explaining it Christocentrically. In the final analysis, profane history is the condition of possibility for the history of Christ, which is also the history of God, just as natural history in its materiality and vitality is the condition of possibility for the emergence of finite spirit.

Wolfhart Pannenberg, in our second example, has also formulated his thesis around the relationship between revelation and history:

1. God's self-revelation has not been carried out directly, as a kind of theophany, but indirectly, through God's works in history.
2. Revelation has no place at the beginning but at the end of the revelatory history.
3. Historical revelation is open for all who have eyes to see; it has a universal character.
4. The universal revelation of God's divinity was not yet realized in the history of Israel, but only in the fate of Jesus of Nazareth, inasmuch as that fate anticipates the end of all that happens.
5. The Christ event does not reveal the divinity of the God of Israel as an isolated event, and it is only comprehensible from the viewpoint of the history of God with Israel.
6. The formation of non-Jewish concepts of revelation in the Christian churches of pagan origin expresses the universality of eschatological self-revelation in the fate of Jesus.

7. The word of God relates to revelation as preaching, as precept, and as story.[14]

Now let us compare this with the way the theology of liberation approaches the double problem defined above with regard to Christian historical transcendence. We will take it step by step, beginning with the experience of Latin American believers—of course, it is not exclusively their experience—especially that of the poorest and most oppressed sectors, and of those Latin American believers who have been compelled by their faith to commit themselves politically in order to win freedom through a process of liberation.

History as a Whole

Granting that there is a difference between what could be salvation history and what is real history as it is lived empirically, we can say that deep down believers see these two histories as unified, that is, united in what might be called the great history of God. This perception presupposes that history is presented as a whole, and within that history are two parts. The first is what can be called salvation history, which certainly is not limited to sacramental, cultic, or strictly religious life. The second, which has a more profane appearance, is also part of the great history of God with humanity. If we are asked whether profane history takes its meaning from salvation history and is subordinate to it, we respond by presenting the problem in deeper terms. Salvation history and so-called profane history both belong to a single history that they serve: God's history; what God has done with all of nature; what God does in human history; and what God wants to result from God's constant self-giving, which can be imagined as going from eternity to eternity. In this sense, the salvation history that culminates in the person of Christ is subordinate to the greater history of God. We could say that this concept gives living expression to Paul's experience when he saw God's secret plan "to lead history to its fullness," that through the Messiah would come the unity of the universe, the things in heaven and things on earth (Eph. 1:9–10).

For all things are yours whether Paul or Apollos or Cephas or the world or life or death or the present or the future—all belong to you, and you belong to Christ, and Christ belongs to God. (1 Cor. 3:21–23)

When all things are subjected to him, then the Son himself will also
be subjected to the one who put all things in subjection under him,
so that God may be all in all. (1 Cor. 15:28)

This affirmation of God's history as the true history embracing everything that happens in history does not identify salvation history with the
autonomy of the profane. The affirmation comes to us through popular
religion and also through pre-Christian religious traditions, which take
it for granted that God has made and continues to make human beings
along with everything else that exists. Christian preaching inserted itself
within an earlier religious tradition, which in some places is still very active, that sees God's action among human beings a part of nature. The gods
of the *Popol Vuh*[15] and the still prevalent cosmovisions of peoples like the
K'ekchi'[16] serve as background to this acceptance of a single God who
begins by making earth and heaven, who is still behind natural events, and
who is in some degree also behind historical events.

    In this history of God, Christian faith gives absolute primacy to the
salvific event of Christ, but this does not imply a caesaropapist and/or re-
ligionist subjection of profane history to the specificity of Christ as head
of the church and therefore to the church as continuation of the work
of Christ. It does, however, imply a subordination to what can be called
the historical-cosmic Christ, called to make history as a whole effectively
God's history, which on earth means establishing the Reign of God. The
historical Jesus of Nazareth, as presented and interpreted throughout the
New Testament from his historical origins and life to his resurrection and
lordship over the universe and history, is the key to the historical-cosmic
Christ. Therefore, the Reign of Heaven is, in a first moment, a seed sown
in the fields of the world and in history, to make of them a history of God,
of a God who is definitely all in all. In this first moment the field is not
subjected to the seed, but the seed to the field; or, as the other evangelical parable puts it, the leavening of the Reign is modestly and effectively
mixed into the dough of the world to make it ferment and rise.

    Latin American popular religiosity expresses this with an absolute natu-
ralness in the way believers live out their relation to nature and relationships to other people. To be committed only to the religious aspect of the
Reign, without concern for its essential reference to the world and history,
would be a clear betrayal of God's history; it would leave the field of history to God's enemies. Thus, there is no reductionism, either reducing God's
history to the history of Christian salvation in its restricted sense or much

less reducing God's history to the history of political, social, economic, or cultural events. Rather, it is an attempt through Christian faith and action in the midst of the world—which has its own autonomy just as Christian faith and action have—to build God's history, in which Christ's action and human actions, the dictates of faith and of reason, come together in their different forms and different levels of reality.

This way of expressing the problem of Christian historical transcendence may seem rather abstract. In reality it is not. In the conceptual formulation, which may miss the mark, we must not forget that the experience belongs to the believers who see everything as a unity in which they are directly involved and which must be respected. This unity is based on the profound conviction that there is only one God and Father, only one creation, only one savior, only one Reign of God, only one eschatology, only one world, and only one humanity. The things of God and the things of humanity, therefore, must not and cannot be separated; that would mean confusing God with humanity. Jesus himself, who as Christ will bring all things together in himself, enters history as the one who has come to serve human beings and to give his life for them. The church, in turn, must also fulfill its mission by placing itself at the service of human beings and giving its life and institutionality for them, knowing that this is the fulfillment of God's great history. The example of Jesus' life remains the fundamental criterion showing how God enters the service of humanity.

To structure salvation history and the history of the world into what we have been calling God's history does not imply accepting a separation and duality between the first two, subsumed in the higher unity of the third. God's history is nothing but the structural unity of salvation history and the history of the world. The history of the world should determine salvation history in many ways; salvation history should determine the history of the world in many ways; and God's history is at play in both. Thus, the history of the world, rightly analyzed and discerned—herein lies the importance that Clodovis Boff attributes to socioanalytical mediation[17]—presents salvation history with its specific task for each moment, to which in part, without diminishing its specificity in each case, salvation history should be shaped by this fundamental mission. But at the same time, the history of revelation, rightly interpreted—herein lies the importance that Boff attributes to hermeneutical mediation[18]—tries to orient the history of the world to the demands of God's history, which is also manifested in different ways in the information conveyed by revelation, in the signs of the times, and even in the most basic conditions of material nature. Therefore, God's self-giving to humanity continues, not only in the limited arena of a salvation history in its restricted sense, but in the total arena of history. Salvation history takes axiological priority in this total arena, because it is the preeminent way in which God's self-giving becomes present, especially in the figure of Jesus and in the revealed word; however, as we shall insist later, Jesus becomes present and intervenes in a special salvific way as the fundamental mediator of God's history in seemingly profane places such as that of the poor in this world.

Grace and Sin

Closely related to the first point is the problem of what is natural and what is supernatural in this whole history of God.

This formulation of the problem is itself somewhat disconcerting. Is the diversity of God's different forms of self-giving greater than the unity that comes from the fact that it is one God, self-giving in different ways? This question is even more valid if we ask it not about the sanctification and the divinization of persons but about God's presence and intervention in history. Are Moses' actions in bringing the oppressed people out of Egypt and God's presence in that action different from the giving of the law or celebrating religious rites? Are Jesus' actions in the feeding of the hungry multitude and God's presence in that action different from expelling the merchants from the temple or proclaiming the Reign of God and institutionalizing the Eucharistic supper? Are we right to describe the more "profane" cases as God's natural intervention and the more "religious" cases as supernatural intervention?

Latin American popular belief does not see, let alone reflexively affirm, one type of natural intervention and another type of supernatural intervention. At most, believers may distinguish between them in terms of miracles but not in terms of a supernatural communication over against a natural communication by God. They may see some things as more or less distant from God, or God as less present in them, but they do not clearly separate the work of grace and the work of nature; that is, they do not separate the natural from the supernatural. They accept, for example, that God becomes present in the sacraments in what we might call a more religious way, but they know that the same God of the sacraments is present in their lives and destinies and in the course of historical events. Everything is included in the category of God's will. Sometimes they may think fatalistically that something happened because it was God's will; other times they may see clearly that an action is against God's will—not only or mainly in the arena of personal actions but in the course of historical events.

For this reason they raise the question in different terms. The fundamental difference is not between nature and the supernatural; since they are part of the whole history of God who, in creating human beings, raises them to personal participation in God's own divine life, the difference is between grace and sin. Some actions kill (divine) life, and some actions give (divine) life; some belong to the reign of sin, other to the reign of grace. Some social and historical structures objectify the power of sin and serve as vehicles for that power against humanity, against human life; some social and historical structures objectify grace and serve as vehicles for that power in favor of human life. The former constitute structural sin; the latter constitute structural grace. Hans Urs von Balthasar rightly sees that "the New Testament is a confrontation between two types of existence: that which is subjected to sin (*hamartia*) and that which is liberated from sin through Christ."[19] But he judges Medellín unfairly for speaking of unjust and oppressive structures as constituting a situation of sin when he says that "situations can be unjust, but they are not in themselves sinful."[20] Some situations may not be sinful, but they can be an objectification of sin, and they can themselves be sin when they are a positive negation of an essential aspect of the God of life. To think that sin exists only when and insofar as there is personal responsibility is a mistaken and dangerous devaluation of the dominion of sin. The theology of liberation encourages people to change specific structures and to seek new ones, because it sees sin in some and grace in others. In the former, it sees the negation of God's will and self-giving, while in the latter it sees the affirmation and realization of God's will and self-giving.[21]

This does not mean that the classical question about the natural and the supernatural is an idle question, only that it is not the first question. The first question is what there is of grace and of sin in humanity and in history, but a grace and sin seen not primarily from a moral viewpoint, let alone from the fulfillment of laws and obligations, but from the perspective of that which makes God's life present among human beings. God's presence is what makes possible the fulfillment of laws and obligations, not the other way around. It is not the law that saves but faith and grace, a faith and grace that operate and are objectified in history.

No special discernment is needed to make the judgment that there is objective sin in the situation that the people of Latin America are living. It is all around us. It has been recognized by Medellín and Puebla, it has been denounced a thousand times by the bishops, and it is clearly recognized by what can be called the *sensus fidei* of the poor. For the oppressed believers in Latin America, injustice and whatever brings death and denies dignity to the children of God are not merely historical effects or even a legal failing; they are sin in a formal sense, something that formally has to do with God. The death of the poor is the death of God, the ongoing crucifixion of the Son of God. Sin is the negation of God, and the negation of sin moves, sometimes in unknown ways, toward the affirmation of God, toward the presence of God as the giver of life. The perception of a world submerged in ambition, hatred, and domination is nourished by faith and by the Christian sense of those who live their faith simply. It is a way of seeing the sin of the world: Christ came to redeem, and Christians must work to make sin disappear from the world. Sin in the abstract does not lend itself to much study, but it can manifest itself concretely in subtle forms that require more careful theological analysis.

Creation: Presence of the Trinitarian Life

In order to go more deeply into this one history of God, which is fundamentally a history of sin-grace, we can offer some reflections that may seem theoretical, but that shed light on what we have been saying, and can also serve as a practical orientation.

Everything depends on how we understand creation. If by "creation" we mean an efficient act of God in which the creature is a separate effect, having at most a remote resemblance to God, then it is very hard to see the unity of the creature with the creator and to understand God's single history. But creation can be conceived in a different way, as Zubiri so often pointed out in his classes. Creation can be seen as the taking-form *ad extra* of the Trinitarian life itself, a freely willed taking-form but of the Trinitarian life itself.[22] It would not be an idealistic exemplary causality but an act of communication and self-giving by the divine life proper. This taking-form and self-communication has degrees and limits, so that each thing, within its own limits, is a limited way of being God; and this limited way is nothing other than the nature of each thing. God's communication, the taking-form *ad extra* of the divine life, has gone through a long process that has been oriented toward the taking-form of that divine life in the human nature of Jesus, and ultimately toward the "return" of all creation to its original source. In that long process, we see the purely material form of creation, the form of life in its different stages, and finally the form of humanity and its history. Humanity as a formally open essence and history in its essential openness are the realities in which that taking-form of the Trinitarian life is present more and more, although always in a limited way—open but limited, limited but open.

This would be the "theologal" character of all things, and especially the theologal character of humanity and history. It would not be simply that God is in all things, as essence, presence, and potency depending on the character of those things. It would be that all things, each in its own way, have been formed according to the triune life and refer essentially to that life. The theologal dimension of the created world, which should not be confused with the theological dimension, would reside in that presence of the Trinitarian life, which is intrinsic to all things, but which in human beings can be apprehended as reality and as the principle of personhood. There is a strict experience of this theologal dimension, and through it there is a strict personal, social, and historical experience of God.[23] This experience has different degrees and modes; but when it is a true experience of the real theologal dimension of human beings, of society, of history, and in a different measure, of purely material things, it is an experience and physical proof of the triune life itself, however mediated, incarnated, and historicized.[24]

From this perspective we see more clearly not only the unity of God's history but also the fundamental dimension from which to reflect on the problem of grace and sin. All created things are a limited way of being God, and the human being in particular is a small God because the human being is a relative absolute, an acquired absolute. What happens is that this limited way of being God is open in principle. This openness must be seen dynamically, but that dynamic openness is precisely the growing presence of the divine reality in the creature. When this dynamism remains limited merely because at a certain level of creaturehood no more of the self-giving is offered, it is not yet sin but only a deficient presence of the divine, although that deficiency can only be measured in comparison with more elevated and less deficient forms of presence. But when the dynamism is limited, now not only in natural evolution but by deliberate negation in the historical process—whether personal or social—that by absolutizing the limit impedes and even explicitly negates the dynamism of the Trinitarian life (although it cannot destroy it), then we have a case of sin in its formal sense.

The absolutization of this limit, in the personal and social, has two aspects. First, it impedes the renewed presence of God's "more," which marks the privative but not formally negating element toward the God who wants to become more present. Second, it makes a created limit absolute and divine, and so in this sense positively denies God and falls into idolatry. In sin, although it may appear paradoxical, there is an affirmation of God insofar as the sinner is oriented to a good that is the presence of God; but there is an even stronger negation of that affirmation, because it presents something as a full and definitive presence that really is only a partial and transitory presence of God, thus denying a "more" that is the historical presence of the transcendent. To put it differently, idolatry, by making absolute what is limited, closes and denies the divine presence that is in all historical things. This closing in on a limit is precisely what negates the presence of that "more" and that "new" through which transcendence becomes present in the form of personal revelation. Thus, a divine character is attributed to what is not divine, but rather limited, because a limit is made absolute. But that attribution and that absolutization are only possible through the presence of the divine from the theologal dimension. Therefore, we must speak not so much of atheism but of idolatry, of making absolutely absolute that which is only relatively absolute. That is how grace becomes sin.

This idea, which may seem so abstract, is easy to exemplify in real and pastoral life. Archbishop Oscar Romero, in his fourth pastoral letter, "The Church's Mission amid the National Crisis,"[25] seeks to unmask the idolatries of our society. He exposes from this perspective the idolatry that assumes the absolutization of wealth and private property, the absolutization of natural security, and the absolutization of one's party or organization. In wealth and power, it is easy to see aspects that have to do with the presence of God, but the historical absolutization of wealth and power converts them into idols to which all other human possibilities are sacrificed. In the individual human person and her freedom, something is also present that has to do very directly with the God who becomes present and operates in history, but the absolutization of the self and its freedom converts them into idols, makes grace appear like sin. In institutional mechanisms and objective realizations, too, one sees God's potency to achieve a more humane and open history by means of structures, institutions, and social bodies that open human beings more and more to themselves and to others, but their idolatrous absolutization converts the limit into a positive obstacle and a negation of something that is always greater than any objective realization of any subjective intention.

If we look at things this way, it is possible to conceive God's history as both a history of grace and a history of sin. At times there is a greater or lesser presence of the divine life, of grace; and there is also sometimes privation, sometimes even negation, of grace.

Unjust Poverty

The problem, then, is to discern what there is of sin and of grace in a specific historical situation. We must ask with all rigor what the sin of the world is today or in what forms the sin of the world appears today. This sin is different from personal sins but is often conditioned by them and continues or prolongs them. Here is where liberation theology, situated at the heart of the passive and active praxis of the poor, has spoken its word and has shaken the conscience of the church, and in some ways also the conscience of the world.

If we look at the reality of the world as a whole from the perspective of faith, we see that the sin of the world is sharply expressed today in what must be called unjust poverty. Poverty and injustice appear today as the great negation of God's will and as the annihilation of the divine presence God wills among human beings. Both poverty and injustice are empirical phenomena whose universality the first world, the source of traditional theologies, has been reluctant to see. Without losing their empirical character, which must be analyzed with the aid of scientific mediations, the very same phenomena appear in the light of faith as a fundamental event in the history of God with humanity. The scriptural perspective of historical transcendence takes very seriously the realities of the poor and their unjustly inflicted poverty; the social, economic, and political structures on which their reality is based; and the complex ramifications of hunger, illness, imprisonment, torture, murder, and so on. Their empirical character is never lost from view, but they are interpreted in God's light, as revealed in scripture, in tradition, and in the continuing inspiration of the Spirit. They are all negations of the Reign of God, and one cannot sincerely proclaim the Reign of God while either turning one's back on these realities or covering them up in order to hide one's shame. It is not necessary to pursue this point, which has already been sufficiently emphasized by the experience of the believers, by the magisterium of the church, and finally by the theological elaboration of the experts.

At the same time we must ask what there is of grace in this historical moment. The answer from the perspective of historical transcendence, especially in the New Testament, is that the poor themselves, impoverished and oppressed by injustice, have become the preferred locus of benevolence and grace, of God's faithful love. To look at things first and foremost from the viewpoint of the poor is one of the essential characteristics of Christian historical transcendence: the crushing down that leads to exaltation, the death on the cross that leads to resurrection, the suffering that leads to glory, the least of these who are the greatest in the Reign, the poor who are promised beatitudes. These examples are the historical ways in which the God of Jesus becomes present among human beings and in the march of history. These examples are specifically Christian signs that the New Testament offers in abundance as the typical forms of Christian transcendence. For good reason, the theology of liberation has repeated as one of its fundamental texts of inspiration—promising good news to the poor, liberty to the captives, sight to the blind, release to the oppressed (Isa. 61:1–2)—the Old Testament words that the evangelist attributes to Jesus in order to show the accomplishment of the Old Testament in the New: "Today this scripture has been fulfilled in your hearing" (Luke 4:21).

Therefore, we are not only speaking of the poor and their growing awareness of salvation history, which the church has neglected throughout the centuries; we are speaking, first, of their desire that the church follow the will of Jesus and, second, of their active participation in gradually turning the proclamation of the Reign into a historically palpable fact. The poor have been evangelized; they have been conscientized and have decided to use their Christian power for their liberation. Just as European Christians were once led supposedly by Christian inspiration to intervene in politics, in that case without scandal and with the clear support of the ecclesiastical authorities, this sometimes leads the poor to political commitments. These political commitments often coincide with that of the revolutionary sectors, which puts them in contact with ideologies that can affect them, just as the earlier European and Latin American Christians were affected by capitalist ideologies. But that does not mean that they have exchanged the inspiration of their faith for the interpretation of ideologies, as if one were equivalent to the other; on the contrary, they have made the ideologies themselves more open, both in practical application and in relation to the Christian faith.

For this reason, liberation theology is accused of converting the evangelical poor into a social class and the struggle for liberation into a class struggle. In doing so, it is said to favor Marxism and anticapitalist tendencies, a point that seems particularly important to the institutionalized church. The theology of liberation is said to be not only influenced by Marxism but at its heart subordinated to it. The accusation is entirely mistaken, from both a methodological and the pastoral viewpoint.

It is wrong from a *methodological viewpoint* because it mistakes the part for the whole, the subordinate for the principal. For example, to speak of liberation theology as Marxist inspired, and to take one of the works of Jon Sobrino as the prime example as Cardinal Ratzinger has done, is a striking methodological error.[26] Marxism may be present to different degrees in other theologians, but in Sobrino's theology its presence is absolutely marginal. The presence of Marxism in the whole of liberation theology is derivative and subordinate, in the first place, and, in the second, it has diminished over the years. Moreover, to insist on the viewpoint of the poor, although that may sometimes favor the revolutionary struggle, does not make of them a social class. Viewing the poor in a stricter sense actually calls for a break with the model of social classes, which is based on ownership of the means of production, and as a theological interpretation, it overwhelms the narrow model of the proletariat as such. From this viewpoint, the theology of liberation sometimes represents a strong critique of what would otherwise be a sociological theory unchallenged historically by differences in reality.

From the *pastoral viewpoint*, we need to distinguish between the clear preferential option for the poor and the subsequent political options that specific social groups may choose once they have understood their obligation to the oppressed majorities. Here there is a very clear progression, from being moved by faith to work on behalf of the poor to choosing the best way of doing so. The first is a purely Christian option, and thus requires little external mediation, one in which Christian historical transcendence becomes clearer. The second leads to two subsequent options: to work on behalf of the oppressed majorities from a methodologically more religious viewpoint (nourishment from discernment, conversion, etc.) or from a more political viewpoint (support or affiliation with groups that try to promote the cause of the poorest in diverse ways). The church has something to say on this option, but clearly it must speak with respect for the autonomy of strictly political positions, without assuming that the political options most in line with the preferences and needs of the institutionalized church are necessarily the options most favorable to the Reign of God and the popular majorities. Let us remember, just in passing, how often the church has interpreted actions that went against its temporal political or social power as going against the will of God, when in reality they were inherently good actions that eventually brought great benefit to the church.

Power

Christian historical transcendence, as it incorporates both Old Testament and New Testament historical transcendence, relates to power in a unique way. The Old Testament tradition would seem inclined to use God's power in the form of state or quasi-state power; the New Testament tradition, following lines clearly marked out in the Old Testament, would seem to abandon that power and focus more on power in individuals. In the latter tradition, religious power would seem more personal and internal while in the former more structural and public. It was not entirely that way, as we see by the church's secular determination to affirm itself as an institutional power and even as a state power, along the line of a perfect society, just as state societies do. Nevertheless, Christian historical transcendence does not repeat either the personalistic or the institutional schema.

In the present, one can sketch out three historical models, each of which admits of several variations.

There is a first attempt to save Israel by means of power—but *power conceived theocratically.* The hope is that God would save the people and save history, as the kings and lords of this world do, but with a purification of their entirely secular way of doing it. This model is exemplified by Moses, the judges, the kings, the Maccabees, and others. The attempt was based on an essential element of truth: God wills a historical salvation, an integral salvation embracing the whole condition of humanity and of peoples, so that salvation is not reduced to something spiritual or transtemporal. But it also contained an element that would later be seen as invalid and antisalvific; that element hides behind the belief that salvation must come through power—military, economic, political, religious, even miraculous power—that is, power shaped by the powers of this world, even though they may be given a sacred character that establishes them as theocratic power.

With the repeated failure of this attempt, an opposite model appears in history: the way of power not only leads to historical failure and the triumph of evil, but *it makes the way of salvation impossible.* Therefore, it is necessary to abandon the world to the powers of evil and seek salvation and holiness through separation from this world. In doing so, one could merit and one day experience, at the end of "these times," that God would break into history to crush God's enemies, definitively uprooting sin and making a new world for God's children. The fundamental elements of truth in this attempt were the affirmation that God's salvation surpasses and transcends the structure and the possibilities of the strictly political, and the affirmation that the political, however necessary, can never bring the integral salvation that humanity needs. But it had another element, which invalidated that solution; salvation was not seen as something historically operative and present in real human situations, gradually transforming the situations and bringing them closer to a real, though not definitive, presence of the Reign of God. Certainly even the Essenes seem to have seen the need for historical salvation, for they awaited, and in different ways even anticipated, a new presence of God, a triumphant irruption of God over the sin of this world; however, they did not make that hope and anticipation historical but left for later the salvific presence of God among human beings and human things. Although they powerfully signal the truth of the "not yet" and the historical limitation of the "already," they fail to see the positive sense of both the "not yet" and the "already." The same is true of those who hope for salvation only in the next world, reducing it in this world to purely internal or moral dimensions. They attribute such autonomy to the world that they separate it from God's history and leave it at the mercy of those who dominate it, except when those who dominate it limit the wealth and power of those who claim to be seeking God.

The third model is the one that best demonstrates Christian historical transcendence; it seeks *to save history by making God's power present in it*, but the power of God that is revealed in Jesus, and in the ways it is revealed in him. This is a truly historical presence, which really operates in history and seeks to transform it but in a unique way that neither spiritualistically retreats from history nor takes on the forms of theocratic power that easily becomes idolatrous power. It concretizes historically the classical figures of Moses, the Messiah, the king of the Jews, etc., in the figure of the historical servant of Yahweh, not to reduce that figure to a cultic expiation of sins and a plea for grace, but to give it historical embodiment in words and action. Thus, it goes beyond the first two models, incorporating what is true and fundamental in them, but leaving out and negating their ambiguous and false points. It is clear from the New Testament that Jesus did not seek theocratic power; it is also clear that he did not withdraw from the sociohistorical arena, if we look at both his life and his death. His unique way of intervening in history, of making God historically present among human beings, is of course by proclaiming the Reign of God, making it present in himself and setting it in motion. One of the essential elements of this proclamation and this setting in motion of the Reign is the commitment of God's cause to the human cause and, more concretely, the commitment of God's cause to the cause of the poor. It is God in the poor who will save history but in real, poor people who really operate in history when, within their material condition of poverty, they recover their total beatitude of the gift of God.

This is where we should look for the uniqueness of Christian historical transcendence. The newness of this transcendence is its break with what the world has understood as God's "glory," as God's true presence. That "glory," which is also partly visible as the power of the divine majesty in the grandiosity of material nature, has been placed by people in such historical factors as human wisdom, the theocratic miracle, religious law, and the wealth and power of the ecclesiastical institution. But these ways have shown that they do not lead to transcendence as revealed to us in Jesus, but rather immediately they become absolutized limits, and, consequently, they are the sinful negation of God and an obstacle to grace. On the contrary, Jesus has discarded what humanity sees as great and has considered what is despised by the power of this world as sacrament of God. This admired greatness and this contemptible smallness can take different historical forms, but they represent a historical constant: the privileged status of the rich and powerful, and the domination and exploitation of those who have nothing but poverty and weakness. Thus, one must confront the false paths of Christian historical transcendence by opening the path of negation, that is, the negation of the false paths to God, of false gods, and of false messianisms. One must also positively open the true and truly Christian paths of God. These are, in contrast to the others, Christian faith confronting the wisdom of the world, the power of the Crucified One confronting the theocratic miracle, grace and love confronting the religious law, poverty and service confronting wealth and power. All of this can be reduced to the commandment of love but of love understood in Christian terms and adequately historicized.

All of this happens in history. Therefore, both the negation and the affirmation must take flesh in history, and the proof that this is happening is nothing other than persecution. What is foolishness to the Greeks and a stumbling block to the Jews is seen as a threat and met with persecution by those who live by sin. Persecution for the sake of the Reign is credible proof of two fundamental things in the historical praxis of salvation: that the salvation that is proclaimed is becoming present in history, or it would not lead to historical persecution; and that the salvation that is proclaimed is real and truly Christian, or it would not be denied and persecuted by those who represent and objectify anti-Christian values.

Thus, the problem is not that God's power, mediated by human beings, should not be used to improve historical realities; the problem is how to use it according to God's will. Once we have analyzed the concrete situation in which we must act, we know God's will primarily in Jesus. Jesus makes his message present in different ways but remains the fundamental criterion by which to test any action taken in his name.

Spirituality

We have been emphasizing some objective aspects of Christian historical transcendence; when these aspects are present, there is transcendence. But we have not sufficiently stressed that which could be called the personal experience of that Christian historical transcendence. That is the problem of spirituality in the theology of liberation, which is becoming increasingly important to Latin American theologians who are unjustly accused of being too secular and too political.[27] Gustavo Gutiérrez has begun focusing on this subject with the well-known Ignatian concept of "contemplation in action." The action represents the objective element and contemplates the subjective; only when contemplation is achieved in action are we truly on the way to realizing and assuming Christian historical transcendence.

The problem, then, is to determine what action, or fundamental plan of action, most fully represents Christian historical transcendence. From a Latin American viewpoint, and that of the third world in general, such action is fundamentally an action of liberation from all that keeps the Reign of God from becoming present among human beings, from all that keeps God from being made manifest as a power of life and not a power of death. This implies that the greatest problem of the world and the greatest sin of the world are seen as the universal and structural situation that forces most of humanity to live in conditions that St. Thomas himself saw as making it practically impossible to live a human life ruled by moral principles. This is the situation caused by the objective culpability—whether it is a sin of commission or of omission—of the dominant minorities that have made domination, exploitation, and consumerism the gods of their institutional existence. This fundamental plan of action is the place with the greatest possibility today of objectively manifesting the will and presence of the God of Jesus. This is not the only sin that is in the world, but it is the fundamental source of many other sins, which must be measured in terms of this one. If the problem is understood on a global scale, then it is clear that the fundamental challenge to the Christian mission of proclaiming and realizing the Reign of God lies in combating this historical sin, which is objectified in easily visible ways, and overcoming it so that the path to a new situation can be opened. This sin is the negation of the fatherhood of God, of the human kinship revealed in the Son, and of the love that the Spirit has spread throughout the world. This sin is the negation of humanity in its most fundamental rights; this sin is the source of violence, conflict, and division; this sin blocks the path of God toward humanity and humanity toward God.

In another sense, we are speaking of a universal liberation. It is an integral liberation expressed not only in terms of economic or political problems but also a universal liberation. The poor must be liberated from their poverty, but the rich must also be liberated from their wealth. The oppressed must be liberated from their condition of domination and the oppressors from their dominant condition. And so on. The preferential Christian option is clear in this contrast, without denying its universality: it is an option for the poor, for the oppressed.

But if we want this liberation to be real, that is, not only forgiving sin but taking it away, we must use not only analytical but also practical mediations. Here and only here is where the theology of liberation finds it necessary to use Marxist analysis and, sometimes, forms of praxis that can be considered Marxist. We shall not enter into discussion of this point. Everything said so far shows that the problem of historical transcendence can be presented without reference to Marxism and without subjecting Christian ideas to Marxist ideologies. But it is worth noting that when the theology of liberation seeks the conceptual assistance of Marxism, it does not subject its discourse to Marxist discourse but the other way around. It tries in this way, with greater and lesser success, to do what every other theology has done with other "ideologies"—sometimes scandalizing the magisterium and sometimes with tacit hierarchical approval, at least after a period of caution—that is, to strengthen its theological discourse with elements that do not close off transcendence but make it possible.

If this is the fundamental action in which we must be contemplative, then we must ask briefly what the Christian characteristics of this contemplation are. The fundamental point is given in action, because it would be an error of subjectivism to try to contemplate God where God does not want to be contemplated or where God cannot be found. The parable of the Good Samaritan (Luke 10:25–37) is clear on this point: the true neighbor is not the priest or the Levite, who pass by the suffering of the marginalized and wounded, but the Samaritan, who takes responsibility for him and offers him material care, thus resolving the situation in which he is unjustly involved. This apparently profane, apparently natural act, one taken apparently without awareness of its meaning, is much more transcendent and Christian than all the prayers and sacrifices that the priests could make with their backs turned to the suffering and anguish around them.

Moreover, contemplation can and must be scrutinized to see whether it is of God or something idolatrous. There are dangers in action, but there is no less danger in contemplation. We have repeatedly been warned against the types of contemplation that divert our gaze and our purpose from the action in which God seeks to become really present: in Jesus' saying, "Not everyone who says Lord, but those who do the will of the Father"; in many scriptural warnings of the Old and New Testaments, especially those of John who identifies (contemplative) light with acts of love and (God-concealing) darkness with hateful or unloving acts (1 John 1:5ff); and, finally, by the great contemplative figures,

Once we have identified the needed action, both in the general plan of Christian life and in its particular diversifications, we must try to see some of the specific characteristics of contemplation itself. The contemplative in action must be truly contemplative, must try to find God subjectively in what he or she is doing objectively. There may be anonymous Christians, there may be unthematic experiences of God, but that is not the ideal; ideally the richest objectivity becomes the fullest subjectivity.

This contemplation should be undertaken from the most appropriate place. The "where" from which one seeks to see decisively determines what one is able to see; the horizon and the light one chooses are also fundamental to what one sees and how one sees it. The where, the light, and the horizon in which one seeks God are of course precisely God but God mediated in that place chosen by God, which is the poor of the earth. This mediation of the poor does not limit, but rather strengthens the power of God as it is presented in scripture, in tradition, in the magisterium, in the signs of the times, in nature itself, in the march of history, and so on. Contemplation depends on a spirituality of poverty; that is one way of interpreting what it means to be poor in spirit, knowing how to live with the spirit of poverty and identifying with the cause of the poor, understood as God's cause. From this perspective of the poor, one sees new meanings and new inspiration in the classical heritage of the faith. Since this is a task rarely undertaken in the course of history, at least at the level of theological reflection, new things appear here that have been unnoticed by those who sat on the high mountaintops, the better to scan God's horizon. The ones who see God most and best are those who have received God's self-revelation.

> I thank you, Father, Lord of heaven and earth, because you have hidden these things from the wise and the intelligent and have revealed them to infants; yes, Father, for such was your gracious will. All things have been handed over to me by my Father; and no one knows who the Son is except the Father, or who the Father is except the Son and anyone to whom the Son Chooses to reveal him. (Luke 10:21–22)

This text can be read in several ways,[28] but one is applicable to what would be a necessary condition for Christian contemplation of God's historical transcendence, for an understanding of what there is of God in history.

It is a confused prejudice to judge the degree of contemplation by whether the object of contemplation appears more or less sacred, more or less internal, more or less spiritual. That would mean assuming that God is more present, more readily heard or contemplated in the internal silence of idleness than in committed action. This may not be so, and there is no reason why it should be so. It may be that it is on the road to Emmaus that one finds the person one was looking for in the past or in the memory of sacred actions; or on the road to Damascus a false and Pharisaic religiosity may be broken in favor of a contemplation and conversion qualitatively incomparable with any prior experience. It is not certain that Christian transcendence can be found in the temple better than in the city, in concern for oneself than in concern for others. A really Christian praxis—which takes the people in greatest need as the starting point of the search for the way to remove the great sin of the world and to implant divine life in the human heart and in the nucleus of human structures—brings with it great richness because of the urgency and depth of its demands, the shared experience, the understanding that these are the very cleavages by which one can most rapidly and profoundly reach the Spirit of Christ that inspires his people.

All this should not overshadow what must be emphasized emphatically: there is a great need for contemplation, and contemplation demands certain conditions without which there is little possibility of discovering what true action should be. Some of these conditions are explicitly revelatory. It is not only erroneous but heretical to try to learn from praxis what God is saying because although God speaks and has spoken "in many and various ways" (Heb. 1:1), God has spoken definitively through the Son, and all revelation and tradition must be placed in this context. Conditions of personal life should be remembered as well, because although God is made manifest even to the greatest sinner, that manifestation usually begins through conversion and purification; it is the pure in heart who see God best (Luke 5:8). Psychological and methodological conditions remain important as well; immersion in action is a rich source of reality, but contemplation requires special moments in which to gather up and consciously deepen the collision between the word of God heard in revelation and the urgent problems that reality raises in the mediation of its very self.[29]

Contemplation in action can only mean the contemplation that can be done and should be done when one is acting. This does not only mean contemplating the action one has taken but transforming one's past actions or future intended actions into what is contemplation strictly speaking, an encounter with what there is of God in things, and an encounter with God in the things. There is not, therefore, an open door to activism, or to abandonment of all forms of spiritual retreat, much less of liturgical celebration. On the contrary, it seeks to make explicit in word, in communication, in living, what one has found less explicitly in action. We know that it is found in action: first, because Jesus promised that it would be so in Christian commitment to those in greatest need; and, second, because the discernment of contemplation enables us to contrast that which is from God with that which is against God. Thus, for example, it is when the celebration of the word, penitential gatherings, or Eucharists are invested with all the personal and community needs that arise from the work of the participants (*opus operantis*) that the gratuitous efficacy of those celebrations (*opus operatum*) is fully given and received. Thus, in this contemplation, there is an effort to actualize what is already present—that which is already present is the fundamental principle of its actualization, but it requires a prepared subjectivity for its full actualization.

That completes the framework of what should be a full discussion of Christian historical transcendence. The subjects outlined here should be more rigorously analyzed, and other subjects should also be discussed, especially the church as a privileged place for demonstrating Christian historical transcendence.[30] Here we have tried to show the importance of the problem and some elements for its solution or, at least, for subsequent discussion. Pannenberg has written, "History is the most elusive horizon of Christian theology."[31] One sees from the article in which that sentence appears that for Pannenberg history is the most globalizing horizon, not only for theology, but for revelation itself. That is very true. It is a history that embraces both the historicity of real people and the real history of empirical events, a history that is not an *Urgeschichte* or an *Übergeshichte*, but a history whose empirical character is itself transcendent, that is, open to God because God has first become present within it.

Thus, historical transcendence is not exclusively a subject of liberation theology, but this theology has a unique way of understanding the formal meaning of Christian historical transcendence. In these pages, I have tried to suggest some expressions of that unique understanding. In doing so, I have tried to point out the uniqueness and the universality of the theology of liberation and, at the same time, its novelty and its traditional character. The purpose was not to expound what the theologians of liberation have thought on this point but only to show a possible way of conceptualizing the problem. Much more remains to be done through biblical, hermeneutical, dogmatic, and pastoral studies, but liberation theology's continuing vitality offers the hope that those studies will be realized.

Notes

[1] See bibliography for relevant texts.

[2] Hans Urs von Balthasar, in International Theological Commission, *Teología de la liberación* (Madrid, 1978), 181.

[3] Ibid.

[4] J. Ratzinger, "Vi spiego la teologia," 30 *Giorni* (March 1984): 49.

[5] Clodovis Boff, *Teología de lo Político* (Salamanca, Spain: Sígueme, 1980).

[6] Ibid., 27–29.

[7] Catholic Church, *Eu ouvi os clamores de meu povo* (Salvador, Bahia : Editora Beneditina, 1973).

[8] Cf. the works of X. Zubiri, *Sobre la esencia* (Madrid: Sociedad de Estudios y Publicaciones, 1962); *Inteligencia sentiente* (Madrid, 1980); *Inteligencia y logos* (Madrid: Sociedad de Estudios y Publicaciones, 1982); *Inteligencia y razón* (Madrid: Sociedad de Estudios y Publicaciones, 1983).

[9] Von Balthasar, 170.

[10] M.-D. Chenu, "Les signes des temps," *Nouvelle revue théologique* 87, no. 1 (January 1965): 29–39; M. McGrath, "Los signos de los tiempos en América Latina hoy," in *Los textos de Medellín* (San Salvador: UCA Editores, 1977), 137–58.

[11] Editor's Note: Parts II and III of "Historicidad de la salvación Cristiana" (respectively entitled "Historical Transcendence in the Old Testament," and "Historical Transcendence in the New Testament") have been omitted in this emended edition of Ellacuría's essay. The complete unabridged English translation can be found in *Mysterium Liberationis*.

[12] K. Rahner, in *Theological Investigations* V (London: Darton, Longman & Todd, 1966), 97–114.

[13] Editor's Note: Ellacuría uses the term "desnuminiza," which invokes the Greek root of "mind" (nous) and the philosophical distinction between the phenomenon and noumenon.

[14] W. Pannenberg et al., *La revelacion como historia* (Salamanca, Spain: Sígueme, 1977), 117–46.

[15] *Popol Vuh: Las antiguas historias del Quiché,* Adrián Recinos, trans. (San Salvador: UCA Editores, 1980).

[16] C. R. Cavarrús, *La cosmovisión k'ekchi' en proceso de cambio* (San Salvador: UCA/Editores,1979).

[17] Boff, 31–144.

[18] Ibid., 135–285.

[19] Von Balthasar, 179.

[20] Ibid.

[21] X. Zubiri sees a need to speak of historical sin as well as personal sin and original sin. Cf. X. Zubiri, *Naturaleza, historia, Dios* (Madrid: Editora Nacional, 1963), 394.

[22] Editor's Note: The term *"plasmación,"* enormously difficult to translate here, is rendered "taking-form." The Spanish verb, *plasmar* (as the Greek root) has to do with molding, forming, shaping (e.g., a pot of clay), or even giving expression to or reflecting. The

difficulty of translation correlates to the difficulty of the notion: an act of creation that is not efficient or exemplary causality, a distinction between creator and created, but not a separation.

[23] On these points, cf. Zubiri's posthumous book (edited by Ellacuría), *El hombre y Dios* (Madrid: Alianza Editorial, 1984).

[24] Editor's Note: Ellacuría uses the term *"probación"* (translated as "proof").

[25] Cf. Oscar Romero, *Voice of the Voiceless* (Maryknoll, NY: Orbis Books, 1985), 114–61; on idolatries,see 133–36.

[26] Ratzinger, "Vi Spiego la teologia."

[27] Cf. G. Gutíerrez, *We Drink from Our Own Wells* (Maryknoll, NY: Orbis Books, 1984); J. Sobrino, "Espiritualidad y liberación," *Diakonia* 30 (June 1984): 133–57; Ignacio Ellacuría, "Christian Spirituality," see chapter 11 of this volume.

[28] Marie-Emile Boismard and Arnaud Lamouille, *L'Evangile de Jean* (Paris: Editions du Cerf, 1977), 169–70.

[29] Editor's Note: Here Ellacuría uses the term *"mismidad,"* an important term in his philosophy that refers to the "sameness" or continuity in something dynamic like history or reality.

[30] The problem of the popular organizations in El Salvador, as reflected in Óscar A. Romero et al, *Iglesia de los pobres y organizaciones populares* (San Salvador: UCA Editiores,1979), is one place to observe this problem in a practical way. The publication analyzes a pastoral letter from Monseñor Romero and Monseñor Rivera on this issue. More generally, all the bibliography on the church of the poor is relevant here.

[31] W. Pannenberg, *Basic Questions in Theology*, trans. George Kehm (Philadelphia: Fortress Press, 1970–71).

Bibliography

North Atlantic:

Alfaro, Juan. *Esperanza Cristiana y liberación del hombre.* Barcelona: Editorial Herder, 1972.

Alonso Díaz, José, y otros. *Fe y justicia.* Verdad e imagen 59. Salamanca: Sígueme, 1981.

Bultmann, Rudolf. *Geschichte und eschatologie.* 3rd ed. Tübingen: J.C. B. Mohr, 1979.

Cullmann, Oscar. *La historia de la salvación.* Colección pensamiento Cristiano 10. Barcelona: Ediciones 62, 1967.

Darlap, Adolf. "Teología fundamental de la historia de la salvación." In *Misterium Salutis* I, vol. 1. Madrid: Ediciones Cristiandad, 1969, 49–204.

Metz, Johannes Baptist. *Zur Theologie der Welt.* Mainz: Matthias-Grünewald Verlag, 1968.

Moltmann, Jürgen. *Teología de la esperanza.* Verdad e imagen 48. Salamanca: Ediciones Sígueme, 1977.

———. *Umkehr zur Zukunt.* München: Siebenstern Tschenbuch Verlag, 1970.

Pannenberg, Wolfhart. *Grundfragen systematischer theologie.* Göttingen: Vandenhoeck & Ruprecht, 1967.

Rahner, Karl and Johann Baptist Metz. *Hörer des Wortes.* München: Kösel-Verlag, 1963.

Rahner, Karl. "Weltgeschichte und Heilgeschicte." En Schriften *zur theologie* V, 115–35. Einsiedeln: Benziger, 1962.

Robinson, James M. and John B. Cobb. *Theologie als geschicte.* Zürich-Stuttgart: 1967.

Sölle, Dorothee. *Teología política.* Estudios Sígueme 3. Salamanca: Ediciones Sígueme, 1972.
Latin America:
Alves, Rubem A. *Cristianismo, ?opio o liberación?* Salamanca: Ediciones Sígueme, 1973.
Assman, Hugo. *Teología desde praxis de la liberación.* Salamanca: Sígueme, 1973. In English, *Theology for a Nomad Church.* Maryknoll, Orbis Books, 1975.
Boff, Clodovis. *Teología de lo político: sus mediaciones.* Verdad e imagen 61. Salamanca: Ediciones Sígueme, 1980.
Boff, Leonardo. *Jesucristo y la liberación del hombre.* Madrid: Ediciones Cristiandad, 1981.
————. *Teología del cautiverio y la liberación.* Teología y pastoral. Madrid: Paulinas, 1978.
Comblin, José. *Théologie de la pratique révolutionnaire.* Encyclopédie Universitaire: Philosophie et Théologie. Paris: Editions Universitaires, 1974.
Dussel, Enrique D. *Histoire et théologie de la libération: perspective latino-américaine.* Collection Développement et Civilisations. Paris: Éditions Économie et Humanisme, 1974.
Ellacuría, Ignacio. *Teología Política.* San Salvador: Ediciones del Secretariado Social Interdiocesano, 1973. In English, *Freedom Made Flesh.* Maryknoll: Orbis Books, 1976.
————. "Tesis sobre la posibilidad, necesidad y sentido de una teología latinoamericana." In *Teología y Mundo Contemporáneo,* edited by A. Vargas-Machuca, 325–50. Madrid: Ediciones Cristinadad, 1975.
————. "Fe y justicia." In Ignacio Ellacuría, y otros, *Fe, justicia y opción por los oprimidos.* Colección Tercer Mundo, 9. 11–78. Bilbao: Española Desclée de Brouwer, 1980.
————. "Pueblo Crucificado. Ensayo sobre una soteriología histórica." In Hugo Assmann, et al., *Cruz y Resurrección Presencia y Anuncio de una Iglesia Nueva.* Colección Teología Latinoamericana 7, 49–82. México, D.F.: Centro de Reflexión Teológica, 1978. [See Chapter 8.]
Gutiérrez, Gustavo. *Teología de la Liberación.* Salamanca: Ediciones Sígueme, 1972. In English, *A Theology of Liberation.* Maryknoll: Orbis Books, 1973.
————. *Teología desde el Reverso de Historia.* Lima: Centro de Estudio y Publicaciones, 1977.
————. *Beber en su Propio Pozo.* Lima: Centro de Estudios y Publicaciones, 1983. In English, *We Drink from Our Own Wells.* Maryknoll: Orbis Books, 1984.
Instituto Fe y Secularidad. *Fe Cristiana y Cambio en América Latina.* Salamanca: Ediciones Sígueme, 1973.
Libâno, João B. *Discernimento e Política.* Coleção Vida Religiosa: Temas Atuais 7. Petrópolis: Editora Vozes, 1977.
López Trujillo, Alfonso. *Liberación Marxista y Liberación Cristiana.* Biblioteca de Autores Cristianos 354. Madrid: Editorial Católica, 1974.
Scannone, Juan Carlos. *Teología de la Liberación y Praxis Popular: Aportes Críticos para una Teología de la Liberación.* Salamanca: Ediciones Sígueme, 1976.
Segundo, Juan Luis. *Liberación de la Teología.* Cuadernos Latinoamericanos 17. Buenos Aires: Ediciones Carlos Lohlé, 1975. In English, *The Liberation of Theology.* Maryknoll: Orbis Books, 1976.
————. *El Hombre de Hoy ante Jesús de Nazaret.* Madrid: Cristiandad, 1982.
Sobrino, Jon. *Cristología desde América Latina.* Colección Teología Latinoamericana 1. México: Ediciones CRT, 1977. In English, *Christology at the Crossroads.* Maryknoll: Orbis Books, 1978.
————. *Jesús en América Latina: Su Significado para la Fe y la Cristología.* San Salvador: UCA Editores, 1982. In English, Jesus in Latin America. Maryknoll: Orbis Books, 1987.
————. Resurrección de la Verdadera Iglesia. Santander: Sal Terrae, 1981. In English, *The*

True Church and the Poor. Maryknoll: Orbis Books, 1984.

Vidales, Raúl, Luis Rivera Pagán y otros. *La Esperanza en el Presente de América Latina.* Colección Economía-teología. San José, Costa Rica: Departamento Ecuménico de Investigaciones, 1983.

Zweifelhofer, Hans. *Bericht zur Theologie der Befreiung.* München: Kaiser, 1974.

Roman Catholic Magisterial Documents:

Vatican II, Gaudium et spes (1965). See, "Pastoral Constitution on the Church in the Modern World." In *The Gospel of Peace and Justice,* ed. Joseph Gremillion (Maryknoll: Orbis Books, 1976), 243–335.

Second General Conference of Latin American Bishops, *The Church in the Present-Day Transformation of Latin America in the Light of the CouncilI* (1968). See *Liberation Theology: A Documentary History,* ed. Alfred T. Hennelly (Maryknoll: Orbis Books, 1990), 89–119.

Pope Paul VI, *Evangelii nuntiandi* (1975). See, "On Evangelization in the Modern World." In *Liberation Theology: A Documentary History,* ed. Alfred T. Hennelly (Maryknoll: Orbis Books, 1990), 187–94.

Conférence des évêques de France, *Libération des hommes et salut en Jésus-Christ* (1975).

Third General Conference of Latin American Bishops, *Evangelization in Latin America's Present and Future.* See, *Puebla and Beyond: Documentation and Commentary,* ed. John Eagleson and Philip Scharper (Maryknoll: Orbis Books, 1979).

— Translated by Margaret D. Wilde

7

Salvation History
(1987)

*Ignacio Ellacuría began seriously reflecting on the theme of salvation in the es-
says that would eventually be collected into his first book, Teología política (1973)
[Freedom Made Flesh (1976)]. There he announced a thesis that would pervade
his theological thought: "salvation history is a salvation in and of history." In the
late 1970s, especially in "The Crucified People" (see chapter 8 in this collection),
through the mid-1980s and the publication of "The Historicity of Christian Salvation" (see chapter 6), until his final major essay, "Utópia y profetismo desde
América Latina: un ensayo concreto de soteriología histórica" (1989) ["Utopia and
Prophecy in Latin America" (1991)], Ellacuría continued to address salvation in
terms of his distinctive framework, historical soteriology. In view of this, the current
essay, "Salvation History," is significant both for the way it advances the arguments
from his earlier essays and for the way it introduces new themes that will play a
crucial role in his final essay. Most importantly, in this essay he draws on his Zubirian philosophy, as well as the biblical witness, to develop a theology of history
that understands "that everything historical has to do with salvation."*

*This essay unfolds in five sections. Ellacuría focuses in the first section on the
way theology construes salvation, contrasting naturalistic views of salvation and
his own historical approach. Drawing on the orientation of Vatican II, he critiques
the naturalistic tendency that ignores history and reifies salvation, and grounds his
theology of salvation in the "extraordinary metaphysical density" of the reality of
history. In the second section he complements Rahner's understanding of the transcendental openness of the human subject ("supernatural existential") with his understanding of the "the elevated, transcendental openness of a gratuitous historicity"
where "salvation is present in every historical event" either in the form of acceptance
(grace) or rejection (sin). "History itself is the fundamental possibility of salvation,"
he argues in the third section, but only the possibility insofar as salvation "depends
on the freedom of God and the freedom of human beings." This implies the full*

engagement of human freedom in salvation both as the overcoming of sin and the realization of a new human being and a new earth. But, as he probes in the fourth section, what can the salvation of history mean given the overwhelming presence of evil in history? It is not the failure of God's promise but of our human response. This leads to his brilliant discussion in the fifth section on the divine and human subjects of salvation and his full view of history now "elevated to a new plane, that of the communication and gift of God's Trinitarian life."

From a Naturalistic to a
Historical Consideration of Salvation

Hellenic, Platonic, and Aristotelian philosophy was for centuries the preferred theoretical framework in which to interpret all reality, including the reality of relationships between God and human beings. Salvation was thus profoundly dehistoricized, with grave consequences both for historical praxis and for the interpretation and effectiveness of the Christian faith. The philosophical mold of Greek thinking overpowered the material shaped by it. In the transition from what was fundamentally a biographical and historical experience, with its own theoretical interpretation, to a metaphysical formulation, historicity was diluted in favor of a static essentialism.

Even those who carried out this interpretive metamorphosis of salvation never doubted that it had come through a historical process, although because of historical limitations that they did not understand and reflect on, they did not think of it as essentially historical. Salvation had occurred (accidentally) in history, but it was not (essentially) historical. If it was hard for them to understand the historicity of human beings, it was even harder to understand that there could be a history of God. Thus, even accepting in the homiletic presentation of salvation that God had been communicating with humanity in different degrees and different ways, this was more a matter of need than of something required by the reality itself. It was beyond their understanding that relations between God and humanity had to be essentially historical, not because it was so hard to understand, but because they had almost dogmatically accepted a set of ideas, which they considered the most reasonable and right, which made that understanding difficult and even impossible. The paradigm of rational interpretation was the explanation of nature with its own metaphysical categories. With regard to nature, history had no reality and no (scientific) reasonableness.

History especially lacked scientific reasonableness. Science could only deal with the universal. What could not be permanently and uniformly repeated fell outside the domain of knowledge; it was reduced to mere opinion. The avatars of personal life stories and events of the history of peoples could serve as examples and motivators, but they were not an adequate basis for a solid knowledge on which to establish an understanding of the world and human behavior. Even when people wanted to develop an ethic of human behavior or a civic policy, they sought out the permanent, what nature dictated, the natural law written once and for all in the heart and mind of universal humanity. History and the historical had done more to confuse the clear and shining certainty of reason, based on nature, than to help describe the essence of human nature.

The consequence of this treatment of history for theological understanding was that the basis of theological knowledge had to be found in a dogmatic rather than a biblical theology. Revealed facts and words were accepted as the principles from which theological deduction begins. It could not be otherwise, if these facts and words were considered as the supernatural action of God—but with a double limitation. These facts and words were reduced to objective, fundamentally closed intellectual formulations, and behind the discursive and deductive mediations of reason, they in turn became rational formulations of absolute validity that could abandon the principle from which they came. This process is due to the forgetting of the Bible, to reading it without an adequate hermeneutic, and to the oversized influence of dogmatic treatises upon which the church's magisterium and catechesis were really based—with some small exceptions in the areas of liturgy, homiletics, and spirituality, which were considered minor disciplines in the theological curriculum. Thus, the fullness of revelation was terribly impoverished, breaking its spontaneous communication with human history.

An equally important consequence is that in ignoring the real density of history, people turned the whole problem of sanctifying salvation into an ontic question, almost entirely reified. The paradigm of nature led to the identification of reality as thing, of essence as substance. Under the powerful influence of this interpretive paradigm, it was not possible, or at least not easy, to recognize that even nature does not permit a reified and substantialist interpretation. This distortion made it impossible to recognize the metaphysical order of historical reality. Thus, the sanctifying communication of God with humanity could hardly be understood, not only when dogmatic theology was being done, but by means of reified categories such as substances and accidents, principal efficient or instrumental causes, matter and form. Again, the effect of all this on the human consciousness, on strictly personal attitudes, on the march of history, was something accidental—something that did not even need to be considered. Thus, infant baptism came to be understood as the supernatural divinization of the child, despite the child's absolute lack of awareness of the event. The infant could receive grace as an objective gift, which conferred definitive transformation even in an accidental way, because the substance was always unchangeable. Not even personal life stories, let alone the history of peoples, were considered to be the most appropriate place for the revelation of God or for the realities that were directly in need of salvation.

All this seems even stranger because it directly contradicts the religious experiences of all humanity, the language of sacred texts, and the reality expressed in that language. It is in personal life stories and in the history of peoples that God has been really present, although this does not exclude ontic transformations. Even original sin appears as the voluntary rejection of a gift and of consciously understood possibilities, rather than as a transformation of corporal frailty and mortality into a supernatural immortality, which in the best of cases one would have experienced if it were not for sin. This does not mean that there must necessarily be an awareness of grace in thematic and certain terms, but it does mean that this awareness, to the extent that it exists in terms of objectification and certainty, would be more related to a free design of God (the personal and historical dimension) than to a real transformation of human structures (the ontic dimension).

This absolutizing and reductionist reification is most blatant in the dehistoricization of Jesus himself. On the one hand, there is an obvious acceptance of the importance of the birth, life, death, and resurrection of the man from Nazareth in explaining the mystery of salvation; but on the other hand, the metaphysical and theological meaning of these historical events in all their historicity is soon set aside, and overwhelming emphasis is placed on what is outside history, or at least it is interpreted ahistorically. Thus, the historical data, or better stated the historical, biographical, and social course of Jesus' life is stripped of real density and salvific meaning; and in its place, questions such as the metaphysical structure of his person, his double nature, the hypostatic union, etc., become all-important. It is not that they are unimportant. The problem is that in this process the historical becomes natural, the existential becomes essential, and thus they cease to be a decisive element enabling Jesus' followers, in their personal life or in the community of the church, to historicize his life, knowing that what is important is not some ontic transformation, which is hard to prove and whose effectiveness in the march of history is entirely accidental.

This reductionism has never occurred in an absolute way in the history of the church as a whole. It was rather a prevailing tendency, apart from which, and even within which, the ineluctably historical nature of salvation was made present. It could not be otherwise, because salvation and revelation not only have a history, they are historical. To deny this explicitly would have been a very grave distortion in the understanding of the faith. But the effort to reflect on and thematically overcome this imbalance of the ontic over the historical came mainly at Vatican II; there, without dismissing what might be valid concerning the ontic treatment of God and humanity, new light was shed on what must be included in order to wrestle with the relationship between God and humanity. This new balance is especially visible in the general way in which the Council dealt with problems, even when they were formulated as dogmatic constitutions, and it is clearly reflected in the new procedures for the formation of priests and pastoral agents (*Optatam totius*, 16) who should take the holy scriptures as the soul of all theology.

With this new orientation, Vatican II was responding especially to the needs of a history of salvation, that is, to needs arising from the Christian faith and life. But it was also responding to the signs of the times, one of which is a discovery of the theoretical and practical importance of the historical as one attempts to penetrate, interpret, and transform a reality that is essentially historical. The human being is a historical reality, a historical essence. History is a reality of extraordinary metaphysical density and the relations of human beings with God, established in freedom, are constitutively historical. In this way believers and the church are better able and more disposed to understand the role of history in shaping Christian life, and the role that the Christian life has and should have in shaping history. This has opened the way to understanding—and acting in accordance with—what history has contributed to salvation and what salvation has contributed and must contribute to history.

The History of Salvation

History is the privileged location of revelation and salvation, as God has freely willed them, not only de facto, but by the very nature of things. In this context, we describe as formally historical whatever becomes truly real in virtue of an option taken either by an individual subject for itself or others, or by a social subject. History is present wherever possibilities are actualized—not only where potencies are acted out—by means of an option (Zubiri). Certainly the relationships between nature and history in human beings are complex, because in them nature opens up to history and history in turn acts on nature, increasing its capacities. Thus, new possibilities are opened up to human persons and humanity itself, so that while the reality and life of persons and all humanity are always the same reality and life, they never remain the same. It is in this historical reality, thus understood, that revelation and salvation become present as a supervenient gratuitousness added to the fundamental gratuitousness of creation.

Indeed the fundamental condition of revelation as such and of the faith that responds to it is the existence of an intelligence and a will, of an apprehension of reality and an ensuing option. The existence and nature of this intelligence and this will arise out of a natural process, formally evolved and governed by the natural forces of evolution, assuming that God has willed that the spatial-temporal expansion of creation take place in an evolutionary manner. Confronted by reality that surrounds it, this human intelligence can see in reality, and especially in human reality, something that manifests what God is. The human being appears when nature, now understood as matter, has given its all in qualitative terms. By making theoretical and practical use of that nature, and experiencing himself as reality, in principle the human being has everything needed to know what God has chosen to reveal of Godself. But even this, which we can call the natural revelation of God, necessarily has a history—especially from the human side. On nature's side, it is inappropriate to affirm the same; properly speaking, there is no such a thing as natural history but only a natural evolution. But on the human side, the always incomplete grasp of what is nature implies a process, a differentiation of viewpoints, an improved use of human gifts themselves, a multiplication and structuring of possibilities in the strict sense. There may also be eyes blind to certain dimensions of reality, obscure interests that obstruct a right and full understanding of that reality, to the point where human beings themselves are undeniably closing off possibilities of intellection and realization; at that point, if left alone, they are unable to see even fundamental aspects of reality and especially of God's self-revelation in that reality. Thus, we would say that even the so-called natural revelation and human moral realization have a history: they are historical. It has to be that way because humanity and society are essentially historical realities.

But it is even more obvious that a possible second communication from God, as truth illuminated and reality given, must take place in history,

in the sense that history is not an established, predetermined process—
not even in the indeterminist understanding of nature as purely material.
Established, predetermined processes can only communicate something
new if the receivers of the communication have renewed their ability to
receive, as a result of an option not merely at random, not because the
process itself allows for something radically new. Historical processes in
contrast, whether or not they force the so-called laws of nature, open up
the domain of the strictly new and thus the possibility of communicating something strictly new, rather than something extrinsically appended.
The strictly new, as a result of a strictly historical process, is interwoven
with a past that becomes present not only in the form of memory but as
real possibilities and acquired abilities; yet, on the other hand, this *novum*
supervenes and irrupts in what is already given and elaborated as an un-
foreseeable and gratuitous future.

History in effect is transcendental openness, because it embraces both
the openness of reality and the double, unified openness of the intelligence and the will of apprehension and option. This openness, which in
each person is the elevated, transcendental openness of the "supernatural
existential" (Rahner), becomes, in history as a whole, the elevated, transcendental openness of a gratuitous historicity. We must accept this gratuitous, transcendental historicity, willed by God as a principle and therefore
a basic principle of history, as necessary if we want to affirm at the same
time that the elevation of history to God is not something extrinsically
appended and that this elevation nevertheless goes beyond what history
alone can do. History itself is transcendentally open, and God is already
present, at least in an inchoate way, in that transcendentality. But that very
transcendentality, although only by means of analogy, becomes present in
any reality. The different transcendentality, which in fact appears in history, is an elevated and doubly gratuitous transcendentality, which we only
recognize as such in a reflective and thematic way when a whole series
of historical events—historical persons, words and works—come together
and become rooted in that primary transcendentality. This happens not
only to isolated individuals, or even to the aggregate of isolated individuals,
but also in that unique type that is history, because it is history itself, and
not only the individuals within it, that is called to be salvation history. The
subject of this history is all humanity, the human species understood in
all its breadth, complexity, and unity; this historical subject, not only collective but unitary, is the bearer of transcendentally open historicity—but
not apart from historical works because these will be the objectification
of either a "yes" or a "no" to God's communication. All historical works,

to different degrees, are either the objectification of grace (the working together of the divine gift and human action), or the objectification of sin (where human action is dominated by evil and objectifies it, while rejecting the offer of grace).

Due to the metaphysical density of historical reality and its essential openness, history, both personal and social, becomes the best place (metaphysical density) and the only possible place (openness), for a doubly gratuitous revelation and salvation that allow human persons and all humanity to participate in God's own Trinitarian life—and not merely the place where through creation and conservation we can see the presence, essence, and potency of God. It can be affirmed that every creative act is a manifestation *ad extra* of God's own Trinitarian life (Zubiri), but not all created things can live that Trinitarian life. That is only possible for human beings, and for them it is only possible in history. The history of God (Darlap) is not formally present in the evolution of nature but in the history of humanity.[1] Human beings have understood and spoken much about God in contemplating nature, but that is because the manifestation of God in nature has been accumulating historically in human traditions, which in fact comprise a single tradition if the subject of that tradition is the human *phylum* as such (Zubiri). But where the gratuitous newness of God is most evident, and most enriching for humanity, has been and is through strictly historical communication to specific persons, to all kinds of prophets, and to whole peoples with whom different covenants were being established.

For Christians, obviously, God has carried out this highest degree of historical communication in the human and historical life story of Jesus of Nazareth nearly two thousand years ago, although that communication had real and interpretive antecedents as well as real and interpretive consequences: Jesus lives by the Jewish tradition, and by many other traditions as well, and Jesus continues to live in the tradition of many other peoples and other persons. Think for example of the historical development of the words and life of Jesus in the dogmatic expression of Paul. But the historical Jesus lived in a specific place and time, no matter how much or how little we know of it, and it must be understood and analyzed as a historical reality and not as an ahistorical reality that is not fundamentally affected by historicity. The same is true of any other moment before or after Jesus. At the same time we must not forget that Jesus himself announces a second coming in which this history will be historically culminated and pass into a different stage, where the historicity of each human being and all humanity will not be totally abolished but will take a different form.

This should not lead us to confuse history with pure subjectivity. It is one thing to define what is formally historical, and something different to describe historical reality in all its integrity. Even when we define the historical as the optional actualization of possibilities, we must remember that both option and possibilities are rooted in very specific material forms. Moreover, this historical formality in its real integrity embraces the whole of reality, both what is given naturally and what is institutionally objectified. History is not to be confused with nature, but assumes and embraces it. To confuse what is formal and differentiated within the historical with what is its concrete and total reality would lead to an idealism of history and freedom that contradicts the concrete mode in which the historical is present. An idealistic conception of history leads to a spiritualistic conception of salvation history, so that the latter is substantially reduced and, worse yet, displaced from its place of action, which is the whole of history in its concrete reality, with its presuppositions and its results.

But historical reality, because it is open in so many ways and because it is the specific field of human freedom, presents its own problems for divine revelation and communication. Before all else, historical reality, despite its unlimited openness, is finite.

Indeed, communicating the absolute mystery of God to a finite reality in process presents many limitations and complications. By definition, both in the order of reality and of understanding, there must be a fundamental incomprehensibility of God's absolute reality, which, for human beings, is constitutively the quintessential mystery. In addition to the mysterious infinitude of divine reality is the divine freedom with which the mystery is communicated. Human reason cannot foresee; nor can human actions or behavior merit when and to what extent divine mystery chooses to communicate itself to human beings. Because of that infinitude and that absolute freedom, no specific historical moment can claim the possibility of totally encompassing the mystery, not even if human beings were to reach the limits of their ability. Even Jesus did not have that fullness, first, because there is a progression, a growth in his own life (Luke 2:52), a process of fulfillment at least in existential communication; and, in the second place, because for the historical Jesus some fundamental questions regarding revelation and the divine communication remained unanswered (Mark 13:32; Matt. 24:36). This does not change Jesus' place as the definitive criterion for God's salvific communication. And although the end of history with its final judgment will bring the consummation of human beings and the fulfillment of divine communication, even so the absolute mystery of God will remain out of reach, awaiting the coming of the new *aeon*, history without time, closer and closer to the giver and the receiver.

In the interpretive context of the plurality and diversity of histories, throughout the more than four million years of humanity, it is an exceedingly complex task to discern what things announce and facilitate the coming of God and what things conceal and obstruct it. History is old; many of its years can be, and are in fact, more propitious than others as a way to encounter God. There are primitive, promising, and mature forms; there can be archaic, modern, and postmodern forms; some are almost immutable, and others rapidly changing. The universal, salvific will of God is not manifested or made present in the same way at different moments of history or in different peoples. Even the Jewish people, with a special promise and an unbreakable covenant, ceased to be the exclusive or privileged subject of the divine offer, when considered along with human acceptance (Rom. 9–11). On the other hand, that salvific will can be expressed where we least expect it; even a pagan can be the provisional messiah sent by God to save his people (Isa. 48:12–19) or to punish the enemies of the people. Thus, it is not easy to decide, especially not before Christ but even afterwards, who are the ones sent by God to give more life to those who do not have it and who are the false prophets who often say "Lord, Lord" but are not acceptable to God and are not messengers of God's word and life—especially if we do not, as we should not, make a sharp separation between what is given in nature and what is a gift of grace. The complex march of history does not allow for a univocal evaluation of events, because we have to distinguish the dynamics of those events from their results, understanding that not everything fits into a specific moment, just as not every food is digestible at a given time.

Along with this intrinsic problem of divine communication, due to the formal nature of history, considering both what history is in itself and in relation to absolute mystery, there are also the limitations of historical self-understanding. History is strictly material, and it is subject to forces and interests of sectors that cannot only cast a dark shadow over it but even lead it to sin against the light. The forces and dynamics of history and the agents who participate in it can conceal and disfigure the communication of God. The history that is called to be the Reign of God can become, in some times and places, the reign of evil and sin. The history that is called to be an arena of liberation and freedom can become an arena of domination and servitude. The shadows may not entirely extinguish the light but may dim it to the point where it becomes difficult to find the way. The forces of death may momentarily—in a historical moment that may last for centuries—impose themselves on the forces of life to the point where almost the whole earth becomes a place of desolation. In these conditions, historical self-understanding inclines toward gigantic ideologizations that are diametrically opposed to the revelation and disclosure of the truth, precisely because it has earlier fallen into idolatries that absolutize the relative and relativize the absolute. The fathers of the lies, who may themselves be culpably self-deceived and self-justified, take control of the collective consciousness and move it toward new idolatries, which in turn generate new and deceptive ideologizations. What Jesus' eschatological discourse proclaims about the days of evil is not something that will only happen at the end of time. In the end, what happens in history can only be what has been gestating within it. The last days have already begun because there are no unbridgeable gaps in historical processes; every person and every generation lives in anticipation of the judgment, although it may come in different degrees and different ways. Not that we are already in the last days, when history is called to become suprahistory, but rather that we are always in history as a final trial, where what is not miraculous looks like a miracle, what is not revelation seems like revelation, what is not divine communication appears to be so, and, above all, one who is not the messiah appears to have laid claim to that role. And inversely, unbeknownst to most human beings, even so-called believers, what gets overlooked is the true miracle, authentic revelation, the most profound divine communication, and the most enriching historicization of messianic faith. History, the location par excellence for the revelation and glorification of God, is also a place of concealment and perdition.

Salvation and History

History itself is the fundamental possibility of salvation because it has been willed as such by God. It is only the possibility because that which is really saved depends on the freedom of God and the freedom of human beings. History itself is the manifestation and always-open presence of God, and it can be so in an always-faithful way to the point where it can be called, and can become, the Reign of God. But how is salvation being made present in history?

We can only verify the kind of salvation that is being made present in history from the standpoint of the salvation announced by Jesus Christ. This does not mean that all salvation, even in the strict meaning of salvation, comes from the historical Jesus by means of direct or indirect causality. There is salvation before Jesus and after Jesus; but that does not mean that this salvation is not always in reference to him or that there is salvation apart from him. The many biblical affirmations that there is salvation only in Jesus must be taken together with many other affirmations that assure us of the presence of the savior God in many people who never explicitly knew of the existence of Jesus or committed themselves personally to him as revealer and savior. Despite this, in order to speak with certainty about who and what is saved, of what are the criteria and the paths of salvation, the Father has chosen the Son as the mediator of salvation by his enlivening Spirit.

From this perspective, we can say that the first gift of salvation to history is the overcoming of sin. History has the fundamental double possibility of being a history dominated by sin or dominated by grace. This is true both in the behavior and in the being of every person as well as in the collective behaviors and institutional structures of different social groups. Indeed although we can recognize the presence of grace in many places and in very different ways, we can also recognize the very extensive and intensive presence of sin with its corresponding absence of grace and with the consequent need for salvation.

This presence of sin in personal life is dramatically highlighted throughout the Old and New Testament revelations. The Letter to the Romans shows it systematically, precisely in relation to the salvation of individuals and peoples. There we have a fairly complete account of the sins that gain control of individuals, until they become sinners by nature: "They were filled with every kind of wickedness, evil, covetousness, malice. Full of envy, murder, strife, deceit, craftiness, they are gossips, slanderers, God-haters, insolent, haughty, boastful, inventors of evil, rebellious toward parents, foolish, faithless, heartless, ruthless" (Rom. 1:29–31). These are sins that degrade human nature, that keep human beings from being human, but they are also sins that deny grace, the saving presence of God in human beings; they not only erase human life but also divine life. They make the Christian life, as Jesus proclaimed it in the Sermon on the Mount, impossible. Comparing the reality of human life to the human experience of the divine life that Jesus proclaimed in different places, we can see how far human beings are from God, how much they need salvation and the conversion it entails. That explains Jesus' constant call to conversion because of the nearness of the Reign: to proclaim the arrival of the Reign meant pushing for conversion, and conversion is needed in order for its transforming power to break into the human heart.

The presence of sin in collective life is also indisputably proclaimed in the revelation of both the Old and the New Testaments, so much so that history is presented more as a history of condemnation than of salvation. In the Jesus tradition itself, sin—understood as a rejection of his saving offer—is linked to the destruction of the city (Jerusalem) and, in the perspective of the time, to the apocalyptic destruction of the world. This is not because so many people sinned but because, as a result of their sins, the city and the world are themselves a denial of God. The fact that this affirmation and denial of God are related to the basic needs of human beings, not only in the general sense of God's presence in his creatures but much more specifically as the denial or affirmation of Jesus' presence in persons and realities that seem to be purely natural, is made clear in Jesus' own symbolic formulation of the definitive word about human beings and the world, that is, the final judgment (Matt. 25:31–46). It will be a judgment on the nations, a judgment on the peoples, and not only on each individual. Thus, Vatican II in *Gaudium et spes*, following the church's long tradition, insists on analyzing and condemning the sins of the world at length, both within each nation and in international relations. The life and action of Jesus cannot be carried forward without working to overcome these sins that are objectified in institutional structures, in collective behaviors, and in the manner that the processes, which determine the shape of history in which human beings live out their own existence, are constituted.

In the face of this history of condemnation, salvation history must become more and more present. Salvation must overcome condemnation. If salvation, as the absence of sin and the presence of God, could increase its power in the human heart and in the laws of history, it would erase the most negative aspects of history. This presupposes a certain historical and biographical gradualism, but that does not mean giving in to fatalistic acceptance. Salvation itself, in deeds and words, is a denunciation of sin and a struggle against it. It is not only forgiveness and understanding; it is also effective action and, of course, a decision to act. Here, too, the example of Jesus sets the decisive standard for the action of salvation in history. He is not only always intolerant of sin but also often of the sinner as well, whenever the sinner shows the marks of impenitence and abusiveness toward the weak. The prophetic line of the Old Testament is not set aside by Jesus who ends up being a victim of his confrontation with sin and with those who have made sin their habitual way of relating to others. Sins are not only to be forgiven but taken away from the world, not only through the transformation of hearts but through the creation of new structures.

From a more positive angle, a new human being and a new earth are what salvation brings to humanity so that all will be reconciled and definitively recapitulated, so that

God will be all in all. When this finally happens, it will be the consummation of salvation.

The new human being is a converted and transformed human being. However, human beings are not only converted and transformed in their hearts—receiving hearts of flesh to replace their hearts of stone—but in the whole of their actions, both toward others and in their permanent objectifications. Salvation is at work when there is conversion and transformation. The rich Zacchaeus is converted when, through Jesus' presence, he has a change of heart and a change of behavior. That is even truer in the gospel. Conversion is not only the absence and even the rejection of sin, but it is a superabundance of grace: where sin reigned, grace now reigns; where the power of sin and evil prevailed, the power and grace of the Spirit now prevail. But this does not happen in an abstract way or purely by intentions, but rather concretely and materially. The words and the life of Jesus do not leave much room for abstraction, even recognizing that literalness is not the best kind of faithfulness. The words and the life of Jesus also do not leave much room for pure intentionality, because even though pure intention is a mark of the follower of Jesus, it is so together with the incarnation of works with their own weight and significance.

In speaking of new human beings, the Christian message highlights the need to pass through death. This is not only biological death, which places human beings and their problems in a different dimension; it is the death of former persons, in their inclinations as well as their actions. There is a break with the old way of life, and even more profoundly, a break in life itself; sin is no longer the principle of life, but grace. This is not just a matter of reforming habits but a leap to something new, to a new way of being human, made by a new person who emerges after the death and burial of the old one.

And we are talking not only of new human beings but of a new earth. There are no human beings without earth; there is no newness of humanity without a new earth. By earth we mean here the whole social and historical world in which human beings live. We could say that new human beings make the earth new, but it is also true that a new and good earth makes new and good human beings. We have already seen how much the shape of human life depends on the social structure in which human beings develop, which for them is never neutral but a principle of humanization or dehumanization, a principle of life or death, a principle of sin or grace. The earth too must pass through death in order to become new. It would not be so if we were still in the idyll of paradise. But in place of paradise, human beings have made and are still making an inferno. Thus, death is needed to mediate between the old earth and the new earth. What this change brought by death means, in social and historical terms, is something that cannot be determined theologically. We can only hazard the guess that it must have a certain subversive and revolutionary character, not in the current sociological and historical meaning of those terms, but in the deeper sense of the need for essential changes. Both the renewal of human beings and of the earth, without which history cannot be saved, require mediations: interpretive and effective mediations (C. Boff). It is history that needs salvation, and history has its own institutional objectification, its own laws and dynamics, its own forces, its own autonomy that must be respected because it responds to its own reality. Although we cannot catalogue, let alone systematize these mediations here, it will be helpful to point out some of them for their importance and as examples of other kinds of mediations.

First, there is the mediation of culture. This is a classical problem in the theorization and praxis of the Christian message. Faith has always been presented in cultural clothing, and at the same time it has claimed to transform cultures. The success or failure of this double operation can be judged very differently in each case, but the challenge is there. Without the salvation of culture, the renewal of the earth is impossible, and the renewal of human beings is very difficult. In some of the historical forms it has taken, and still takes, culture can be seen as a form of salvation. Through cultures, including not only their religious and moral but also interpretive and recreational aspects, the universal salvific will of God has been saving human beings, in the order of revelation as well as of sanctification (Darlap). This affirmation can be relativized but not denied, if we accept the universal salvific will of God and his universal fatherhood, and if we consider the best achievements of all cultures. But at the same time, that salvific will and action need to be made more present and visible in the different cultures. This requires an inculturation of the faith. The inculturation of faith not only enriches, purifies, and even renews cultures, but it also enriches, purifies, and renews the faith itself. Every faith is carried by a culture; this culture makes it present and effective, on the one hand, but also limits and obscures it. In the case of Christian faith, which claims to be absolutely universal, it can only show its full salvific universality when it is clothed and unclothed in each and every one of the cultures of the earth. Only in this way would it fully be able to save the cultures and with them the self-interpretive, evaluative, and guiding frameworks of each people and all humanity. The salvation of history happens through the salvation of cultures.

Economic and sociopolitical systems represent another of the great carriers of salvation in history. Without an appropriate satisfaction of basic needs, and without a fully established respect for fundamental human rights, we cannot speak of salvation in history and of the salvation of history. On the contrary, we must speak of oppressed and repressed persons and whole peoples, whose cries have reached the ears of God and filled God with indignation, as we see repeated so often in scripture and recently in the magisterium of the church. Thus, it is not a purely social or political problem, but a theologal problem, in the strict sense, having to do with the salvific will of God and the establishment of the Reign of God among human beings. Of course, the prevailing socioeconomic and political system determines whether in each nation and in all humanity there will be a just social order in which the needs and rights of all, and preferentially the majorities, are satisfied and respected. Nor can we speak here of a new earth and new human beings if the economic and political systems, in themselves and to a greater degree, are the result of sin, of the desire for riches, power, and domination—where they objectify that evil and configure the life of both oppressors and oppressed. Within an oppressive system, it may be possible that some of the oppressed become new human beings who struggle for their brothers and sisters and for a more just order, even to the point of giving up their lives. But that does not diminish—rather it strengthens—the need to transform the economic and political structures, which have become absolute idols to whom the dignity of human life is sacrificed, sometimes by means of exploitation and other times by consumerism. The two great economic systems prevailing today, capitalism and Marxism, are not exactly carriers of the salvation of history. At most they can be considered stages in a process, stages that must be surpassed by passing through death toward higher forms of humanity. The same is true of political systems. The message of salvation and salvific actions have much to contribute to all these if they are truly effective.

In the third place, we must be aware of the social forces, whatever form they may take in different times and places, that operate most visibly in history. Certainly, one cannot reduce history to politics or economics. We should not even think, at least in the history of salvation, that in the last analysis politics or economics dominate and/or determine everything else (Althusser). Thus, in speaking of social forces or agents we must also think of those that make up culture in the broadest sense. Salvation should also operate through all these social agents and forces. To that end, as a first step, they must become historical subjects, determinants of the course of history, without ever forgetting the ways in which all personal or collective freedom is conditioned. The fact that these agents and forces are absolutely, or almost absolutely, subject to history is a sign of how far history is from being a reign of freedom and of self-giving love. But even when they claim to have become the active subject of history, we cannot say that salvation is already present. Because without the transformation of that subject, evil and not grace will continue to reign. In addition, because the subject of history is usually a collectivity, it remains an open question which collective and under what conditions this collective can best contribute to the salvation of history, so that that salvation—without being reduced to the historical—should be made manifest in it. Yet the ongoing problem is that someone is needed to historicize salvation.

The open question as to which culture, which economic and political system, and which collectivity in this historical moment are the best mediators of salvation as it is described in the message of Jesus goes beyond the scope of this essay. Nevertheless, the question is not so open that just any answer will suffice. The message of Jesus, preceded by the Old Testament and other forms of revelation, followed by the sending of his own Spirit, and set over against historical events, clearly shows many of the things that cannot be tolerated and the general outline of a utopia that should be historicized. It also shows a location and a criterion, the preferential option for the poor, which if they are used well can guide and strengthen the presence of salvation in history.

Each human person, humanity, and human institutions can be saved in different ways. Only human beings and humanity can be first intrinsically elevated and then culminated and transformed by what we can call the divinizing communication of the Trinitarian God. However, that divinization should not only flow into human life and action and into its historical objectifications; its presence and depth are at least indirectly a criterion by which to measure the divinization. The children of light do not produce works of darkness, and good trees do not give bad fruit. Rather, bad fruit and darkness show that they do not come from the God of life but from the gods of death.

Is There Salvation in History?

Anyone who looks with critically realistic eyes at the different scenarios of history can only wonder how we can say that history has already been saved. The coming of Jesus does not appear to have turned history into a history of salvation. It does not seem as if salvation, insofar as it comes from Jesus, has made enough of an impact as to divide history into what came before and after his birth. It might have seemed so when history was confused with Western civilization and during the ten centuries or more when Western civilization was dominated more by ideology than by Christian faith. Even then, without denying the great contribution of faith to improving history, we were far from being able to speak of a human history, let alone a divine history. And if that was true in the times and places where Christian ideology dominated the culture and social structures, the view from a broader perspective in space and time would have to be more pessimistic.

We might think that the peoples most influenced by the Christian faith, especially in its Protestant form, still spearhead the movement of history. But this self-complacent view goes against the present state of humanity, as it was so strongly condemned by Vatican II in *Gaudium et spes,* by Paul VI in *Populorum progressio,* and by Medellín and Puebla. The extreme poverty in which more than half of humanity lives, the permanent state of war, the brutal inequality among members of the human family, the hundreds of thousands of victims of repression, even by governments that call themselves Western and Christian, the civilization of terror as a fundamental means of avoiding the total destruction of human life, the moral disintegration, the idolatries of power, money and pleasure, the greed and hostile alienation among peoples, cultures, and nations, etc. All this seems to support the assertion that evil holds sway over good or that we can barely speak of salvation in history, certainly not the salvation of history. The presence and effectiveness of Jesus' work would have to be reduced to a small ferment, incapable of leavening a loaf more dominated by evil than by good, in spite of some scientific and technical progress and some social movements that have tried to bring about a more just and human world, where all are respected as children of God and brothers and sisters in Jesus Christ.

This situation calls for a Christological focus. Did Jesus fail, during his mortal life, in the proclamation and realization of the Reign of God? Did that experience of failure force him to describe the task of realizing the Reign in less historical terms? Was it necessary to resort to an imminent parousia in which a triumphal second coming would correct the failure of his humble first coming? Was it necessary to think of salvation without its own historicity; as something that could only happen in subjective interiority; and, above all, as coming in an existence after history? Is history nothing more than the testing ground for human beings, deciding what will be their eternal destiny beyond time and space in the only place where salvation is fully present? Can the Reign of God preached by Jesus only be fully realized beyond history, so that salvation is offered in history but not promised to history itself?

Jesus' experience in history, and the experience of the Christians who follow his work, apparently leads to the conclusion that salvation, although incipient, is not yet within reach in all its fullness. Not even the whole life of Jesus, before his death, recognizes the totality of the salvific process; only with his resurrection and exaltation are we able to speak fully of salvation, through the communication of divinity to humanity. The logic that led Kant to postulate the immortality of the soul, in order to harmonize the just life with the happy life, can be used here to affirm Jesus' promise of eternal life: the assurance of eternal life for the elect, where the greatest possible communication from God to his creature takes place, is the fundamental point of salvation. Salvation par excellence comes beyond history, after the resurrection of the whole human being. This can only be affirmed in faith, but it must be maintained even in the darkest moments of life and history, when it seems as if God has abandoned his elect and even his own Son, and when it seems as if all history is dominated by the powers of evil.

But salvation is not ahistorical. Salvation must be made present in history. The historical failure of salvation does not prove its historical uselessness. History has not ended. In the hearts of most human beings, there is a yearning for things to improve and a utopia, precisely along the line and in the project reflected by the Reign. That yearning, that hope, that protest against injustice and sin, that getting to work, are good signs among others that salvation is trying to break into history. The Apocalypse, last of the revealed books, dramatically expresses this as the struggle between the faith of the righteous and the power of the empire. It is not only about the struggle of the newborn church against the Roman empire but also highlights the permanent struggle on which talk of salvation history should focus: the struggle between Christ, the principle of good and salvation, and Satan, the principle of evil and condemnation. In the struggle of history, the lamb will conquer in spite of his sacrifice and death. The tenacious struggle of the powers of evil against good, and more specifically against the good of salvation as proclaimed, lived, and realized by Jesus, shows the powerful intention of that good to be historical, to be present in history; otherwise, the power of evil could simply ignore Jesus' forceful message of salvation.

But it is not and never was so. The power of the world, through flattery and co-optation, tries to overcome the force of the gospel in different ways, as it has done ever since Constantine, or, alternatively, to crush it, as it crushed Jesus, the early Christians, and all authentic Christians, to the point where persecution has become a sign of authenticity. But that persecution, which is at bottom a recognition of the power of salvation, can never eliminate it and cannot keep its small seed from growing, so that in the maturity of history it becomes the great tree that gives its shadow of life to everyone else, to the multitude.

For that reason, the fact that salvation has not reached a satisfying fullness in history is not a definitive proof of its failure. Rather it proves that human beings, especially those specifically called to proclaim and historicize salvation, have failed in their mission. In the covenant, God's promise has not failed, but rather humans' responses have failed. Today we must reread from that perspective all the demands that Yahweh makes on his people, especially on their religious and political leaders. We do not need another covenant—in this sense the new covenant is definitive but not closed; what we need is to put into practice what God requires of human beings in order to bring about salvation, both personal and historical salvation.

The Historical Subject of Salvation

Certainly all humanity is the passive historical subject of salvation. All humanity, and to a proportionate degree all creation, has been called to salvation. Although this salvation could have taken different forms, it conforms to the nature of what is to be saved and according to the decisions made by human beings—in relation to which the Trinitarian God remains lovingly free, not only abstractly free. The incipient and different kind of divinization that is already occurring in every creature seeks fulfillment, within each one's limits and within the divine will. To affirm otherwise would be to deny the Trinitarian character of God and, even more clearly, the primacy of God's love and his universal salvific will. This does not negate the real possibility of condemnation, that is, of rejecting the salvation offered by God; nor does it necessarily imply that salvation, insofar as it is historical, is fully realized in each of its moments and in every person. Also, the fullness of salvation, understood as eternal salvation, that is, as the full gift of Trinitarian life to human beings, is only possible for an open essence (Zubiri) and is only consummated beyond death. But this does not hinder that same salvation, in a different degree and a different form, from being made present in history, not only in the human heart, but in all of history including physical nature itself, which sings the glory of God and is the worthy dwelling place of every kind of life and should not be ecologically destroyed. Everything is to be saved, although in different ways.

The active subject of salvation par excellence is God and God's mediator Jesus Christ. God is the beginning and end of human salvation and
has offered it definitively to humanity in the incarnation, life, death, and
resurrection of the Son. To seek total salvation apart from God would be
idolatry. False gods not only cannot give total salvation, they become the
principle of condemnation. Nothing and no one can take the place of
God or of Christ in the history of salvation. Salvation by definition is the
ever-increasing presence of God in human life and in human history. God
is the principle of holiness and happiness, principle of fullness and progress,
Alpha and Omega of human beings and of history. The truth of this God
is the incarnate *Logos*, and the way to God's life is Jesus alone, who died
and was resurrected for our sins and our salvation.

This appeal to the Trinitarian God as the beginning and end of salvation and to Jesus Christ as its mediator is the basis of the unity of history,
on the one hand, and of its distinctiveness, on the other. There is only one
history, which arises from the loving and salvific will of the only true God,
of the Trinitarian God as true God, so that one should do away with the
real separation between a profane history and a history of salvation, in spite
of the many distinctions that must be made within the history of revelation and of salvation (Darlap). What happens is that the unity of historical
reality is structural and not substantive, and it presupposes many different
elements. Between the monistic concept of history, which explains the
unity of history as a differentiating process of a single substance, and the
dualistic concept, which denies the essential unity of history and affirms
at most a certain parallelism between salvific events and profane events, it
is necessary to understand history as a structural unity in which the qualitative diversity of its elements is absorbed into the structural unity of its
deepest reality. The structural concept preserves the unity of history and
the diversity of its different elements without separation. If in thinking
about the history-of-salvation, we make the somewhat risky distinction
between history and salvation for the sake of mental clarity, then we can
distinguish between more formally historical elements and more formally
salvific elements. We can also speak of a more formally historical subject
and a more formally salvific subject. However, if in this distinction we
want to preserve, as we should, the structural unity of a single history, expressed precisely by the "of" in history-of-salvation, the salvific elements
should be pointed toward the historical elements and the historical toward
the salvific; the same is true of the subject of history and the subject of
salvation. In the latter case, this means that the subjects of history are really
subjects of salvation, as long as they are making a history of salvation and

not of condemnation, while the subjects of salvation are really subjects of history, when they put into motion and orient the way of salvation and not of condemnation.

The one salvation history can be a history of grace and a history of sin, but this is more realistic than affirming the duplicity of two histories: a profane history that is supposedly purely natural and a sacred history that is supposedly purely supernatural. On this point, we can take a model of interpretation from the double nature of Jesus, human and divine, in the profound unity of a single, all-encompassing reality of both. If Jesus' acts of eating, sleeping, taking walks, etc., were formally salvific, then so-called profane realities are also salvifically rooted in the structural unity of history. They may have a positive or negative influence with respect to salvation, but they also have a positive or negative influence with respect to history. The material part of a human being does not cease to be human just because it is not the psychic part of the person or confused with the human soul (psyche). In the same way, the historical (human), just because it is not exclusively salvific (divine), does not cease to be salvation history formally.

This distinction without separation allows us to conceive of actions and subjects as more specialized between the formally salvific and the formally historical. The church with its array of salvific actions is the subordinate subject of salvation, under the principal subject that is God and God's mediator Jesus Christ with the Holy Spirit. But not everything in the church is salvific; nor is everything salvific enclosed within the limits of the visible church. Many actions of the church have led and still lead to condemnation; the same is true of many members of that collective subject, the church. We need only look at the past and the present of the church, as seen in its actions and omissions and in specific subjects (including bishops and popes). At the other extreme, there are active subjects of salvation and many salvific actions that do not take place within the visible church. Often the best neighbor, the one who most loves and makes present the merciful God of love, is not the priest, not the scribe, not even the fellow Jew, but the Samaritan. The traditional patristic recognition of the "naturally Christian soul" is especially relevant in this perspective. The sanctifying and operative grace of God is not transmitted exclusively (although it is formally) through the channels of the visible church or through the sacraments alone. There are other religions that are vehicles of salvation, although they can be of condemnation as well. The objective criterion of discernment, since his coming, is the historical existence and the word of Jesus.

With regard to the active subject of the historical, within the structural unity of salvation history, the question is even more open, both in theoretical-cultural terms and in social relations. Nevertheless, there is a certain criterion. Although we can say in some way that everything good, true, beautiful, worthy, etc., can and must be included in a history of salvation, the structural moment of salvation plays a guiding role in evaluating and selecting the elements that can form a structural unity with salvation as Christ proclaimed it. For example, it might seem that the more wealth certain individuals possess, the better their chance of salvation, but in principle it is quite the contrary: wealth is a permanent danger to salvation, and in fact greed becomes not only a source of separation from God formally but something that distorts history and leads it toward oppression.

It might seem, at the other extreme, that political and cultural movements cannot be assimilated into the history of salvation because of their opposition to certain forms of the institutional church. But such movements might sometimes do more for the historicization of the Reign and even for the liberation of the poorest, at least initially, than has been done in this important area of salvation by certain sectors of the church. At certain times, those ecclesial sectors have become worldlier and have been shaped in some ways by the historical forces of condemnation rather than by the force of salvation. For example, some people have thought that Aristotelianism, purified by the presence within it of some elements of salvation stemming from the Christian faith, has served the interpretive history of salvation very well. The same might be said of many other historical characters and movements more or less present in today's world. Inversely, we might reject theories and practices that seem good for or distinct from salvation, no matter how profane and autonomous they may appear, because they cannot be reconciled with the one history, that is, the history of salvation. The fact that even the magisterium of the church has made mistakes along this double line of accepting and rejecting should not keep us from seeing the fundamental fact: that everything historical has to do with salvation, and that there are historical aspects that may work against salvation and in that sense are unacceptable. The opposite is not true because there is nothing in salvation—and nothing should be presented as salvific—that might be harmful to history on its way to fullness, on its liberating march toward freedom, understood as nothing less than the freedom of the children of God. That this has in fact happened simply shows the difficulty of the historical process and the limitations of the principle subject of history subordinated to salvation.

So there are some subjects that work in a specialized way for the salvific character of history and others that work more for the historical character of salvation. We usually think of the former as religious subjects and the latter as lay. The difference between them is more functional than structural, because in the structural unity of salvation-history, the historical effort presupposes an intrinsic orientation toward salvation, and the salvific effort presupposes an intrinsic orientation toward history; nevertheless, the functional difference is real. The underlying reason for this is that history, as it is symbolized in the description of paradise, is from the beginning the place chosen by God for all possible self-communication. Thus, there is not only a potential elevation of history but an actual beginning of that elevation, although in a progressive way, so that in each case one finds the elevation of the times. The fact that God's gift to that history has been free and gradual does not contradict that the operative gift has already been given, insofar as it was possible in the context of the organic and psychic development of humanity as it advanced within the animal kingdom.

It could have been otherwise, but by all the evidence of revelation, God did not want it otherwise. Therefore, those who follow the historical vector of the increasing gift of God to human beings as a principle of divinization, knowingly or not, are not only saving history but making possible a greater gift of God in history. Those who resist that vectorial force are not making another history apart from salvation history, a neutral and profane history, but rather are trying, within the same salvation history, to help the forces of evil and sin prevail over the forces of good and grace. Clearly the very *Logos* through which all things were made, which is the life of the world, is the same *Logos* that gave itself from the beginning and became incarnate in the historical Jesus rather than some ahistorical creature. Precisely the unconfused continuity between the creator *Logos* and the savior Jesus is the best proof and guarantee that the history nourished by the *Logos* and the salvation nourished by the Spirit of Christ form a structural unity that permits us to speak of a single salvation history.

It has always been difficult to accept this differentiated unity. Either one side is upheld monistically in a way that reduces the other to an extreme, so that they negate one or the other, or they are maintained in more or less parallel dualisms. The ancient controversy over accepting Mary as mother of God because she was only the mother of Jesus' humanity illustrates this difficulty. Nevertheless, the best Christian tradition has incorporated, as intrinsic to salvation history, elements that do not appear to be formally salvific. Certainly there is the humanity of Mary, whom we confess as mother of God, but there is also the materiality of the sacraments, without which there can be no supernatural transmission of their sacramental grace: bread becomes the body of Christ without losing its notes but still retains its appearance as bread; water becomes the carrier of baptismal grace and is considered to be elevated to carry out that function intrinsically. In the same way, history must be considered as a whole. History can engender salvation, as is true in the case of Mary or of sacramental materiality, if God so wills it and to the degree that God wills it. This does not happen extrinsically to history, because history itself, with its own structure, brings forth salvation from its womb without changing its structural elements and maintaining all its appearance as historical reality.

This of course presupposes that history has been chosen by God as the midwife of salvation and that in that election, it has been radically elevated to the mission for which it is chosen. It also presupposes that the salvation brought forth in history works within history itself, which is already prepared for its radical elevation but which, without this explicit presence of salvation, does not even know, at least explicitly, the extent and meaning of its own salvation. Thus, history is doubly dependent on salvation. History by itself is not salvific, but rather becomes so by the design and will of God; and history only becomes salvation history through the historic appearance of salvation within it, through the historicization of salvation.

From this viewpoint, to maintain the classical language, we can say that the natural is material nature, and the supernatural is history. History is the supernature of nature. This does not deny that salvation affects material nature itself in some way—the dogma of resurrection—but this happens because it is in history that salvation formally occurs. History would only be supernature in a purely metaphysical sense if it were not for its gratuitous elevation by God, but because of that elevation, history is supernature in a strictly theologal sense: all history is elevated to a new plane, that of the communication and gift of God's Trinitarian life. This communication and gift can be rejected by individual human beings, or by peoples and their institutions, but this does not keep history from being supernature or the historical from being supernatural; in that case it would be not a simple moral failure but a true sin, a rejection of God's grace. Thus, salvation is present in every historical event; and within its dual possibility as grace and as sin, all history is salvation history.

Note

[1] Though not noted in the original text, the reference is to Adolf Darlap, *Histoire du salut et révélation* (Paris: Éditions du Cerf, 1969).

—Translated by Margaret D. Wilde.

8

The Crucified People

An Essay in Historical Soteriology
(1978)

In March of 1977, the Jesuit priest Rutilio Grande was assassinated near the town of Aguilares where he was pastor. This commenced a wave of repression against peasants, unionists, catechists, and priests, who were tortured, kidnapped, and murdered. A death squad even threatened the murder of all Jesuits who did not leave the country within thirty days. In the year this essay appeared, 1,063 people were arrested and 147 murdered by security forces for political reasons. These facts frame the 1978 appearance of this most widely republished and most memorably titled of all of Ellacuría's writings.

If "the crucified people" is Ellacuría's most lapidary phrase, the essay of that name stands as one of his most penetrating and influential. Indeed, though not as arresting or poetic as the title, the subtitle is also important, for it highlights the theological watershed that Ellacuría was crossing. He writes that in a consideration of the crucified people "we could say that we find … the whole of Christology and ecclesiology in their character as historical soteriology." Historical soteriology not only thinks about salvation but actively promotes salvation, inviting Christians to embody a saving praxis. The essay begins with an important reference to theological method and the "double-hermeneutical perspective" in which historical reality is viewed through its corresponding key in revelation, even as revelation is interpreted "from the history to which it is addressed." Ellacuría then establishes the importance of the cross in salvation history and applies his double-hermeneutical perspective to the death of Jesus and "the crucifixion of the people." He concludes with his famous argument for considering the crucified people as "a principle of salvation for the entire world," an argument developed as a poignant biblical reflection on the songs of the "servant of Yahweh" found in the prophet Isaiah.

If we are to understand what the people of God is, it is very important that we open our eyes to the reality around us, the reality of the world in which the church has existed for almost two thousand years, since Jesus announced the approach of the Reign of God. This reality is simply the existence of a vast portion of humankind, which is literally and historically crucified by natural oppressions and especially by historical and personal oppressions. This reality prompts in the Christian spirit inescapable questions: What does the fact that most of humankind is oppressed mean for salvation history and in salvation history? Can we regard suffering humankind as saved in history when it continues to bear the sins of the world? Can we regard it as savior of the world precisely because it bears the sins of the world? What is the relationship with the church as sacrament of salvation? Is this suffering humankind something essential when it comes time to reflect on what the people of God is and what the church is?

Posing these questions indicates the historical gravity and theological importance of the issue. Many Christological and ecclesiological topics are wrapped up in this question; in fact, we could say that we find here the whole of Christology and ecclesiology in their character as historical soteriology. How is the salvation of humankind achieved starting from Jesus? Who continues in history that essential function, that saving mission that the Father entrusted to the Son? The answer to these questions can give historical flesh to the people of God and thus avoid dehistoricizing this basic concept and also avoid spiritualizing or ideologizing it falsely. Historical soteriology provides an essential perspective in this regard.

Historical soteriology here means something referring to salvation as it is presented in revelation. But the accent falls on its historical character and that in a double sense: as the realization of salvation in the one and only human history, and as humankind's active participation in that salvation, in this case, the participation of oppressed humankind. Which historically oppressed people serve as the continuation, par excellence, of the saving work of Jesus, and the extent to which they does so, is something to be uncovered throughout this essay. That task is one of the things required of historical soteriology and clarifies what such a soteriology must be. To begin with, it must be a soteriology whose essential reference point is the saving work of Jesus, but it must likewise be a soteriology that historicizes this saving work and does so as the continuation and following of Jesus and his work.

The analysis will be carried out from only one angle: the one that places in unity the figure of Jesus with that of oppressed humankind: his passion and death. There are other angles, but this one is essential and merits study by itself—in it, all life flows together, and from it, history's future opens.

The Passion of Jesus as Seen from the Crucified People: The Crucifixion of the People as Seen from the Death of Jesus

Here we have something required by theological method as understood in Latin American theology: any situation in history should be considered from its corresponding key in revelation, but revelation should be approached from the history to which it is addressed—although not every moment in history is equally valid for providing a proper focus. The first aspect seems obvious from the angle of Christian faith, even though it conceals a problem: that of finding the proper equivalence so as not to confuse the key for one situation as one proper to another. The second aspect, which has a circular relationship with the previous one, is not so obvious, especially if we mean that the situation enriches and actualizes the fullness of revelation, and if we maintain that not every situation is the most conducive to having revelation offer itself in fullness and authenticity.

In this instance, we confront two crucial poles with regard to both revelation and situation. Treating them together clarifies a basic problem: the historicity of the passion of Jesus and the saving character of the crucifixion of the people. In other words, both the historical character of the salvation of Jesus and the saving character of the history of crucified humankind are clarified, once it is accepted that in Jesus salvation is given, and in humankind this salvation is realized. Therefore, the meaning of both the passion of Jesus and the crucifixion of the people are enriched, and that means an enrichment of who Jesus is and who the people are. However, that approach faces a very serious problem: making sense of the seeming failure involved in the crucifixion of a people after the definitive proclamation of salvation. Involved here is not only the failure of history, but also what the vast majority of humankind means in history, and even more important, the historical task of its salvation.

Hence, the focus here is primarily soteriological. The accent will fall not on what Jesus and the people are but on what they represent for the salvation of humankind. Of course, we cannot separate what are called the ontological from the soteriological aspects, but we can accent one side or the other. Here the accent will be on the soteriological aspects, keeping in mind that the aim is not to reduce the being and mission of Jesus, or the being and mission of the people, to the dimension of historical soteriology, though it must be said that neither being nor mission is properly illuminated if soteriological reflection is left aside.

If this warning is important for avoiding one-sided reflections on Jesus, which are so only if they are absolutized, it is also important for avoiding confusion about the historical role that falls to the oppressed people in their struggles in history. This role does not come down to simply that which stands out when it is likened to the passion and death of Jesus. Neither Jesus nor the crucified people, as they will be considered here, are the only salvation of history, although the salvation of history cannot reach fulfillment without both of them, even with respect to salvation in history. The former is clear and acknowledged, as long as the structural complexity of human history is taken into account; the latter is clear for believers, at least with regard to the first term, but it must be proven to nonbelievers. This should be done in such a way that the clear contribution of the crucified people to salvation is the historical verification of Christian salvation; at the same time, it should not be turned into a sentimentality and mystification that would hinder the political organization of the people and their effective contribution to liberation in history.

To propose salvation on the basis of the crucifixion of Jesus and the people assumes the same scandal and the same madness, especially if we wish to give to salvation a content that can be verified in historical reality, where *verifiable* does not mean *exhaustible*.

Today from a Christian standpoint, it is not scandalous to say that life comes from the death of Jesus in history, even though it was indeed a scandal for those who witnessed that death and had to proclaim it. Nevertheless, we must recover that scandal and madness if we do not want to vitiate the historical truth of the passion of Jesus. We must do that in three dimensions: with regard to Jesus himself who only gradually was able to comprehend the true path toward proclaiming and realizing the Reign of God; with regard to those who persecuted him to his death because they could not accept that salvation involved taking particular positions in history; and, finally, with regard to scandal in the church, which leads the church to avoid passing through the passion when it proclaims the resurrection.

It is indeed scandalous to propose the needy and the oppressed as the historical salvation of the world. It is scandalous for many believers who no longer think they see anything striking in the proclamation that the death of Jesus brought life to the world, but who cannot accept in theory, and much less in practice, that today this life-giving death goes by way of the oppressed part of humankind. It is likewise scandalous to those who seek the liberation of humankind in history. It is easy to regard the oppressed and needy as those who are to be saved and liberated, but it is not easy to see them as saviors and liberators.

It is only fair to acknowledge that there are movements in history that regard the oppressed as the radical subject of salvation and especially the subject of the liberation of peoples in history. We have, for example, this well-known text of Marx's from "Toward the Critique of Hegel's Philosophy of Law":

Where, then, is the *positive* possibility of German emancipation?

Answer. In the formation of a class with *radical chains*, a class in civil society that is not of civil society, a class that is the dissolution of all classes, a sphere of society having a universal character because of its universal suffering and claiming no *particular* right because no *particular wrong* but *unqualified wrong* is perpetrated on it; a sphere that can invoke no *traditional* title but only a *human* title, which does not partially oppose the consequences but totally opposes the premises of the German political system; a sphere, finally, that cannot emancipate itself without emancipating itself from all the other spheres of society, thereby emancipating them; a sphere, in short, that is the *complete loss* of humanity and can only redeem itself through the *total redemption of humanity*. This dissolution of society as a particular class is the *proletariat*.

The proletariat is only beginning to appear in Germany as a result of the rising *industrial* movement. For it is not poverty from *natural circumstances* but *artificially produced* poverty, not the human masses mechanically oppressed by the weight of society but the masses resulting from the *acute disintegration* of society.

Heralding the *dissolution of the existing order of things*, the proletariat merely announces the *secret of its own existence* because it *is* the *real* dissolution of this order.

This text is clear proof that the oppressed have been regarded as an element of salvation when it comes to revolution. Yet, we must say that there is a deep religious inspiration in this text, which shows through the terminology. It does not, however, represent the whole of Marxist thought—much less its historical praxis—on the question. Marxist attacks on the *Lumpenproletariat* as hindering the revolution, moreover, signal a viewpoint that, if read without rigor, could leave a vast sector of crucified humankind outside the course of history. We cannot enter into this point now, but we should not forget it. If it has been Marxist theory's genius that for historical reasons it attributes to the dispossessed a primordial role in the overall rescue of humankind, and in the building of the new person and the new earth, this does not mean that it has posed in all its universality and intensity, that is in its overarching scope, the contribution of the dispossessed to the integral salvation of human history.

Whether or not it is a scandal to hold that the passion and crucifixion of Jesus and of the people are central for human salvation, it is clear that precisely because of its implausibility as salvation, the passion of Jesus casts light on the implausibility of the people's crucifixion as salvation, while this latter prevents a naive or ideologized reading of the former.

On the one hand, the resurrection of Jesus and its effects in history are a hope and future for those who live in a time of passion. Certainly Jesus maintained hope in the definitive victory of God's Reign, to which he devoted his life and for which he died. Behind Luke 22:15–18 (and its parallel, Mark 14:25), despite the redaction done by the early community, we can reconstruct a double prophecy of the death of Jesus: after his death, Jesus will again celebrate the Passover and will organize a banquet in the Reign of God, which of necessity must arrive. His death will not prevent the salvation to come, and he himself will not remain imprisoned by death forever. Hence, as Schürmann says, the inbreaking of the Reign and Jesus' violent death are not to be separated. Jesus' death is inseparably connected to the eschatological and historical coming of the Reign, and for that purpose the resurrection means not only a verification or consolation but the assurance that this work must continue and that he remains alive to continue it.

This hope of Jesus was not of such a nature that the passion ceased being so, all the way to his anguished cry of abandonment on the cross. His struggle for the Reign, and his certainty that the Reign of God would triumph definitively, did not prevent him from "seeing" the connection between his personal days of tears, between the momentary failure of the coming of the Reign, and the glory of final victory. That is why he is an example for those who look more like the wretched of the earth than like its saviors. In being condemned personally, Jesus had to learn the road to definitive salvation—a salvation, let us repeat once more, that was essentially a matter of the coming of God's Reign and not a personal resurrection separate from what had been his earthly preaching of the Reign.

On the other hand, the ongoing passion of the people and all that it entails—the historical reign of sin as opposing the Reign of God—do not permit an ahistorical reading of the death and resurrection of Jesus. The fundamental flaw in such a reading would lie in uprooting the Reign of God from history and relegating it to a stage beyond history, so that it would no longer make sense to continue within history the life and mission of Jesus who announced the Reign. That would be a betrayal of Jesus' life and death, which was entirely devoted not to himself but to the Reign. Moreover, identifying the Reign with the resurrection of Jesus would leave unfulfilled Jesus' message that predicted persecutions and death for those who were to continue his work. When Paul speaks of what is still wanting in the passion of Christ, he is rejecting an ahistorical resurrection that ignores what is happening on earth. It is precisely the reign of sin, which continues to crucify most of humankind, that obliges us to historicize the death of Jesus as the historical Passover of the Reign of God.

Theological Importance of the Cross in Salvation History

An ascetic and moralizing focus on the Christian cross has distorted the importance of the cross in history and led to a rejection of everything that has to do with it. Such a rejection is fully justified if it is not simply a matter of the immature outburst of people liberated from their emotional fantasies. The renewal of the mystery of the cross has little to do with gratuitous repression, which places the cross where one wants it and not in its real site, as though what Jesus had sought for himself was death on the cross and not the proclamation of the Reign.

Even more dangerous is the effort to evade the history of the cross in those theologies of creation and resurrection that at most make of the cross an incident or an isolated mystery that mystically projects its efficacy over human relationships with God.

A "naturalistic" view of creation, as faith inspired as it might regard itself, is ignorant of the novelty of the Christian God revealed in salvation history. It even ignores the fact that Israel did not come to the idea of the creator God through rational reflection on the course of nature, but rather through theological reflection on what had happened to the chosen people. Von Rad has shown clearly that it is in the political struggles of the Exodus that Israel becomes aware that Yahweh is its savior and redeemer, that this salvation has been conceived as the creation and launching of a people, and that faith in a God who creates the world is a subsequent discovery that occurs when the historical experience of the people of Israel in the failure of the exile gradually points it toward a universalizing consciousness, which demands a universal God, creator of all humans. Hence, a faith apart from history, a faith apart from historical events, whether in the life of Jesus or in the life of humankind, is not a Christian faith. It would be at best a somewhat corrected version of theism.

Neither is it a Christian position that takes its support exclusively from the faith experience of the Risen One and ignores the historical roots of the resurrection. That temptation is an ancient one, and most probably came up even in the early communities, forcing them to emphasize very soon the continuity of the Risen One with the Crucified One. Otherwise, people live with the false assumption that the struggle against sin and death is over with the triumph of the resurrection. The Reign of God again would be reduced to something in the future, which either does not require human effort because it is imminent, or reduces the Reign to the resurrection of the dead because it is a long way off. If the life of the Risen One victorious over death is the future of salvation for Christians and for a new humankind, as Pannenberg points out, the life of the Risen One is the same life as that of Jesus of Nazareth who was crucified for us, so that the immortal life of the Risen One is the future of salvation only insofar as we abandon ourselves to obedience to the Crucified One who can overcome sin.

Hence, from a Christian viewpoint, the immediate connection between creation and resurrection is false whatever the understanding of the original "image and likeness," the historical process of death and resurrection. Every process in history is a creation of the future and not merely a renewal of the past. The fallen human is not restored, but rather the new human is built up; that new human is built up in the resurrection of one who has struggled against sin to the death. To put it another way, eschatological hope is expressed equally as Reign of God and as resurrection of the dead, which for Pannenberg—who is not exactly a liberation theologian—means that the Reign of God is not possible as a community of human beings in perfect peace and total justice, without a radical change of the natural conditions that are present in human life, a change that is called the resurrection of the dead. He also says that the individual destiny and the political destiny of human beings go hand in hand.

Thus, the resurrection points back toward the crucifixion: the Crucified One rises, and rises because he was crucified; since his life was taken away for proclaiming the Reign, he receives a new life as fulfillment of the Reign of God. Thus, the resurrection points back toward the passion, and the passion points back toward Jesus' life as proclaimer of the Reign. As is well known, that is the sequence followed in putting the gospels together. The need to historicize the experience of the Risen One leads to a reflection on the passion story, which occupies a disproportionately large space in the gospel accounts and which, in turn, requires historical justification in the narration of the life of Jesus. In any case, the gospels as a whole seek to give theological weight to two facts that are part of a single reality: the fact of Jesus' failure in the scandal of his death and the fact of the persecution that the early communities soon undergo.

Hence, the gospels do not treat an expiatory masochism of a spiritualizing sort but the discovery of something real in history. It is not a matter of grief and mortification, but of making a break and a commitment. Jesus' death makes it clear why really proclaiming salvation runs up against the resistance of the world and why the Reign of God struggles against the reign of sin. That is made manifest both in the death of the prophet, the one sent by God, and in the ravaging and death of humankind at the hands of those who make themselves gods, lording it over humankind. If a spiritualizing approach to the passion leads to an evasion of that commitment to history that results in persecution and death, a historical commitment to the crucified people makes it necessary to examine the theological meaning of this death and, thus, to go back to the redeeming passion of Jesus. Reflecting historically on the death of Jesus helps us to reflect theologically on the death of the oppressed people, and the latter points back toward the former.

The Death of Jesus and the Crucifixion of the People Are Realities of History and the Result of Actions in History

Historical Necessity of Jesus' Death

We may admit that the death of Jesus and the crucifixion of the people are necessary but only if we speak of a necessity in history and not a merely natural necessity. It is precisely their nature as historical necessity that clarifies the deep reality of what happens in history, at the same time as it opens a space for the transformation of history. That would not be the case if we were dealing with a merely natural necessity.

The scriptures themselves point out this necessity when they try to justify the passion of Jesus, and they even formulate it as a kind of principle: "Did not the Messiah have to suffer (*edei pathein*) all this so as to enter into his glory?" (Luke 24:36). But this "having to" undergo "so as to" reach fulfillment is a historical "having to." It is historical not because the prophets had announced it but because the prophets prefigured the events in what happened to them. Through what happened to the prophets, this necessity is grounded in the opposition between the proclamation of the Reign and the fact that sin is obviously a reality in history. The resistance of the oppressive powers and the struggle for liberation in history brought them persecution and death, but this resistance and struggle were simply the consequence in history of a life in response to God's word. That long experience, explicitly recalled by Jesus, leads to the conclusion that in our historical world arriving at the glory of God requires passing through persecution and death. The reason could not be clearer: If the Reign of God and the reign of sin are two opposed realities, and human beings of flesh and blood are the standard bearers of both, then those who wield the power of oppressive domination cannot but exercise it against those who have only the power of their word and their life, offered for the salvation of many.

Hence, this is not the biological image of a seed dying in order to bear fruit or of a dialectical law that demands undergoing death in order to reach new life. Of course, there are scriptural texts that speak of the need for the seed to die; these texts point toward the necessity and the dialectical movement of this necessity, but they do not make it "natural." Making it natural would entail both eliminating the responsibility of those who kill prophets and those who crucify humankind, thereby veiling the aspect of sin in historical evil. It would also imply that new life could emerge without the activity of human beings who would not need to be converted internally or to rebel against what is outside. It is true that biological images of the Reign sometimes emphasize how the growth is God's work, but we cannot, thereby, conclude that human beings should cease caring for the field of history.

Necessity in history, on the other hand, forces us to emphasize the determining causes of what happens. Theologically speaking, the fundamental cause is expressed countless times in scripture: passing from death to glory is necessary only given the fact of sin, a sin that takes possession of the human heart, but especially a sin in history that collectively rules over the world and over peoples. There is, in Moingt's phrase, a "theologal and collective sin," and it is to that sin that the proclamation of the death of Christ for our sins refers, not directly to our individual and ethical sins; it is a "collective reality," grounding and making possible individual sins. It is this theologal and collective sin that destroys history and hinders the future that God would want for history; this collective sin is what causes death to reign over the world, and, hence, we must be freed from our collective work of death in order to form once more the people of God. It is Moingt himself who goes so far as to say that redemption is simultaneously "the political liberation of the people and their conversion to God."

This historical necessity differs in respect to death than it does to glory: while it is necessary to go through death to reach glory, glory need not follow death. Thus, there is one attitude for struggling against death and another for receiving life. In both cases, there is something external to the individual human being. The evil of the world, the sin of the world, is not simply the sum of particular individual actions; nor are these foreign to this sin that dominates them. Likewise, the forgiveness and transformation of the world are things that human beings initially receive so as to then offer their own contribution. The external aspect is different in the case of evil and of good, of sin and grace; sin is the work of human beings, and grace is God's work, although it is something that operates within and through human beings, and, thus, there is no question of passivity. Although God gives the growth, the effort of human beings is not excluded but in fact is required, especially for destroying the objective embodiment of sin and then for building up the objective embodiment of grace. Otherwise, necessity would not have any historical character but would be purely natural, and the human being would be either the absolute negation of God or a mere executor of presumably divine designs.

The "necessary" character of Jesus' death is seen only after the fact. Neither his disciples nor he himself saw as a principle, not even through reflection on scripture, that the proclamation and victory of the Reign had to go by way of death. When it happened, the surprised minds of the believers found in God's designs, manifested in the words and deeds of the scriptures—Moses and the prophets—the signs of the divine will that made death "necessary."

This "necessity" is not based on notions of expiation and sacrifice. In fact, when the Servant of Yahweh in Deutero-Isaiah is used to explain the meaning of the death of Jesus, the thread of discourse is not "sin-offense-victim-expiation-forgiveness." This framework, which may have some validity for particular mindsets and which expresses some valid points, may turn into an evasion of what must be done in history in order to eliminate the sin of the world. In times when consciences were oppressed or felt oppressed by a Christianity centered on the idea of sin, of guilt, and of eternal condemnation, it was utterly necessary that there be a framework of forgiveness in which an offended God forgave sin and wiped out condemnation. But even with its valid points, this framework does not emphasize either the collective embodiment of sin or human activity that is "necessary" in history—destroying injustice and building love. A new theology of sin must move beyond the expiatorial frameworks but should not permit the existence of sin itself to be forgotten. To forget it would, among other things, leave the field open to the forces of oppression, which are overwhelmingly dominant in our world, and it would also neglect the area of personal conversion.

Implications

Emphasizing the historical character of the death of Jesus is fundamental for Christology and for a historical soteriology, which as such would take on a new meaning.

The historical character of the death of Jesus entails, to begin with, that his death took place for historical reasons. New Christologies are increasingly emphasizing this point with good reason. Jesus dies—is killed as the four gospels and Acts so insist—because of the historical life he led, a life of deeds and words that those who represented and held the reins of the religious, socioeconomic, and political situation could not tolerate. That he was regarded as a blasphemer, one who was destroying the traditional religious order, one who upset the social structure, a political agitator, and so forth, is simply to recognize from quite distinct angles that the activity, word, and very person of Jesus in the proclamation of the Reign were so assertive and so against the established order and basic institutions that they had to be punished by death. Dehistoricizing this radical reality leads to mystical approaches to the problem, not by way of deepening, but by way of evading. We cannot simply settle the matter of the "died for our sins" by means of the expiatory victim, thereby leaving the direction of history untouched.

It likewise implies that Jesus followed a particular direction in history not because it would lead to death or because he was seeking a redemptive death, but rather because that was what truly proclaiming the Reign of God demanded. Whether the emphasis be on the soteriological character of Jesus' death, as in Paul, or on the soteriological character of the resurrection, as in Luke, it cannot be forgotten that the historical Jesus sought for himself neither death nor resurrection but the proclamation of the Reign of God to the point of death, and that brought resurrection. Jesus saw that his action was leading to a mortal confrontation with those who could take his life, and it is utterly inconceivable that he did not see the probability, and even proximity, of his death along with their reasons.

Indeed, in a broad sense, he was better (and earlier) aware of the salvific value of his person and his life than of the salvific value of his death. He does not begin by focusing his activity on waiting for death but on the proclamation of the Reign. Even when he sees death as a real possibility, he does not hesitate in that proclamation or shrink back from his conflict with power. Putting all the saving value on his death cannot be reconciled with his life and the demands he places on his disciples; it cannot be said that there is in Jesus a gradual shift from life to death as the center of his message, since in the many texts about following him as being difficult and contradictory, the accent is on the continuity of life with death and not on death as a break with regard to the way of salvation that his life represents.

Salvation, therefore, cannot be made exclusively a matter of the mystical fruits of Jesus' death, separating it from his real and verifiable behavior. It is not merely a passive and obedient acceptance of a natural fate, let alone a fate imposed by the Father. It is, at least at a basic level, an action that leads to life by way of death, in such a way that in the case of Jesus what is salvific cannot be separated from what is historical. Consequently, Jesus' death is not the end of the meaning of his life, but rather the end of that pattern that must be repeated and followed in new lives with the hope of resurrection and thereby the seal of exaltation. Jesus' death is the final meaning of his life only because the death toward which his life led him shows the historical and theological meaning of his life in tandem. It is, thus, his life that provides the ultimate meaning of his death, and only as a consequence does his death, which has received its initial meaning from his life, give meaning to his life. Therefore, his followers should not focus primarily on death as sacrifice, but rather on the life of Jesus, which will only really be Jesus' life if it leads to the same consequences as his life did.

Historical soteriology is a matter of seeking where and how the saving action of Jesus was carried out in order to continue it in history. Of course, in one sense, the life and death of Jesus is over and done, since what took place in them is not simply a mere fact whose value is the same as that of any other death that might take place in the same circumstances, but was, indeed, the definitive presence of God among human beings. But his life and this death continue on earth, and not just in heaven; the uniqueness of Jesus is not in his standing apart from humankind, but in the definitive character of his person and its saving omnipresence. All the insistence on his role as head to a body, and on the sending of his Spirit, through whom his work is to be continued, point toward this historical current of his earthly life. The continuity is not purely mystical and sacramental, just as his activity on earth was not purely mystical and sacramental. In other words, it is not in the cultic, not even the celebration of the Eucharist, that is the *totum* of the presence and continuity of Jesus; there must be a continuation in history that realizes what he realized in his life and as he realized it. We should acknowledge a transhistorical dimension in Jesus' activity, just as we should acknowledge it in his personal biography, but this transhistorical dimension will only be real if it is indeed transhistorical, that is, if it goes through history. Hence, we must ask who continues to carry out in history what his life and death was about.

The Crucified People, Principle of Universal Salvation

We can approach the question by taking into account that there is a crucified people whose crucifixion is the product of actions in history. Establishing that may not be enough to prove that this crucified people is the continuation in history of the life and death of Jesus. But before delving into other aspects that demonstrate that such is the case, it would be a good idea to take the same starting point as that concerning the saving value of Jesus' life and death.

What is meant by crucified people here is that collective body that, being the majority of humanity, owes its situation of crucifixion to a social order organized and maintained by a minority that exercises its dominion through a series of factors, which, taken together and given their concrete impact within history, must be regarded as sin. This is not a purely individual way of looking at every person who suffers due to unjust actions by others or even because such a person is sacrificed in the struggle against prevailing injustice. Although looking collectively at the crucified people does not exclude such an individual perspective, the latter is subsumed in the former, since the collective is the historical location of the individual's realization. Nor is the viewpoint here one of looking at purely natural misfortunes, although natural evils play a role, albeit derivatively, insofar as they take place in a particular historical order.

To regard a collective body as subject of salvation is not foreign to the scriptures but is in fact its original thrust. For example, as J. Jeremias points out, an individual can only become a servant of Yahweh insofar as he or she is a member of the people of Israel, since salvation is offered primarily to the people and within the people. The communal experience that the root of individual sins is within the presence of supraindividual sin, and that each one's life is shaped by the life of the people in which he or she lives, makes it connatural to experience that both salvation and perdition are played out primarily in this collective dimension. The modern insistence on individualizing human existence will be faithful to reality only if it does not ignore its social dimension, which is not the case in the frenzied individualism and idealism that is so characteristic of Western culture, or at least of its elites. All the selfishness and social irresponsibility borne by these notions is but the reverse proof of how false this exaggeration is. There is no need to deny the collective and structural dimension in order to give ample space for the full development of the person.

If this assertion of collective salvation is not arbitrary from a theological standpoint, it is even less so in terms of the real situation. It is something confirmed in historical experience now viewed from the standpoint of soteriology. One who is concerned as a believer about the sin and salvation of the world cannot but affirm that in history, humanity is crucified in the concrete form of the crucified people. By the same token, one who reflects as a believer on the excruciating reality of this crucified people must inquire what there is of sin and the need for salvation there. In view of this reality, which is so extensive and so serious, considering the particular cases of those who do not belong to the crucified people becomes a secondary matter, although we should here repeat that the universalist and structural approach by no means has to do away with the individualistic and psychological approach but simply provides it with a framework rooted in reality. What Christian faith adds after it is really clear that there is a crucified people is the suspicion that, besides being the main object of the effort of salvation, it might also in its very crucified situation be the principle of salvation for the whole world.

This is not the place to determine the extent and the nature of the ongoing oppression of the bulk of humankind today or to carry out a detailed study of its causes. Although it is one of the fundamental realities that should serve as a starting point for theological reflection, and although it has been scandalously ignored by those who theorize from the geographical world of the oppressors, it is so obvious and widespread that it needs no explanation. What it does need is to be lived experientially.

Now although there are undeniably "natural" elements in the present situation of injustice that defines our world, there is also undeniably a side that derives from actions in history. Just as in the case of Jesus, we cannot speak of a purely natural necessity because the oppression of the crucified people derives from a necessity in history: the necessity that many suffer so a few may enjoy, that many be dispossessed so that a few may possess. Moreover, the repression of those in the vanguard of the people's interests follows the same pattern as the case of Jesus although with different meanings.

Without doubt, this general formulation should be historicized. It does not happen everywhere in the same way or for the same reasons, since the general pattern of the oppression of humans by humans takes on very different forms both collectively and individually. In our universal situation today, oppression has some overall characteristics in history that cannot be ignored, and those who do not take a stand on the side of liberation are culpable, whether actively or passively.

Thus, within this collective and overall framework, more specific analyses must be carried out. While maintaining the universal pattern of people crucifying others in order to live themselves, the subsystems of crucifixion that exist in both groups, oppressors and oppressed, should also be examined. As has often been pointed out, in a number of ways among the oppressed themselves, some put themselves at the service of the oppressors or give free rein to their impulses to dominate. This serious problem forces us to get beyond simplistic formulas with regard to both the causes of oppression and to its forms, so as not to fall into a Manichean division of the world, which would situate all good in the world on one side and all evil on the other. It is precisely a structural way of looking at the problem that enables us to avoid the error of seeing as good all the individuals on one side and as evil those on the others side, thus leaving aside the problem of personal transformation. Flight from one's own death in a continual looking out for oneself and not acknowledging that we gain life when we surrender it to others, is no doubt a temptation that is permanent and inherent in the human being, one that structures and history modulate but do not abolish.

The focus on the death of Jesus and the crucifixion of the people, the fact that they refer back and forth to each other, makes both take on a new light. The crucifixion of the people avoids the danger of mystifying the death of Jesus, and the death of Jesus avoids the danger of extolling salvifically the mere fact of the crucifixion of the people, as though the brute fact of being crucified of itself were to bring about resurrection and life. We must shed light on this crucifixion out of what Jesus' death was in order to see the salvific scope and the Christian nature of this salvation. To that end we must examine the principles of life that are intermingled with the principles of death; although the presence of sin and death is overwhelming in human history, the presence of grace and of life is also very prominent and palpable. We must not lose sight of either aspect. Indeed, salvation can only be understood as a victory of life over death, a victory already announced in the resurrection of Jesus but one that must be won in a process of following his steps and understanding the meaning that those steps have in him.

Jesus' Death and the People's
Crucifixion in Terms of the Servant of Yahweh

One of the approaches that the primitive Christian community used in order to understand Jesus' death and give it its adequate value was the figure
of the Servant of Yahweh as described in Second Isaiah. This fact entitles
us to appeal once more to the Suffering Servant in order to see what, in
one of its aspects, the death of Jesus was, and especially what, in one of its
aspects, the crucifixion of the people is.

Thus, this section will have three parts. In the first, we shall list some
of the characteristics of the Servant as proposed in Second Isaiah. In the
second part, we shall align these characteristics with the concrete reality
of Jesus' life and death. Finally, in the third part of this section, we shall
draw up a corresponding list of what are or ought to be the characteristics of the oppressed people if they are to be the continuation of Jesus'
redemptive work. The first two parts will be orientated toward the third:
thus, even if we do not manage to prove that the oppressed people are
the historical extension of the crucifixion and of the Crucified One, we
will have indicated at least the route to be followed if that people is to
conform its death with that of Christ—keeping account, meanwhile, of
the distinction between the two realities and of the different functions
incumbent upon each.

Characteristics of the Servant of Yahweh

We will analyze the Suffering Servant of Yahweh from the perspective of
the crucified people. Every reading is done from a situation more than
from a preunderstanding, which is in some way determined by the situation. Those who claim to be able to do a neutral reading of a text of
scripture commit a twofold error. First, they commit an epistemological
error by believing it possible to do a nonconditioned reading. They also
commit a theological error by scorning the most apt locus of any reading, which will always be the principal addressee of the text in question.
This addressee is different at each historical moment, and the hypothesis
with which we are working is that at this particular moment of ours, the
addressee of the Suffering Servant Songs is the crucified people—a hypothesis that will be confirmed if indeed the text sheds light on what the
crucified people is, and if, conversely, the text is enriched, and endowed
with currency, by the reality that is this historical addressee. This is not the
place for a discussion of the epistemological and theological justification of

this methodological procedure—which does not exclude the most careful utilization of exegetical analyses but only subordinates them. Suffice it to have enunciated this procedure in order not to go astray in our analysis of the text at hand.

Our analysis will prescind from whether the "Servant" is a collective or individual personage, a king or a prophet, and so on. None of this is relevant for our purpose, since what we formally intend here is to see what the text says to the oppressed people—what the text declares to this historical addressee. What we propose, of course, is not an exhaustive treatment, but an indication of the basic lines of the text in question.

The theology of the Servant proposes that the encounter with Yahweh occurs in history and that that encounter thus becomes the locus both of Yahweh's intimate presence with the people and of the people's response and responsibility (Joachim Jeremias). The unity prevailing between what occurs in history and what God seeks to manifest and communicate to human beings is, in the text of Second Isaiah, indissoluble. We need only recall the references we find in that text to the humiliation of Babylon, or to the triumph of Cyrus, in order to have overwhelming proof of this. This is the context in which the four Suffering Servant Songs must be read.

The First Song (Isa. 42:1–7) speaks of the election of the Servant. He is a chosen one, a favorite of Yahweh: upon him God has placed his spirit. The finality of this election is explicitly proclaimed: "He shall bring forth justice to the nations." Indeed, not content with this quite explicit formulation, the sacred writer emphasizes and amplifies it:

> A bruised reed he shall not break,
>   and a smoldering wick he shall not quench,
> Until he establishes justice on the earth;
>   The coastlands will wait for his teaching. (Isa. 42: 2–4)

In question, accordingly, is an objective implantation of right—especially, of justice in the real, concrete sense of justice to be done to an oppressed people. It is a matter of creating laws in which justice, rather than the interests of the mighty, has the preeminence, although account is also kept of the need to interiorize the love of justice. That is, what is at stake is a new human being who would truly live and experience right and justice. Likewise, there is a universal gaze upon the nations and the "coastland"— that is, the scope does not remain a purely Judaic ambit. Finally, all of this will be God's response to that which peoples deprived of justice and right await, what they "hope" for—a response to be implanted by the Servant who will never waver or be shaken in his mission.

The election, the choice, is God's. Political as the Servant's mission may appear at first (there is no talk of restoring worship, converting sinners, or the like, but only of the implantation of right), this is what is wanted by that God who "created the heavens and stretched them out," by the God who consolidated the earth. After all, it is that God who has chosen the Servant in order to cause justice to be, in order to do justice:

> I, the Lord, have called you for justice,
>   I have grasped you by the hand;
> I formed you, and made you
>   as a covenant of the people, a light for the nations. (Isa. 42:6)

And the Song repeats, with explanation, what it is to do justice:

> To open the eyes of the blind,
>   to bring out prisoners from confinement,
>   and from the dungeon, those who live in darkness. (Isa. 42:7)

Thus says the Lord, for the "Lord" is his name. That is, God's very being for humanity is expressed here, and God's proclamation of the future contrasts with what has been occurring.

The Second Song underscores the nature of this election by God. God has chosen someone whom the mighty despise, who seemingly lacks the strength to have justice reign over the world, and who, nevertheless, has God's backing and support:

> Yet my reward is with the Lord,
>   my recompense is with my God ...
> Thus says the Lord,
>   the redeemer and the Holy One of Israel,
> To the one despised, whom the nations abhor,
>   the slave of rulers;
> When kings see you, they shall stand up,
>   and princess shall prostrate themselves
> Because of the Lord who is faithful,
>   the Holy One of Israel who has chosen you. (Isa. 49:4, 7)

The purpose of the election is the building of a new land and a new people: "To restore the land and allot the desolate heritages" (Isa. 49:8). The people will emerge from their state of poverty, oppression, and darkness into a new state of abundance, liberty, and light. And the reason for God's intervention through his Servant is clear:

> For the Lord comforts his people
> and shows mercy to his afflicted. (Isa. 49:13)

This notion, that God is on the side of the oppressed, and against the oppressor, is fundamental in the text and refers to an entire people and not merely to particular individuals:

> I will make your oppressors eat their own flesh,
> and they shall be drunk with their own blood
> as with the juice of the grape.
> All the world will know
> that I, the Lord, am your savior,
> your redeemer, the Mighty One of Jacob. (Isa. 49:26)

The Third Song takes a new step, setting in relief the potential importance of suffering in the people's march toward liberation. The long experience of being crushed can lead to the loss of trust, but the Lord will be a support in that suffering and put an end to it, giving victory to someone seemingly defeated:

> The Lord God is my help,
> therefore I am not disgraced;
> I have set my face like flint,
> knowing that I shall not be put to shame. (Isa. 50:7)

A great hope arises, a hope bearing on the future of the afflicted and persecuted. The suffering of these is not in vain. God stands behind them. And this is a hope that they shall touch with their hands, and that will transform their lives altogether:

> Those whom the Lord has ransomed will return
> and enter Zion singing,
> crowned with everlasting joy;
> They will meet with joy and gladness,
> sorrow and mourning will flee. (Isa. 51:11)

But it is the Fourth Song that most explicitly and extensively develops the theme of the Servant's passion and glory. Primarily, the situation of the Servant is counterposed with the Servant's real capacity for salvation:

> See, my servant shall prosper,
>   he shall be raised high and greatly exalted.
> Even as many were amazed at him—
>   so marred was his look beyond that of man,
>   and his appearance beyond that of mortals—
> So shall he startle many nations,
>   because of him kings shall stand speechless;
> For those who have not been told shall see,
>   those who have not heard shall ponder it. (Isa. 52:13–15)

It is here that the description of the persecution of the Servant in his mission of "implanting right" acquires characteristics very similar to those that the oppressed people suffer today:

> He grew up like a sapling before him,
>   like a shoot from the parched earth;
> There was in him no stately bearing to make us look at him,
>   nor appearance that would attract us to him,
>
> He was spurned and avoided by men,
>   a man of suffering, accustomed to infirmity,
> One of those from whom men hide their faces,
>   spurned, and we held him in no esteem.
>
> Yet it was our infirmities that he bore,
>   our sufferings that he endured,
> While we thought of him as stricken,
>   as one smitten by God and afflicted.
>
> But he was pierced for our offenses,
>   crushed for our sins;
> Upon him was the chastisement that makes us whole,
>   by his stripes we were healed.
> We had all gone astray like sheep,
>   each following his own way;
> But the Lord laid upon him
>   the guilt of us all.

Though he was harshly treated, he submitted
   and opened not his mouth . . .
Oppressed and condemned, he was taken away,
   and who would have thought any more of his destiny?

When he was cut off from the land of the living,
   and smitten for the sin of his people,
A grave was assigned him among the wicked
   and a burial place with evildoers,
Though he had done no wrong
   nor spoken any falsehood.

If he gives his life as an offering for sin,
   he shall see his descendants in a long life,
   and the will of the Lord shall be accomplished through him.
Because of his affliction
   he shall see the light in fullness of days.
Through his suffering my servant shall justify many
   and he shall divide the spoils with the mighty,
Because he surrendered himself to death
   and was counted among the wicked;
And he shall take away the sins of many,
   and win pardon for their offenses. (Isa. 53:2–12)

This text, which is fundamental for any theology of salvation, any so-teriology, admits of various readings because it can illuminate different problems. In the problem at hand, it is impossible to ignore the applicability of the description in the text to what is occurring today among the crucified people. A reading that has become traditional sees a prefiguration of Jesus' passion here. But this is no reason why—all "scriptural accommodation" notwithstanding—we should close our eyes to how it possesses a real description of what is today a vast majority of humanity. From this outlook, we may underscore certain historico-theological moments in this impressive song.

In the first place, the personage we contemplate is a figure shattered by the concrete, historical intervention of human beings. We have a person of sorrows here, someone accustomed to suffering, who is carried off to death in helplessness and injustice. Scorned and contemned by all, he is someone in whom there is no visible merit.

In the second place, not only is this figure not regarded as a potential savior of the world, but, quite the contrary, he is regarded as someone who might have leprosy, someone sentenced to death, someone wounded by God, someone brought low and humiliated.

In the third place, he appears as a sinner—as the fruit of sin and as filled with sins. Accordingly, he was given burial with the wicked and with evil-doers. He has been reckoned among sinners, because he bore the burden of the sin of so many.

In the fourth place, the believer's view of things is a different view. The Servant's state is not due to his own sins. He suffers sin without having committed it. He has been pierced for our rebellions and crushed for our crimes—wounded for the sins of the people. He has taken on sins that he has not committed: thus, he is in his desperate situation because of the sins of others. Before his dying for sins, it is those sins that lead to his death; they are what kill him.

In the fifth place, the Servant accepts this lot, this destiny. He accepts the fact that it is the weight of sins that is bearing him off to death, al-though he has not committed them. By reason of the sins of others, for the sins of others, he accepts his own death. The Servant will justify so many because he has taken their crimes on himself. Our punishment has fallen on him, and his scars have healed us. His death, far from being meaningless and ineffective, removes, provisionally, the sins that had been afflicting the world. His death is expiation and intercession for sins.

In the sixth place, the Servant himself, crushed in his sacrificed life and in the failure of death, triumphs. Not only will others see themselves justified, but he will see his offspring and will live long years. He will see light and be satiated with knowledge.

In the seventh place, it is the Lord himself who adopts this condition. God takes our crimes on himself. Indeed, we read that the Lord actually wished to crush the Servant with suffering, and deliver his life over in expiation for sin, although afterwards he will reward him and give him complete recompense. This is very strong language. But it admits of the interpretation that God accepts as having been wished by himself, as salu-tary, the sacrifice of someone who has concretely died for reason of the sins of human beings. Only in a difficult act of faith is the sacred writer able to discover, in the Songs of the Servant, that which seems to the eyes of history to be the complete opposite. Precisely because he sees someone burdened with sins that he has not committed and crushed by their con-sequences, the singer of these songs dares, by virtue of the very injustice of the situation, to ascribe all of this to God: God must necessarily attribute a fully salvific value to this act of absolute, historical injustice. And the attribution can be made because the Servant himself accepts his destiny to save, by his own suffering, those who are actually the causes of it.

Finally, the comprehensive orientation of this Fourth Song, together with that of the three that have preceded—their prophetic sense of a proclamation of the future, and their ambit of universality—prevent a univocal determination of the Servant's historical concretion. The Suffering Servant of Yahweh will be anyone who discharges the mission described in the Songs—and, par excellence, will be the one discharging it in more comprehensive fashion. Or better, the Suffering Servant of Yahweh will be anyone unjustly crucified for the sins of human beings, because all of the crucified form a single unity, one sole reality, even though this reality has a head and members with different functions in the unity of expiation.

For all the accentuation of the traits of suffering and seeming failure, the hope of triumph emerges paramount. And it is a hope, let us not forget, that must have a public, historical character related to the implantation of right and justice. No "substitutive" elements it may have militate against its possessing a historical reality and effectiveness.

Life and Death of Jesus, and the Servant of Yahweh

Before any Christian interpretation of the Suffering Servant had come to be, this figure had already been set in relationship with that of the Messiah. One line of theological reflection saw that the triumph of the Messiah would come only after a passage through pain and suffering, and this precisely because of the existence of sin. It is impossible to ignore the fact that Second Isaiah itself, which so strongly emphasizes Yahweh's love for the people, places harsh reproaches in the mouth of God when it comes to that people's wicked behavior. The mystery of sin and evil continues to make its way toward integration into a more complete interpretation of God's activity in history.

The New Testament does not teem with explicit references to the Servant of Yahweh. The title, *pais Theou*, appears only once in Matthew (12:15) and four times in Acts (3:13–26, 4:27–30). However, the theology of the Suffering Servant of Yahweh, along the lines of suffering and oblation for sins, is of prime importance in the New Testament when attempts are made to explain theologically the historical fact of Jesus' death. The almost complete disappearance of the term may be attributed to the fact that the Hellenistic communities very soon began to prefer the title, "Son of God," to that of "Servant of God," which they less readily assimilated. For Joachim Jeremias, the Christological interpretation of the Servant of Yahweh of Second Isaiah belongs to the earliest Christian communities and corresponds to the Palestinian, pre-Hellenistic stage. Cullmann maintains that the Christology of the Servant is probably the oldest Christology of all.

However, it is not the common opinion of exegetes that Jesus himself was aware of being the Servant of Yahweh spoken of in Second Isaiah. We need not enter into the discussion here, since our concern is to emphasize that the primitive community justifiably saw the theological context of the Suffering Servant in the historical events of the life of Jesus, so that, without being explicitly aware of it, Jesus will have carried out the Servant's mission. It might be objected that the concrete events narrated in the gospels are only the historical flesh placed by the primitive communities on the framework of their theological thought concerning the Servant, in order to historicize that thought. But even in that case—which does not seem, across the board, to represent an acceptable explanation—we would be satisfied with this acknowledgment of the need for a historicization of salvation and of the manner of salvation. If, on the other hand, Jesus himself was aware that he was the full realization of the Suffering Servant of Yahweh, obviously he did not have this consciousness from the beginning of his life, or even from the commencement of his public life, from which we must again conclude that only his real, concrete life of proclamation of the Reign and of opposition to the enemies of the Reign led him to an acceptance, in faith and hope, of the salvific destiny of the Servant: in both Jesus and the Servant, the struggle against sin came before death for sin.

On the face of it, it is difficult to hold that Jesus would have publicly and solemnly manifested the notion that his death was to have a salvific scope (Schürmann). Jesus' preaching and behavior are not oriented toward his future death, and do not depend upon it (Marxsen). A more difficult question is whether he communicated a salvific meaning for his death to his closest disciples, at least on the eve of his passion, if not indeed when they were sent on the mission of announcing the Reign. In order to answer this question, we should of course have had to be present at the Last Supper. We cannot enter in depth into this question here, but we can rely on exegetes' intermediate positions, between Jeremias' literal positivism and Bultmann's historical skepticism. Schürmann, after a lengthy exegetical analysis, concludes as follows: it is a soteriological perspective that best explains the gestures of offering by the one who is going to die and who proclaims eschatological salvation. In these gestures of the Servant performed by Jesus, eschatological salvation becomes comprehensible in the symbolic activity of one who has given the gift of oneself in death as a culmination of that person's entire life, a life that in turn has been a pro-existence—that is, it has always been a life defined by its total commitment to others. An acknowledgement of the salvific value of Jesus' death, after the Resurrection, was possible only on the basis of Jesus' pro-existent attitude, as solemnly expressed in the gestures of the Last Supper and as reconsidered in the light of the scriptures, especially in light of the Suffering Servant. It came to be seen that Jesus' death was necessary, that it was conformable to the scriptures, that it had a salvific value for those who had followed him, and that that value could be extended to the sins of the many.

Running counter to a full self-understanding of his death, on the part of Jesus himself, however, is his cry on the cross as reported by Matthew (27:26) and Mark (15:35), which seems to indicate an absolute abandonment by God and, consequently, a weakening in Jesus' faith and hope. The difficulty presented by this text is so grave that the other evangelists substitute words of trust (Luke 23:46–47) or consummation (John 19:30). Indeed, since it is possible to see, in Jesus' words of abandonment, the first words of Psalm 22, which ends with words of hope similar to those of the Song of the Servant, we cannot be certain that the tenor and sense of the words placed on Jesus' lips by Matthew and Mark is one of dereliction by God. For Xavier Léon-Dufour, Jesus intended to express his state of dereliction, his condition of abandonment, that is death, a death that in and of itself is separation from the living God. However, the experience of abandonment is simultaneously proclaimed and denied in a dialogue expressing the presence of the one who seems absent—a dialogue that abides uninterrupted, even though God seems to have disappeared. Jesus calls Yahweh not "Father" but—the only time he does so in the Synoptics— "God." All of this arouses the suspicion that the "Why have you forsaken me?" remains without immediate response, which will only appear after his death and which the evangelists posit in the voice of the centurion: "Clearly this man was the Son of God!" (Mark 15:39).

Consequently, although Jesus might not have had an explicit awareness of the complete meaning of his death, he would have had the firm hope that his life and death were the immediate announcement of the Reign. In other words, the definitive coming of the Reign was through his life and his death, and between these two there is a continuity that must be accepted, so that his death was the culmination of his life, the definitive moment of his total surrender and commitment to the proclamation and the realization of the Reign. And all of this to the point that the sacrificial and expiatory meaning of the sufferings of the Suffering Servant would be more clear than that of Jesus' death. Only later would that death come to be understood as that of a universal victim of the sins of the world.

In Order That Oppressed People Be the
Continuation of the Redemption of Jesus, the Servant

Obviously, the crucified people is not explicitly conscious of being the Suffering Servant of Yahweh, but as in the case of Jesus, that is not a reason to deny that it is. Nor would the fact that Jesus is the Suffering Servant be such a reason, since the crucified people would be his continuation in history, and thus we would not be talking of "another" servant. Hence, it would be sufficient to show that the crucified people objectively bring together some essential conditions of the Suffering Servant to propose that, even if they are not the Servant in all its fullness, the people constitute the most adequate historical place for the embodiment of the Servant.

If it is acknowledged that Jesus' passion is to be continued in history, it should also be acknowledged that in order to be historical, that continuity can take on different shapes. Leaving aside individual figures, that is, the need for Jesus to continue in each of his followers, the continuation in history by the people should also take on different shapes. In other words, we cannot say once and for all who constitutes the collective subject that most fully carries forward Jesus' redeeming work. It can be said that it will always be the crucified people of God, but as certain as that is, that statement leaves undefined who that people of God is—and it cannot be understood simply as the official church or even as the persecuted church. Not everything called church is simply the crucified people or the Suffering Servant of Yahweh, although correctly understood this crucified people may be regarded as the most vital part of the church, precisely because it continues the passion and death of Jesus.

This historicity does not mean that we cannot come to an approximation of the present-day figure of the Servant. It might vary in different historical situations, and it might represent some of the Servant's fundamental features under different aspects, but it would not thereby cease to have certain basic characteristics. The most basic is that it be accepted as the Servant by God; that acceptance, however, cannot be established except through its "likeness" to what happened to the Jesus who was crucified in history. Therefore, any present-day approximation of the Servant will have to be crucified for the sins of the world; it will have to become what the worldly have cast out, and its appearance will not be human precisely because it has been dehumanized. It will have to have a high degree of universality, since it will have to be a figure that redeems the whole world. It will have to suffer this utter dehumanization, not for its sins, but because it bears the sins of others. It will have to be cast out and despised precisely as savior of the world, in such a way that this world does not accept it as its savior but, on the contrary, judges it as the most complete expression of what must be avoided and even condemned. Finally, there must be a connection between its passion and the working out of the Reign of God.

On the other hand, this historical figure of the Servant is not to be identified with any particular organization of the crucified people whose express purpose is to achieve political power. Of course, the salvation promised to the historical mission of the Servant of Yahweh must be embodied in history, and such a historical objectification must be achieved through an organizing process that if it is to be fully liberating, must be intimately connected with the crucified people. But the aspect through which the crucified people—and not a purely undifferentiated people—brings salvation to the world, continuing the work of Jesus, is not the same as that by which it effects this salvation in historical and political terms. In other words, the crucified people transcends any embodiment in history that may take place for the sake of its salvation in history, and this transcending is due to the fact that it is the continuation in history of a Jesus who did not carry out his struggle for the Reign through political power. The fact that it transcends, however, does not mean that it can be isolated from any embodiment in history, for the Reign of God entails the achievement of a political order, wherein human beings live in covenant in response to God's covenant.

The crucified people thus remains somewhat imprecise insofar as it is not identified, at least formally, with a specific group in history—at least in all the specific features of the group in history. Nevertheless, it is precise enough so as not to be confused with what cannot represent the historical role of the Suffering Servant of Yahweh. To mention some examples with two sides, the first world is not in this line, and the third world is; the rich and oppressive classes are not, and the oppressed classes are; those who serve oppression are not, no matter what they suffer in that service, and those who struggle for justice and liberation are. The third world, the oppressed classes, and those who struggle for justice, *insofar as* they are third world, oppressed class, and people who struggle for justice, are in the line of the Suffering Servant, even though not everything they do is necessarily done in the line of the Servant. Indeed, as was noted at the beginning of this essay, these three levels must by necessity divide—although we cannot here go into studying the ways this division takes place—into some embodiments that are strictly political and others that are not formally political, though they are engaged in history.

This likening of the crucified people to the Servant of Yahweh is anything but unfounded. If we can see common basic features in both, there is moreover the fact that Jesus—or that was the view of the early Christian community—identified himself with those who suffer. That is, of course, true of those who suffer for his name or for the Reign, but it is also true of those who suffer, unaware that their suffering is connected to the name of Jesus and the proclamation of his Reign. This identification is expressed most precisely in Matthew 25:31–46, and, indeed, that passage appears just before a new announcement of his passion (Matt. 26:1–2).

The passage has a "pact structure," says Pikaza, in its two-part statement (I am your God, who is in the little ones, and you will be my people if you love the little ones). The pact takes place through justice among human beings. It is the judgment of the Reign, the universal and definitive judgment, that brings to light God's truth among human beings. This truth is in the identification of the Son of Man, become king, with the hungry, the thirsty, wayfaring strangers, the naked, the sick, and prisoners. The Son of Man is he who suffers with the little ones; and it is this Son of Man, precisely as incarnate in the crucified people, who will become judge. In its very existence the crucified people is already judge, although it does not formulate any theological judgment, and this judgment is salvation, insofar as it unveils the sin of the world by standing up to it; insofar as it makes possible redoing what has been done badly; insofar as it proposes a new demand as the unavoidable route for reaching salvation. This is, lest we forget, a universal judgment in which sentence is passed on the whole course of history. Pikaza notes that Matthew 25:36–41 entails a dialectical vision of the Jesus of history; he has been poor and yet it is he who helps the poor. Seen from the Pasch, Jesus appears as the Son of Man, who suffers in the wretched of the earth, yet is likewise also the Lord who comes to their aid.

Thus, the crucified people has a twofold thrust: it is the victim of the sin of the world, and it is also bearer of the world's salvation. But this second aspect is not what we are developing here in terms of the Pauline "died for our sins and rose for our justification." This present essay, halting at the crucifixion, presents only the first stage. A stage focused on the resurrection of the people should indicate how the one crucified for the sins of the world can by rising contribute to the world's salvation. Salvation does not come through the mere fact of crucifixion and death; only a people that lives because it has risen from the death inflicted on it can save the world.

The world of oppression is not willing to tolerate this. As happened with Jesus, it is determined to reject the cornerstone for the building of history; it is determined to build history out of power and domination, that is, out of the continual denial of the vast majority of oppressed humankind. The stone that the builders rejected became the cornerstone, stumbling block, and rock of scandal. That rock was Jesus, but it is also the people that is now his people because it suffers the same fate in history. Those who once "were not people" are now "people of God"; those who were "viewed without pity" are now "viewed with mercy." In this people are the living stones that will be built into the new house, where the new priesthood will dwell and will offer the new victims to God through the mediation of Jesus Christ (cf. 1 Pet. 2:4–10).

—Translated by Phillip Berryman and Robert R. Barr

Part III

Saving History

9

The Church of the Poor,
Historical Sacrament of Liberation
(1977)

By 1977, Ignacio Ellacuría had published over seventy essays, including more than thirty theological essays, but only three had taken the church as their major focus. That changed in 1977 with the publication of "Church of the Poor, Historical Sacrament of Liberation," the first of fifteen new essays on ecclesiological themes written between 1977 and 1984 and one of the most important chapters in Ellacuría's collection, Conversión de la iglesia al reino de Dios (1984). One might reasonably argue that the shift was inevitable insofar as liberation theology has a pronounced ecclesiological focus, but it was the actual history of El Salvador that moved Ellacuría to begin reflecting more decisively on the praxis and identity of the church and its option for the poor. In particular, this essay was inspired by the death-squad assassination of Ellacuría's fellow Jesuit, Rutilio Grande, and it concludes with a moving tribute to Grande's faith, pastoral praxis, and martyrdom as seen through the eyes of the people he served.

Ellacuría introduces this essay with a paragraph-long "definition" of liberation theology that begins with this striking thesis: "The theology of liberation understands itself as a reflection from faith on the historical reality and action of the people of God, who follow the work of Jesus in announcing and realizing the Reign of God." He then picks up an important thread in post-Vatican II ecclesiology, examining the church as a historical sacrament of salvation. Expanding of this theme and in response to the mistaken understanding of liberation theology's method reflected in the 1977 Declaration on Human Promotion and Christian Salvation published by the Vatican International Theological Commission, Ellacuría then argues that the historical form of salvation is liberation. In the final section of the essay he examines how only a "church of the poor" can be and why it must be "the historical sacrament of liberation."

The theology of liberation[1] understands itself as a reflection from faith on the historical reality and action of the people of God who follow the work of Jesus in announcing and realizing the Reign of God. It understands itself as an action by the people of God in following the work of Jesus and, as Jesus did, it tries to establish a living connection between the world of God and the human world. Its reflective character does not keep it from being an action, and an action by the people of God, even though at times it is forced to make use of theoretical tools that seem to remove it both from immediate action and from the theoretical discourse that is popular elsewhere. It is, thus, a theology that begins with historical acts and seeks to lead to historical acts, and therefore it is not satisfied with being a purely interpretive reflection. It is nourished by faithful belief in the presence of God within history, an operative presence that, although it must be grasped in grateful faith, remains a historical action. There is no room here for faith without works; rather, faith means being drawn into the very force of God that operates in history, so that we are converted into new historical forms of that operative and salvific presence of God in humanity.

From this perspective the church presents itself, first, as that people of God who carry forward in history what Jesus definitively sealed as the presence of God in humanity. In this essay, we shall examine what the church must be today, historically, in the situation of the third world and, especially, of Latin America. To what degree that presence in the Latin American situation also represents historical universality will become clearer in the following analysis.

The result of this examination can be formulated as follows: The church is a sacrament of liberation and must act as a sacrament of liberation. This formulation, which derives from the feelings (*sentir*) and lives of the believing majority and is an essential element of the faith of a people on pilgrimage in history, is the fundamental premise of these lines. Its purpose is simply to reflect on the living action of the people of God, a reflection that begins from that action and seeks to return to it to strengthen it.

The Church, Historical Sacrament of Salvation

There is nothing new about understanding the church as a sacrament, even less as a sacrament of salvation. Jesus is the primary and fundamental sacrament of salvation, and the church, in continuing and realizing Jesus' ministry, participates, though derivatively, in that same character. The relative newness appears when we speak of the church as *historical* sacrament of salvation. What is the contribution of this historicity to its sacramentality and to salvation, to the salvific sacramentality of the church? To pose the problem in these terms may sound excessively sacral: both the idea of sacrament and the idea of salvation have been reduced and seem to refer to a sacral sphere that has little to do with palpable, everyday reality. Nevertheless, we cannot discard the meaning that lies behind the terms "sacrament" and "salvation." It is necessary, however, to purge them of self-interested sacralization in order to recover their full meaning. That is best done by "historicizing" them, which does not mean reciting their history but establishing their relationship to history.

A historical understanding of salvation cannot theorize abstractly on the essence of salvation. Not only is that abstract theorizing more historical than it appears, and as abstraction can deny the real meaning of salvation, but it is also impossible to speak of salvation except in terms of concrete situations. Salvation is always the salvation *of someone*—and in that person, *of something*. This is so much so that the characteristics of the savior must be understood in terms of the characteristics of that which needs saving. This would seem to diminish the meaning of salvation as the gift of God who anticipates the needs of humanity, but it does not. It does not because the needs, understood in their broadest sense, are the historical path by which we move toward the recognition of that gift that will appear as a "negation" of the needs. From the perspective of that gift, the needs appear as a "negation" of the gift of God, of God's very self-giving to humanity. But beyond that, the needs can be seen as the outcry of God made flesh in human suffering, as the unmistakable voice of God, who moans in pain in God's own creatures or, more exactly, in God's children.

One might say that biblically, salvation is salvation from sin. But this does not deny what we have just said; rather, it confirms it, at least if we appropriately historicize the concept of sin, which is supported by a vigorous and lasting biblical tradition. The concept of sin, in fact, emphasizes the nature of evil that is revealed in human needs and their relationship to whom God is. Thus, it is a historical theologizing of need understood in all its breadth, as we have done here. It is perhaps this perception of evil as sin that has made the history of God among humanity a history of salvation; but for that very reason, salvation, as the presence of God among humanity, is not yet fully effective except in the struggle to overcome the power of evil and sin.

Let us set aside, for the moment, what salvation should be. It is clear, and has been said many times, that salvation in spiritualistic, personalistic, or merely transhistorical terms is not only not self-evident but also implies a false and self-interested ideologization of salvation. Moreover, an exclusive concern for otherworldly and extrahistorical salvation would deserve the reproach of John: those who say they are concerned for the salvation that is not seen, but do not value the salvation that is seen, are liars, for if we do not care about what stands before us, how shall we care about what we do not see? Let us therefore consider what the church must be with respect to salvation, before going on in turn to the historical essence of salvation and what the church's action should be with respect to that salvation. This is the theme of historical sacramentality.

The sacramentality of the church is based on a prior reality: the corporeality of the church. It was ingenious of the early church, especially of Paul, to conceive of the church in bodily terms. We shall not go into the rich biblical and dogmatic bibliography on this concept of the church as a body and as the body of Christ. We shall only point out what this truth of the corporeality of the church, and its bodily nature with respect to Christ, means for the historicization of salvation. Briefly, the historical corporeality of the church implies that the reality and the action of Jesus Christ "being embodied" in the church, so that the church will realize an "incorporation" of Jesus Christ in the reality of history. A few words on each of these two aspects.[2]

"Being embodied" entails a series of interrelated aspects. First, it means that something becomes corporeally present and thus present in reality for a person to whom only a corporeal presence is real. It also means that something becomes more real simply by being embodied; it becomes real by becoming something else without ceasing to be what it was. It also means that something is actualized in the same way that we say the body actualizes a person. It means, finally, that something that could not act before is now able to act. Seen theologically, "being embodied" corresponds to the word, which "took flesh" so that it could be seen and touched, so that it could intervene in a fully historical way in the action of humanity. As St. Irenaeus said, if Christ is Savior by his divine condition, he is salvation by his flesh, by his historical incarnation, by "being embodied" among human beings.

"Incorporation" functions as the activation of "being embodied;" it is becoming a body with that global and unified body that is the material history of humanity. Incorporation is an indispensable condition for effectiveness in history and thus for the full realization of that which is incorporated. Incorporation thus presupposes being embodied, but it also means adhering to the single body of history. It is only possible to speak of incorporation when that which is not historical is historically embodied; but, on the other hand, only an effective incorporation can demonstrate the degree to which something is embodied.

It is clear that Jesus was embodied in history, which means that he took mortal flesh, but that goes beyond the fact of having taken flesh; it is also clear that he was incorporated in human history. Once his historical visibility disappears, it is the task of the church, that is, of everything that represents his historical continuation, to continue being embodied and incorporated. One can say that the true historical body of Christ, and therefore the preeminent locus of his embodiment and his incorporation, is not only the church but the poor and the oppressed of the world, so that the church alone is not the historical body of Christ, and it is possible to speak of a true body of Christ outside the church. This is true, as we shall see, and it leads us to consider that the church is, par excellence, the church of the poor and that, as church of the poor, it is the historical body of Christ. Its very embodiment and incorporation demand and entail an obligatory individualizing concreteness; to be embodied and incorporated is to be engaged concretely in the complexity of the social structure.

We shall analyze this subtheme later on, but let us return now to the church as historical body of Christ:

> The foundation of the church should not be understood in a legal and juridical sense, as if Christ had delivered to a few men a doctrine and a foundational Magna Charta, and kept himself separate from that organization. That is not so. The origin of the Church is something much deeper. Christ establishes his church in order to maintain his own presence in human history, precisely through that group of Christians who form his church. The church is, thus, the flesh in which Christ, through the centuries, makes his own life and his personal mission concrete.[3]

Jesus was the historical body of God, the full actualization of God among humanity, and the church must be the historical body of Christ, just as Jesus was of God the Father. The continuation of the life and mission of Jesus in history, which is the task of the church, animated and unified by the Spirit of Christ, makes the church his body, his visible and operative presence.

This expression, "historical body" should not be seen as over against the more classical "mystical body." The church is the mystical body of Christ insofar as it tries to make present something that is not immediately and totally palpable; even more, and this is something impossible to grasp and express, it is the historical body of Christ insofar as that presence must continue throughout history and must be made effective within it. Just like the historical Jesus, the church is more than meets the eye, but that "more" is and must be present in what is seen; here we have the unity of its mystical and its historical nature. The church's mysticism does not derive from something mysterious and occult, but rather from something that surpasses history within history, from something that surpasses humanity within humanity, from something that forces us to say, "Truly, the finger of God is hidden here." The supernatural should not be conceived as something intangible, but rather as something that surpasses nature in the same way that the historical life of Jesus surpassed what one might "naturally" expect of a man. If the life of Jesus—and what could be seen in that life by being embodied in it—is not supernatural, then the supernatural has no Christian meaning.

One example will clarify the transcendence of this distinction. There is an apparent divergence between the historical salvation proposed in the Old Testament and the mystical salvation proposed in the New. "They were liberated or led out of Egypt" seems a very different point of departure from "they were baptized in Christ." Those who began with a historical experience and a historical-political concreteness, like that of a people who find themselves liberated from the oppression of another people and who receive the promise of a new land in which to live freely, would seem to be a world away from those who begin with a sacramental experience, like that of baptism, with regard to the "mystical" event of the death, burial, and resurrection of the Lord. In the first case, the praxis of faith seems to lead in a direction that could not possibly coincide with the praxis of those who receive the salvific gift of God mysteriously and freely by faith. One of these directions would lead to the mystical body, and the other would lead to the historical body. Since the New Testament would lead to the mystical body, we would take it that mystical salvation is the Christian way.

There is a very real danger in this interpretation, and the early church, or some communities of the early church, took it as real. That is why they felt obliged to round out the more mystical interpretation of Paul by referring to the historical Jesus as transmitted through the synoptic gospels and John. This shows that the salvific or soteriological nature of the death of Jesus is inseparable from his historical nature; the "why did Jesus die" is inseparable from the "why did they kill him."[4] Moreover, the "why did they kill him" has a certain priority over the "why did he die." But, from the perspective of the historical Jesus, we understand that dying with Jesus and being resurrected with him in baptism, according to Paul, are not primarily mystical but primarily historical; they are the most faithful reenactment and continuation of the life of Jesus, and they bring consequences like those that Jesus suffered, as long as the world remains like the world in which Jesus lived. Its "mysticism" derives merely from the fact that the grace of Jesus and his personal call make it possible, for those who live as Christians, to follow the road of death that leads to life, instead of following the road of life that leads to death. Thus, it is not right to set "they were baptized" over against "they were led out of Egypt," because the former is not a purely mystical event or the latter a purely political one.

Now then, it is from this historical corporeality, which does not exclude but demands mystical corporeality, that we should understand the historical sacramentality of the church. From the outset we must repeat that the primary sacramentality of the church does not derive from the effectiveness of what we call sacraments but that, on the contrary, the sacraments are effective insofar as they participate in the sacramentality of the church. Of course that sacramentality derives from the radical and fundamental sacrament that is Christ, and this is true, as we have just noted, not only because Christ is the head of the church—the head-body relationship is not the one we assume in speaking of the corporeality of Christ and the subsequent corporeality of the church—or only because the Spirit of Christ gives life to the body of the church, but also because the church carries forward the life of Jesus, in and by the same Spirit. Sacramentality has been presented with the double mark of mediational visibility and effectiveness. Therefore, when we refer to the sacramentality of the church, we are expecting the church to give visibility and effectiveness to the salvation it announces.[5]

This fundamental sacramentality of the church, because it is historical, requires the church to be present through particular actions, which must be a visible presence and effective realization of what the church is historically and mystically. Certainly the seven sacraments are among those actions and must be historicized, not reduced to cultural mimicry. Those actions, which touch human life at such fundamental points as birth and incorporation into a new community, the struggle with sin, love, death, and so on, show how deeply Christian salvation seeks to be incorporated in history. But these actions, despite their fundamental and often irreplaceable nature, are not the only loci of the sacramentality of the church.

Classical theology, which saw the sacraments as privileged "channels" of grace, acknowledged that they were not the only channels. It acknowledged that the grace of Christ is also made present, visible, and effective through other channels. In other words, the sacramentality of the church can and must be made historically present in other ways. And those other ways, although they may not have all the exclusive marks of the seven sacraments, are no less and may be even more fundamental with respect to the sacramentality of the church. They cannot be considered profane actions of the church, if they are actions that put its salvific mission in practice. We cannot go more deeply into this theme because what concerns us here is the fundamental sacramentality of the church and not the particularity of its sacramental actions.

The church makes real its historic, salvific sacramentality by announcing and fulfilling the Reign of God in history. Its fundamental praxis consists in the fulfillment of the Reign of God in history, in action that leads to the fulfillment of the Reign of God in history.

We do not need to insist, although it must be kept very much in mind, that the church is not an end in itself but that the whole church, in following the historical Jesus, is at the service of the Reign of God. The church must understand itself from two points outside itself, Jesus Christ, and the world, as they become one in the Reign of God; all its action must have that same, non–self-centered orientation. The church faces few temptations more serious than that of considering itself an end in itself and of evaluating each of its actions in terms of whether they are convenient or inconvenient for its survival or its grandeur. It has often fallen into this temptation, as nonbelievers have often pointed out. A self-centered church—and one need only skim through ecclesiastical documents to observe just how self-centered it is—is not a sacrament of salvation; it is, rather, just another power in history, which follows the dynamics of other historical powers. It doesn't even help to say that the center of the church is the Risen Jesus, if that Risen Jesus is deprived of all historicity. It is true that the guiding center of the life of Jesus was in the experience of God, but a God who was historically embodied in the Reign of God. If the church does not incarnate its central concern for the Risen Jesus in the fulfillment of the Reign of God in history, it loses its touchstone and, thereby, its assurance that it is effectively serving the Lord and not itself. Only by emptying itself, in self-giving to the neediest people, unto death and death on the cross, can the church claim to be a historical sacrament of the salvation of Christ.

It is beyond debate that Jesus centered his action and his proclamation, not on himself or even on God, but on the Reign of God. The essence of the complexity of the Reign of God, with all its wealth of nuances, is not beyond debate, but in general it is clear that the Reign of God implies a specific historical world, that is, that the Reign of God cannot be reconciled with just any type of human relationships. The Reign of God, as the presence of God among humanity, goes against everything that, instead of making the God of Jesus Christ present, conceals and even negates that God who is not only the God of religions or the God of the powerful in this world. The Reign of God, rather, upholds everything that makes all people children of the one Father who is in heaven. Few theological expressions are as corporeal and historical as this one of the Reign of God, which refers to God, on the one hand, but also and inseparably alludes to God's salvific presence among humanity. It is the church's task to go on historicizing the demands of this Reign of God in each situation and each moment, because the church itself must take shape as a historical sacrament of salvation, a salvation that consists of implanting the Reign of God in history.

Generally speaking, the realization of the Reign of God in history implies "taking away the sin" of the world and making the incarnate life of God present in human beings and human relationships. It is not just a matter of taking away sin where it is (in the world), but of taking away the sin-of-the-world. What that worldly sin is, the sin that condemns the world, must be determined in each case. The other sins must be interpreted in terms of that sin-of-the-world—without forgetting that all sin leads to the destruction of the sinner and is objectified in one way or another in structures that destroy humanity. It is clear that the annunciation of the Reign entails a very special attention to the nature of humanity in its own human freedom and intimacy, both to defend and to promote it. It is clear, too, that the sin-of-the-world moves in the individual consciousness and will, but that should not cause us to forget the presence of worldly and historical sin. Against this sin-of-the-world, incorporated in individuals and social groups, the annunciation of the Reign proposes a very clear counterexample: that represented by the life of the historical Jesus.

Because this sin-of-the-world has a singular importance in the configuring of history and, thereby, in the shaping of personal lives, the presence of God among humanity takes shape in what we call salvation. Clearly then, that salvation, which generically means salvation from sin, takes a different historical shape according to the specific sin in question and according to the historical situation in which it occurs. That is why there is a history of salvation, because salvation takes different forms in different historical moments, and that is why this history of salvation must be embodied and incorporated in history by assuming the nature of a salvation that is also historical. Now we can better understand why anyone is a liar who claims to be concerned for transhistorical salvation without first being concerned for historical salvation. The latter is the way to the former;

historical salvation is the truth and the life of transhistorical salvation. It is another way of saying that the love of God moves through human love and cannot exist without it.

Liberation as the Historical Form of Salvation

In 1977, the International Theological Commission published a *Declaration on Human Promotion and Christian Salvation*.[6] This amounted to a confrontation with the theology of liberation and grew out of the annual session that was dedicated to the subject in October 1976. The document, although it had some merit and gave a certain academic and professional respect to the theology of liberation, shows a lack of understanding of the epistemological and methodological groundwork of that theology and seems by all means to ignore the best efforts of what might be called the second wave of liberation theology. Its value therefore does not lie in that almost shadow-boxing confrontation but in having given theological legitimacy to what has been the fundamental theme of Latin American theological efforts, although that theme is formulated in the aseptic and historically disengaged terms of human promotion.

Not only does the title of the declaration speak of human promotion "and" Christian salvation but the document affirms,

> This unity of connection, as well as the difference that marks the relationship between human promotion and Christian salvation, in its concrete form, must certainly become the object of new investigation and analysis; that is without a doubt one of the principal tasks of theology today.[7]

So now the radical concern of Latin American theology, which was formerly viewed by the theologians of reaction as a digression and a sociologizing deformation, is recognized as one of the principal tasks of theology today, a task scandalously neglected until now by the dominant theologies. How could they have failed to advance theological principles to resolve a subject that is not only central to any historical situation but essential to the history of salvation and to the Christian message? How could such an essential theme in the history of revelation as that of liberation have had so very little importance in biblical analyses and theological reflections until it was moved forward by the theologians of liberation? Even if they had succeeded only in obliging the "international" theologians to pay attention to this fundamental theme, by providing them with the basic elements of its formulation, that would have been a Christian and theological task of the first magnitude.

But clearly they have done much more than that. We cannot go into a systematization of what they have accomplished here, or even summarize my own modest contribution to a solution for this problem, which has been the fundamental focus and perspective of all my theological work.[8] What we will do here is to pick up some central points, not to discuss the problem in all its breadth, but to hint at ways in which liberation is the historical shape of salvation and not a generic "human promotion" that, in its abstract generality, has little to do with the historicity of salvation but a lot to do with a positive historical disengagement.

To recognize that salvation is related to human promotion does not represent a great advance from the customary praxis of the church or from its own ecclesial self-understanding. Although it may often have misunderstood the meaning of authentic human promotion, we cannot deny that the church has always recognized the need to carry it out in one way or another; nor can we deny that many of its best efforts have been focused on human promotion. A real advance would mean, first, defining what kind of human promotion the church should undertake and only then what concrete kind of human promotion is related to Christian salvation and what the relationship between them is. That is a problem that cannot be posed at the margin of history as if it were a concrete expression of other general themes such as the relation between the natural and the supernatural, between reason and faith, and so forth. Rather, it must be posed historically, that is, looking at what humanity needs to be saved from and looking at how that salvation is inseparable, although it can be differentiated, from Christian salvation. Those people are right, therefore, who pose the problem in terms of faith and justice or, more generally, in terms of salvation and liberation, although sometimes when it is posed in a subtly dualistic way, it leads to contradictions in speaking of justice or liberation as a component, an integral part, an inescapable demand, and so on. They are right because they are using concrete historical terms, but they encounter serious problems insofar as they do not adequately conceptualize unity and do not open the way for a unitary praxis.

This problem cannot be resolved without reference to the life of the historical Jesus, as it is apprehended in the tradition and in the experience of the early communities. Those who accuse Latin American theological and pastoral efforts of excessive historicity—which has nothing to do with historicism—must take into account (as the International Theological Commission does not adequately recognize) the radical importance the second wave of the theology of liberation attributes to the historical Jesus as cornerstone of the understanding of history and of action on it. This turn toward the historical Jesus—where, again, "historicity" should not be understood in an academic sense but in the sense of his embodiment in history—might not have occurred if there had not been a believing praxis in the specific situation of Latin America; just as the rediscovery of biblical liberation might not have occurred if that same believing praxis had not demanded it, which only confirms the theological virtualities of the Latin American theological method. But this does not prevent us from giving primacy to that which is most fundamental in the historical Jesus or from taking this historical Jesus, and the obligation to follow him, as the criterion and norm of historical ecclesial praxis. The inspiration and the achievements of the theology of liberation do not derive directly from other mediations, although these mediations may have drawn attention to the reality from which, in faith, people have sought and found an irreducible newness in the Christian message.[9]

Fundamental aspects of the life of Jesus, like the subordination of the Sabbath to humanity, the unity of the second commandment with the first, the unity of "why did he die" with "why did they kill him," show how we should look for the unity between what Christian salvation is and what historical salvation is.

From this viewpoint we must affirm, once again, that there are not two levels of problems (the profane level, on one hand, the sacred level, on the other); neither are there two histories (a profane history and a sacred history), but rather only one level and one history. This does not mean that in that one history and that one level there are not subsystems that have an autonomy of their own, without breaking the unity but drawing their full reality from that unity. The unity of all the intramundane is structural, and that structural unity, far from imposing uniformity on each of its structural moments, is nourished, we might say, by its plural diversity. There is not a single moment. Nor is there a mere plurality of equal moments; rather there is a single unity, which shapes the particularity of the moments and which in turn is shaped by that same particularity. When unity is seen structurally, when we see the structural unity of history, we need not fear that one autonomous moment will nullify another autonomous moment, although the autonomy of each is subordinate to the unity of the structure. Only a structural model is capable of giving shape to an action that, although it is single, is also diverse; only a structural model can safeguard the relative autonomy of the parts without breaking the structural unity of the whole.

But if there is not a sacred history and a profane history, if what the historical Jesus, gathering together all the richness of revelation in the Hebrew scriptures, came to show us is that there are not two worlds incommunicado (a world of God and a human world); what there is instead—and what the same historical Jesus shows us—is the fundamental distinction between grace and sin, between the history of salvation and the history of perdition. Yes, both in the same history. This is shown by the contrast between two apparently contradictory readings in the Christian scriptures ("he who is not with me is against me" and "he who is not against me is with me"). The fundamental division of the single history resides in being with Jesus or not being with him, in being for him or against him. There are historical contexts in which one of these formulations seems more appropriate: everyone who is not against Jesus is for him. There are other contexts in which the spectrum of choice, so to speak, is narrower, and in that case whoever is not positively with Jesus is against him. One of those contexts is found, without doubt, in the relationship between oppressors and oppressed: only those who are positively with the oppressed are with Jesus, because those who are not with the oppressed are, by commission or by omission, with the oppressors, at least wherever the positive interests of the two groups are in conflict, either directly and immediately, or indirectly and apparently remotely. This "not being with" Jesus or "being against" him, in the very different forms in which it can occur, is what divides history and divides personal lives in two, without leaving neutral space. There may seem to be neutral space insofar as it possesses a specific technical autonomy, but there is not insofar as everything human is linked together, forming a single historical unity with one meaning. From this viewpoint, we have even gone beyond the classic discussion of morally indifferent acts; the acts are not indifferent, although they may seem so, because each one in its concrete reality prepares, slows, or impedes the coming of the Reign.

The apparent impossibility of transforming history, or even the subtle interest in improving history so it would not be transformed, is what has led to the spiritualization, individualization, and transtemporalization of historical salvation. By definition, history is so complex, so long and structural, so earthly, that it seems as if Christian faith, the continuation of the life of a man like the historical Jesus, can do little about it. If he ended up as a failure on the cross, as far as his historical life is concerned, it seems the best thing is to renounce historical salvation and to take refuge in a faith of the resurrection, in a spiritual and individual salvation by grace and sacrament that leads to a final resurrection, for only at the end will there be a salvation or a condemnation of history. But this attitude ignores the real meaning of the resurrection and misunderstands the mission of the church with respect to history.

The resurrection, in effect, is not the transplanting of the historical Jesus to a world that it beyond history. For good reason, the resurrection is expressed in the New Testament less as the reassumption of Jesus' mortal body than that of his transformed historical life. The Risen Jesus extends his transformed life beyond death and beyond the powers of this world to become the Lord of history, precisely because of his incarnation and his death within history. He will never again abandon his flesh and, therefore, he will never abandon his historical body, but rather he continues to live in it so that, when the rest of his passion is fulfilled, the rest of his resurrection will also be fulfilled. Historical death and resurrection will continue until the Lord returns. The Spirit of Christ continues to live and animate his historical body, just as it animated his mortal and risen body.

Only when the church is confused about what it can and should do as church will it be vulnerable to discouragement or, at the other extreme, to the ambition for earthly power. Like the mission of Jesus, the mission of the church is not the immediate fulfillment of a political order but the fulfillment of the Reign of God, and, as a part of that fulfillment, the salvation of any existing political order. By political order we mean here the global institutionalization of social relations, the institutional objectification of human actions, which comprises the public venue of their personal and interpersonal actions. The church does not have sufficient corporeality or materiality to bring about the immediate fulfillment of this political order, which extends to everything from collective knowledge to social organization, from the structures of power to social forces; other entities exist for that purpose.

But the church does have the function of leavening, that is, the ferment that transforms the dough to make of it the bread of life, human bread that gives life to humanity. The church presupposes the dough of the world and its organization as necessary, while the church's appropriate role is to become salt, which inhibits corruption, and leavening, which transforms the dough from within. It is equipped for that task just as Jesus was; and it is not equipped, as Jesus was not, to become a power in this world, which takes pleasure in having the power to subdue its subjects. So the church cannot close in upon itself as if its principal objective were the conservation of its institutional structure and its comfortable place in society; rather, it must open itself to the world, put itself at the world's service in the march of history. The church knows that what is involved in the problem of humanity is not the problem of God as God but the problem of God in history; it also knows that what is involved in the problem of God in history is the problem of humanity. If each individual as a member of the church must realize his or her salvation in relationship with others, the church as a body must realize its own salvation but in relationship with historical structures.

Thus, what the church contributes to the salvation of history is the fundamental sign of salvation history. The church belongs intrinsically to this salvation history and carries within it the visible part that reveals and makes effective the whole of salvation in us. It makes no sense directly or by insinuation to accuse the theology of liberation of proposing only a sociopolitical salvation; even Marxism does not make such a reduction of salvation. What the theology of liberation affirms is that salvation history is meaningless if it does not include the sociopolitical dimension, which is an essential part but not the whole of it. If we include in that dimension everything that has to do with justice and with doing justice, everything that is sin and a cause of sin, there is no way to avoid saying that it pertains fundamentally to salvation history. Obviously, that does not exhaust the full extent of God's action with humanity, which the church must announce and realize, but without it, that action is gravely mutilated.

Now then, this historical salvation must be as responsive as possible to the situation that is to be saved, and in which human beings are immersed, since salvation is fundamentally addressed to them. In the situation of the peoples of the third world, the realization of salvation history is presented primarily in terms of liberation, because their situation is defined in terms of domination and oppression. That oppression can be analyzed by means of different theoretical instruments, but as a fact, and a definitive fact, it is independent of all such instruments. Neither is it a valid objection against the theology of liberation to say that Marxism, for example, also defines that situation in terms of oppression and exploitation and that, therefore, the theologians of liberation are only repeating what others have said rather than speaking from Christian inspiration. This is not valid for two reasons: in the first place, the fact under analysis must be distinguished from how that fact is understood; and second, that fact and the response to it gain a specificity proper to the Christian faith. Thus, the same historical facts the oppressed perceive as unjust oppression, and which Marxism interprets as the exploitation of human labor and as the consequences of that exploitation, are interpreted by faith and theology as the reality of sin and as an injustice that cries out to heaven.

We must bear in mind that what occurs in history, as Zubiri has pointed out, is not the intentionality of human acts, what is called the *opus operans*, but the objective result of those acts, the *opus operatum*. History does not judge or condemn intentions; it does not accuse people of personal sins. What is judged and condemned by history is what matters in history, because it is the only thing that is objectified in history. Whatever in history that is a source of salvation or of oppression is, therefore, that which has been objectified in history, and it is in the realm of those objectifications that liberating action must take place. As we shall immediately see, this liberation in history is not the full extent of the liberating process, but it is an essential part of it because, without liberation, the reign of sin prevails in the place of grace. Only by measuring and experiencing what this situation of permanent and structural oppression means to human beings can we see how central the Christian struggle against oppression is to the essence of salvation history. It matters little at first that that structural oppression is maintained with the trademark and mechanisms of "national security" and such; what matters, for Christian reflection and ecclesial praxis, is the fact of structural oppression itself. When one lives as the majority of the people do (those for whom Jesus, for profound theological and human reasons, felt an undeniable preference), subjected to inhuman situations, it is not hard for the believer to see that what is happening is a new death of God in humanity, a renewed crucifixion of Jesus Christ, who is present in the oppressed. Consequently, the insistence of the theology of liberation on undertaking its reflection from this fundamental *locus theologicus* should not be seen in pietistic terms but in purely Christian and strictly theological terms. If theology as an intellectual act entails a particular set of technical requirements, as a Christian intellectual act, it also entails certain Christian demands that cannot be reduced to accepting certain items of faith. This is what some groups of academic theologians seem not to understand.

It is through incarnation in that situation of oppression (it is very hard to live in a situation of oppression in the first world) that one understands the realities of the duality between oppression and liberation, as they are focused by faith and by theological reflection. Oppression that is not merely natural, that is, that does not follow from the physical laws of nature, thus a strictly historical oppression, is always a sin, that is, something positively unacceptable to God. In other situations, finding "meaning" in the Christian message can be a difficult task. In situations of oppression, the whole of the Christian message offers such an immediate "meaning" that there is nothing to do but pick it up and redirect it. In these situations of oppression, one may perceive how the love of God and human love are at work, and also the negation of the very existence of children of God, brothers and sisters in Jesus Christ. The experience of the proclaimers of liberation, when they read the good news to humble and believing peoples, proves the tremendous force of the liberating word of God. They feel the radical truth of the words of Isaiah and Jesus of Nazareth. The proclaimers and the receivers of the proclamation, in a single shared word, feel the depth of meaning of the whole Christian message for the poor, the persecuted, the oppressed, and those in need. It is not only that the Christian message is preferentially addressed to the poor; it is that only the poor are capable of drawing from that message its full meaning. This is the affirmation of the theology of liberation, and this is what shapes its method of doing theology.

As the word of God is read from this situation of structural sin and structural violence, Christian love presents itself forcefully in terms of the struggle for justice, which liberates and saves crucified and oppressed humanity. The justice asserted by the Christian faith should not be set apart from Christian love in a situation defined by an injustice that makes human life impossible. The struggle for justice, without making justice itself unjust by the methods used, is very simply the historical form of active love. Although not all love can be reduced to doing good to the neighbor, this doing good, if it is generous, if it does not possess boundaries, if it is humble and kind, is a historical form of love. Not all struggles for justice are the incarnation of Christian love, but there is no Christian love without a struggle for justice when the historical situation is defined in terms of injustice and oppression. Therefore, the church, as a sacrament of liberation, has the double task of awakening and fostering the struggle for justice among those who are not committed to it, and of making those who are committed to it carry out the struggle in Christian love. Here, too, the example of the historical Jesus is decisive. In his society, divided and antagonistic, Jesus loved everyone, but he placed himself on the side of the oppressed, and from there he struggled energetically but lovingly against oppressors.

Finally, if we consider the character of universality that the historical cry for liberation from oppression of peoples, social classes, and individuals in our time, it is not hard to see that the church, as a universal sacrament of salvation, must become a sacrament of liberation. This cry of oppressed peoples, when we look at their real characteristics from the viewpoint of revelation, is one of divinity crucified in humanity, the servant of Yahweh, the prophet par excellence; it is the great sign of the times. The historical shape of the church, as a salvific and liberating response to this universal cry, presupposes, first, its permanent conversion to the truth and the life of the historical Jesus and, second, its historical participation in the salvation of a world that can only be saved by following the way of Jesus. The cry of the immense majority of humanity, oppressed by an arrogant minority, is the cry of Jesus himself historically embodied in the flesh, in the need, and in the pain of oppressed humanity.

Certainly there are other forms of oppression besides the sociopolitical and economic, and not all forms of oppression derive exclusively and immediately from that one. Christians would be wrong, therefore, to seek only one type of social liberation. Liberation must extend to everyone who is oppressed by sin and by the roots of sin. It should strive so that both the objectification of sin and the internal principle of sin itself are liberated; it must extend both to unjust structures and the people who do injustice. It must extend both to the inner life of people and to the things they realize in their acts. The goal of liberation is full freedom, in which full and right relationships are possible, among people and between them and God. The way to liberation can only be the way that Jesus followed, the way that the church must carry forward in history, the way in which it must believe and hope as an essential element of human salvation.

The Church of the Poor, Historical Sacrament of Liberation

We have just said that the church must be a sacrament of liberation in the same way Jesus was; adjustments are possible and necessary in the way it carries out its task of salvation but only when they are a continuation of the ways Jesus used. The institutional nature of the church, necessarily derived from its social corporeality, entails clear requirements that only an anarchist idealism can fail to see. But that institutionality does not have to be shaped, as has often happened, in accordance with the institutionality required by the powerful of this world to maintain their power. That institutionality must be subordinated to the deeper nature of the church as a continuation of the work of Jesus. The church must continue to believe in the specificity of the way of Jesus and must not fall into the trap of generic and rational salvations.

Jesus had a unique way of struggling for the salvation and liberation of humanity. It is unique not only for the content of that salvation and liberation, a point we cannot go into here—that is the question of the Christian praxis Jesus asks for—but it is unique because of the way it addresses the salvation and liberation of humanity. Jesus does not view them in a generic and abstract way that leads to human promotion, the defense of human rights, and so forth, but in a unique way. Facing the situation of a divided society, Jesus' way seeks human promotion or human rights from the side of the oppressed, on their behalf, and in struggle against the side of the oppressors. In other words, his action is historical and concrete and goes to the roots of oppression. The church must follow the same pattern and situate itself on the same alternative side, and this is what should correct both its false institutionality and an institutionality placed on the side of the oppressive structures. In our time, base communities are advanced as a way of countering the exaggerated institutionalization of the church. In a brief talk to a German group of base communities, Rahner has said, "Base communities are necessary for the church today. The churches of the future will be built up from below through base communities of free initiative and membership."[10]

It is supposed then, that the force of the Spirit will be more nimble and alive in these communities, so that their initiatives will flow up freely from the base to the head, thus avoiding the excess weight of the ecclesial structures, which can suffocate both personal initiative and Christian inspiration. This leads to opposition between base communities (small groups meeting freely to live their faith and undertake action accordingly) and the institutional structures, which are needed but which are not the proper initiators of all ecclesial activity.

The theology of liberation would pose the problem in different terms. The base communities can serve as a basis of the church of the future because they are *of the base*. This language may sound Marxist, because of the word "base," but the term is used by communities that not only have nothing to do with Marxism but interpret the word "base" exclusively in the sense that they are the basic elements or original cells of the ecclesial organism. From the viewpoint of the theology of liberation, the evangelical "base" of the Reign of God is made up of the poor, and only the poor in community can succeed in keeping the church from indulging both excessive institutionalization and worldliness. The ultimate reason why the institutional church can oppress its own children is not so much its institutional nature, but its lack of dedication to the people of greatest need, in following who Jesus was and what he did. Consequently, it can only resist worldliness by placing itself at the service of the poorest and those of greatest need; and having resisted worldliness, it will no longer fall into all the defects that come naturally to an organization and power closed in on itself.

The base of the church is the church of the poor, and the diverse forms in which it has appeared are derived from and subject to historical conditions. What does it mean to say that the base of the church is the church of the poor?

It is not easy to conceptualize the poor, especially after the softening and spiritualizing of some parts of the Christian scriptures and, even more, after so much exegetical effort to reconcile the Reign of God with the kingdom of this world.[11] But no matter how much we reinterpret scripture to focus on the poor in spirit, on detachment from the things of this world, and so on, we cannot forget that those "spiritual ones" must be poor in substance, which is not impossible for God but extremely improbable and difficult from the viewpoint of evangelical preaching. The need to be poor, to be one with the poor, is an inescapable mandate for anyone who wants to follow Jesus.

But even with these corrections, the fact remains that their purpose is not to exclude any person—all are called to salvation, based on proper and real conversion—but this in no way negates the real preference shown by Jesus. The massive weight of Jesus' dedication to the poor, his frequent attacks on the rich and the dominant, his choice of apostles, the condition of his followers, the orientation of his message, leave little doubt about the preferential meaning and will of Jesus. That is so true that one must become poor like him, with all the historical attributes of poverty, in order to enter the Reign. From the historical reality of Jesus, it is clear, with no possibility of evasion, what he meant by the Reign of God among humanity.

It is from this perspective that one should understand what the church of the poor is. The church, in effect, should configure itself as one that follows and continues the person and work of Jesus.

Consequently, the church of the poor is not that church that, being wealthy and establishing itself as such, concerns itself with the poor. It is not that church that, standing outside of the world of the poor, generously offers its help to the poor. It is, more properly, a church in which the poor are its principal subject and its principle of internal structuring. The union of God and humanity, as it is evidenced in Jesus Christ, is historically a union of God emptied primarily into the world of the poor. Thus, the church, being itself poor, and, above all, dedicating itself fundamentally to the salvation of the poor, could become that which it is and could fulfill its mission of universal salvation in a Christian way. By incarnating itself among the poor, dedicating its life to them, and dying for them, it could constitute itself in a Christian manner as an efficacious sign of salvation for all humanity.

The question of who are the poor, in the real situation of the third world, is not a problem that has to be resolved with elaborate scriptural exegesis, sociological analysis, or historical theories. Certainly it is dangerous to speak of "the poor" as a slogan in front of other, more politicized categories. But as a primary fact, as the real situation of the majority of humankind, there is no room for self-interested equivocations. What makes it worse is that, to a large extent, those poor and their poverty are the result of a sin that the church must struggle to take away from the world. There is no other possible northern star that orients the historically constituted mission of the church, its primordial purpose. This is not only because the poor represent the majority of humanity and, in this sense, are the necessary condition of universality, but, above all, because the presence of Jesus is especially in them, a hidden presence, but no less real for being hidden. It follows that the poor are the historical body of Christ, the historical locus of his presence, and the base of the ecclesial community. In other words, the church is the historical body of Christ insofar as it is the church of the poor; and it is a sacrament of liberation insofar as it is the church of the poor. The reason for that is found both in the celebrated passage of the Last Judgment and in the missionary essence of the church. If the church is truly shaped as church of the poor, it will cease to be a church installed in and attached to the world and become again a predominantly missionary church, that is, open to a reality that will force it to draw on its best spiritual reserves; that will also force it to become Jesus Christ truly present in a special way in the prisoners, in the suffering, in the persecuted, and so on.

The church of the poor, therefore, refers to a basic problem of the history of salvation. Because *poor*, in this context, is not an absolute and ahistorical concept; nor is it a "profane" or neutral concept. In the first place, when we speak here of the poor, we are speaking of a relationship between poor and rich (more generally, between dominated and oppressor), in which there are rich people because there are poor, and the rich make the poor poor, or at least deprive them of a part of what belongs to them. Certainly there is another valid sense of the word *poor*: one who feels or is marginalized by "natural," not historical, causes; but the first meaning is the fundamental one in both its dialectical and its historical nature. In the second place, this relationship is not purely profane, not only because we have already rejected the sacred–profane duality in general, but, more particularly, because its special dialectic is deeply rooted in what is essential to Christianity: loving God by loving humanity, justice as the locus of love realized in a world of sin. Thus, the singular Christian and historical importance of a church of the poor is to break that dialectic for the sake of love, in order to achieve the salvation of both sides together, which are now bound together by sin and not by grace. The very evasion of those who keep saying "the poor you will always have with you" is turned against them, because what it would mean is that, when the visible Jesus disappears, then the poor take his place, making him present in a way that is invisible to the eyes of the world but visible to the eyes of faith.

This conception of the church as church of the poor has great practical consequences. Only a few are mentioned here, in a synthetic and programmatic manner.

The Christian faith must mean something real and palpable in the life of the poor. This may seem obvious, something the church has always attempted but not always achieved. But it is not. It is not, in the first place, because "the poor" has not been understood as we are interpreting it here, that is, as a dialectical and historical concept. And it is not, in the second place, because that real and palpable meaning does not refer only to a problem of individual behavior but also—and just as essentially—to real life in the real structures that form a part of human life as a whole. It refers, therefore, to the sociopolitical aspect of their lives and to those structural sociopolitical realities that decisively shape personal lives.

In more general and more theological terms, let us repeat that "salvation history" must also be a historical salvation. It must also save historically, and it must also be a principle of integral salvation here and now. To understand this, it is sufficient to look at the fundamental criterion of Christian theory and praxis: the historical Jesus. The preference of Jesus for the poor is not a purely affective preference; it is also a real dedication to their achievement of a salvation that is not only a promise of a life beyond earth but is eternal life already present. It is impossible to ignore all the real and historical work that Jesus did for the poor of his time. And it is clear that this historicization of salvation, referring to a people and an oppressed people, has and must have unique characteristics in accordance with the nature of the oppression.

This does not necessarily mean that the poor should be treated as a "class," or otherwise categorized, which diminishes their personal nature. The effective and pressing existence of social realities does not negate the irreducible existence of personal realities. One should not be confused with the other, and it cannot be assumed that a solution at one level will be valid at the other. On the other hand, although to some extent this focus enables us to separate individuals from the category they represent—and in this sense it overcomes or can overcome prejudice—it does not nullify the fundamental option, which is still the liberation of the oppressed, with all the sociopolitical meaning that concept implies.

For that reason the Christian faith, far from becoming an opiate—and not only a social opiate—should establish itself as what it is: a principle of liberation. This liberation must include all things and include them in a unitary manner: there is no liberation if the heart of the person is not liberated; but the heart cannot be liberated when the whole person, which is more than inner being, remains oppressed by collective structures and realities that invade the whole being. If the church should avoid letting more structural concerns turn it into an opiate with respect to personal problems, it should also make sure its more individualistic and spiritualistic concerns do not turn it into an opiate with respect to structural problems.

This places the Latin American church in a difficult position. On the one hand, it brings persecution on the church, as it brought persecution-unto-death to Jesus himself. The Latin American church, more precisely the church of the poor, must be convinced that if it is not persecuted by the powerful in a historical world, it is not authentically and completely preaching the Christian faith. While not all persecution is a sign and miracle proving the authenticity of faith, the absence of persecution by those who hold power in a situation of injustice is a sign, irrefutable in the long range, that the proclamation of its message lacks evangelical courage. But on the other hand, the fact that the church cannot and should not be reduced to a pure sociopolitical force, working exclusively from an ideological locus against unjust structures or giving absolute priority to that work, brings on it incomprehension and attack from those who have embraced personal and political partiality as if it were the whole of humanity. These people do not know the damage they are causing not only to a profound and long-term work of the church but, more importantly, to themselves. They consider themselves servants, when at times they are serving themselves in order to carry out an impossible political project that does not even take into account the whole range of material conditions in which they find themselves.

Thus, the church of the poor does not permit us to make a sharp separation between faith and religion, at least in specific social contexts and in the early stages of a conscientizing process. The distinction between faith and religion, which has a lot of validity in both the general theoretical order and the practical order of specific social environments, must be used carefully in situations like those of Latin America. This distinction, which is theologically well founded, is needed to recover the uniqueness of what is Christian, but it can be manipulated and does not always fit the reality of a church of the poor. It can lead us to underestimate the authentic needs of a cultural situation and can also disembody the faith and dehistoricize it. On the one hand, the distinction can turn faith into something purely individual and purely parochial and not structural; or, on the other, it can bypass the need to embody the faith "also" in religious form, as the "corporeal" nature that the social reality requires. It is true that the Central European emphasis on faith vis-à-vis religion brings in a recovery of fundamental dimensions, but it also entails the danger of individualistic subjectivity and idealization, and also the danger of becoming an option for the elites. An authentic church of the poor must respond to these dangers by understanding and practicing the faith as a historical following of the person and work of Jesus, and also as a historical celebration; both the following and the celebration must respond to the problems and the situation of the oppressed majorities that are struggling for justice.

That is one way of approaching the problem of popular "religiosity," the problem of the "religious" ways of cultivating and celebrating the faith. With all their weaknesses, these ways are needed as a way of responding historically to the historicity of faith itself, and they can be the corrective needed to ensure the continued historical mediation of the historical faith. For example, it is wrong when priests collectively abandon or undervalue the proclamation and living practice of the sources of faith in order to engage in political struggle. To claim that this is "faith" over against "religion" involves a secularization of the faith that goes beyond the need to historicize and politicize it. Evangelization should indeed come before sacramentalization in the proclamation and living practice of the Christian faith, precisely because evangelization is an essential part of sacramentalization. Evangelization can and must be political and historical, but, above all, it is the proclamation of the salvation that is offered and given to us in Jesus.

Therefore, this church of the poor must not become another form of elitism. The very concept of church of the poor goes beyond the elitism of those who see Christianity as way to refinement that only the perfect can enjoy or practice. The church of the poor closes its doors to no one; nor does it diminish the fullness and universality of its mission. It must always conserve the fullness of its force, although this means foolishness to some and a stumbling block to others.

But it also must not leave room for another form of elitism: that which is appropriated from the whole people by the most conscientized, and from the conscientized ones by those who consider themselves the most committed vanguard, and from this committed vanguard by the vertical leaders, who lead from above with preestablished plans, dogmatically monopolize the needs of the people, and set the direction and pace of their resolution. That leads to a preference for the dramatic and quick success of political action rather than the slow growth of the evangelical seed, planted and carefully tended in its own soil.

In the face of these different forms of elitism, the alternative of the church of the poor does not constitute either a stupefying opiate or a stimulating drug. The Christian faith should be neither an eternal opiate nor an apocalyptic and millenarian stimulant; it is a small seed that little by little can become a great tree sheltering all people. Revolutionary haste and desperate eschatology do not respect the reality of either the people or the church. And it is neither just nor evangelical to confuse the select, elitist pace of individuals with the pace of the real people. Lack of faith and confidence in the salvific potential of the preaching of Jesus easily leads away from following Jesus in history to purely political action. That action may be fully justified, and must be shaped by rigorous technical considerations, but it alone does not constitute the Christian faith and cannot substitute for it, although it can sometimes be an incarnating sign of faith in a given situation.

We still need to analyze the possibility of a certain elitism in the gospel itself: people, followers, disciples, apostles, the three, Peter, and more. But however this knotty problem is resolved, we can suppose that the gospel never fails to give ultimate respect to the potential self-giving of a particular social group at any particular time. If the church of the poor is to be shaped by the fullness and energy of the Christian faith, each of the human groups within it and, above all, each person, must receive the infinite respect that Jesus showed in his ministry of evangelization, except in cases of clear exploitation of one person by another.

I do not want to end these reflections on the church of the poor as sacrament of liberation without bringing in the feelings of the peasants evangelized by a prophet of the church of the poor, Father Rutilio Grande, a martyr of that church in El Salvador, who for giving active witness to the Christian faith was riddled by the bullets of oppressors. Here are some of the peasants' testimonies.

> I think Rutilio has fulfilled his priestly mission. . . . He understood the Christian commitment that God wants all people to carry out. He made this commitment by serving others; he related to the

humble people in the countryside and in the city, teaching them the true way of Christianity that we must show to others.

He began to develop a line, putting it in practice with the delegates of the word, and later he began opening a Christian way, committing himself to the people, until one day we saw him killed by the murderous bullets of the enemy, who did not want him to go on working with his people . . . taking him on the way that Christ wanted to show us.

He related to the humble people to show them that the gospel must be lived in struggle, not to leave it in the air, but to be able to overcome injustice, exploitation, and misery. That is why the enemies of the people decided to kill him along with his people.

Because the work of Father Rutilio Grande and the other missionary fathers was the first to lift up this community, that is why the communities feel their spirit evangelically uplifted because they received very deeply when Father Rutilio came to say Mass. That is why the communities have grown in number. When he formed those communities, he left eight delegates there. Now there are eighteen delegates in the community, but delegates who have really understood what it means to follow Christ and why they should not stop for anything that people invent in this oppressed world.

Father Grande and his missionaries also enlightened us that it was good to celebrate the festival of the products that we harvest, like corn. . . . In that festival it didn't matter if people had a suit, good shoes, if they went barefoot, or with sandals made of rubber tires; we were all the same there, there were no class differences.

The challenge to us of Father Rutilio's death is to go forward, not to faint—to see clearly the position of this man, a martyr and prophet of the church. We have to maintain the position that this prophet maintained and, if possible, give our lives in service to others because the grain has to die before we see the fruit.

Meditating on these words of living faith would inspire many reflections. They show very well what a church of the poor can be as a sacrament of universal liberation, which only leaves out those same people who stayed out when Jesus died for all people—the ones Rutilio Grande forgave at his death, as Jesus did, because they did not know what they were doing.

Notes

[1] Although this term denotes a diversity of currents—it would have to, given its own definition as a historical task—I prefer to keep the term for the sake of differentiation.

[2] Cf. X. Zubiri, "El hombre y su cuerpo," *Salesianum* 3 (1974): 479–86.

[3] Oscar A. Romero, *Voice of the Voiceless*, trans. Michael J. Walsh (Maryknoll, NY: Orbis Books, 1985); see the Second Pastoral Letter.

[4] Cf. I. Ellacuría, "Por qué muere Jesús y por qué le matan?" *Misión Abierta* (March 1977): 17–26; on the bibliography cited there, cf. H. Schürmann, *Comment Jesus a-t-il vecu sa mort?* (Paris: Les Éditions du Cerf, 1977).

[5] This point was developed in I. Ellacuría, "Iglesia y realidad histórica," *Estudios Centroamericanos* 331 (1976): 213–20.

[6] I refer here to the French translation, which appeared in *La Documentation Catholique* 1726 (1977): 761–68. (For an English translation, see J. Schall, ed., *Liberation Theology* [San Francisco: Ignatius Press, 1982], pp. 363–83.)

[7] Ibid., 766.

[8] Cf. "Historia de la salvación y salvación en la historia," in *Teología política* (San Salvador, Ediciones del Secretariado Social Interdiocesano, 1973), 1–10; "El anuncio del evangelio a la misión de la Iglesia," ibid., 44–69; "Liberación: misión y carisma de la Iglesia latinoamericana," ibid., 70–90; "Tesis sobre posibilidad, necesidad y sentido de una teología latinoamericana," in *Teología y mundo contemporáneo* (Madrid: Ediciones Cristindad, 1975), 325–50; "Hacia una fundamentación del método teológico latinoamericano," *ECA* (August–September 1975): 409–25; "En busca de la cuestión fundamental de la pastoral latinoamericana," *Sal Terrae* 759/760 (1976): 563–72; "Teorías económicas y relación entre cristianismo y socialismo," *Concilium* 125 (May 1977): 282–90; "Fe y justicia," *Christus* (August and October 1977), 23–33; 19–34.

[9] J. Sobrino, in his *Christology at the Crossroads* (Maryknoll, NY. Orbis Books, 1978) and in many of his writings, has shown in *actu exercito* how the primacy of the historical Jesus can and should be maintained from and for a historical incorporation.

[10] K. Rahner, *Ökumenische Basisgemeinden* (Frankfurt: Aktion 365, 1975).

[11] From here on I am following some reflections that I have already published in "Notas teológicas sabre religiosidad popular," *Revista de Fomento Social* 127 (July–September 1977): 253–60; therefore, the following pages may contribute some ideas on the important subject of popular religiosity.

—Translated by Margaret D. Wilde

10

Theology as the Ideological
Moment of Ecclesial Praxis
(1978)

*On February 22, 1977, Oscar Romero was consecrated Archbishop of San Sal-
vador. That same day, Ignacio Ellacuría was denied entry into the country after a
visit abroad. He was not able to return to El Salvador until August 1978, the first
of two periods of exile (the second lasted from November 1980 until May 1982).
Thus, he was out of the country when Rutilio Grande was assassinated on March
12, 1977. Several months later, when a death squad called the "White Warriors
Union" (Unión de Guerreros Blancos) threatened to murder every Jesuit who did
not leave the country within thirty days, he could only support his brothers from
abroad. Not surprisingly, he kept close tabs on the unfolding political situation. He
experienced from afar the impact of Grande's death on Romero and of Romero's
gathering influence on the church in El Salvador. In this context, experiencing both
personally and vicariously the wave of persecution sweeping over his land, he spent
time with his mentor and friend, Xavier Zubiri, renewing and deepening the framework of his philosophical and theological vision. This essay emerged as a result of
the middle distance afforded by his immediate situation of exile. From that "place"
he grasped the church's urgent duty to rethink its self-understanding. Likewise, he
noticed that this could only happen if theology reconceived its nature and purpose
as an ecclesial discipline in historically real terms.*

*"Theology as the Ideological Moment of Ecclesial Praxis" stands at the intersec-
tion of the disciplines of fundamental theology and ecclesiology. It remains one of the
more technical and important essays that Ellacuría produced. He begins with the
familiar but crucial recognition that theology is not "an absolute and supreme form
of knowledge that floats above the historical vicissitudes of other forms of knowledge
and praxis." Rather, every theology is historically contextualized. Hence, he frames
the doing of theology in terms of "ecclesial praxis"—action on behalf of the Reign*

of God by the people of God, the church. In turn, he locates the ambit of ecclesial praxis within the larger field of "historical praxis," where it enjoys a relative autonomy, but over which it cannot and must not seek direct control. Meanwhile, theology does not ground itself or is an end in itself. Rather, the purpose of theology is to conceptualize the real linkage that graced ecclesial praxis forges between history and the Reign of God. To do this, it must always discern and locate itself within those concrete historical places where "the truth of the Reign of God is most accessible."

One of the most serious methodological concerns of North American theology deals with the place that the theological task occupies in the historical context of ecclesial praxis and the necessary conditions for the theological task to be evaluated as integrally Christian. This essay aims to show how one can respond to that concern and how that response is justified. It deals with one aspect of theological method that needs to be complemented by others. But it is an essential aspect with transcendental consequences for the global orientation of theology.

This essay consists in two fundamental parts. The first part will show the way in which theology, or the theological task, is the ideological moment of ecclesial praxis, while the second part will analyze the necessary conditions for that ideological moment to be fully Christian. The scope of the subject matter demands a plethora of perspectives. As a result, rather than a detailed exploration of each perspective, a clear formulation and precise systematization of the whole will be sought. In this way, the conclusions will be supported as a whole, and we leave for further reflection the revision and in-depth study of each moment within that whole.

Theology, Ecclesial Praxis, and Historical Praxis

The place of theological reflection and its products within the concrete context of historical reality that encompasses them is often forgotten. An ancient assumption continues to weigh on theology. It views theology as an absolute and supreme form of knowledge that floats above the historical vicissitudes of other forms of knowledge and praxis. For example, it is thought and practiced (although less and less) that the work of St. Thomas (Aquinas) can be taken as a definitive theological text that fundamentally covers everything that needs to be known "dogmatically." Theology would then be a pure theoretical knowledge about unchanging realities and, as a result, would have little to do with history.

Although it is sometimes accepted reflexively that theology possesses a practical end, the implications of this intentionality and its determining conditions, even in the case where theology explicitly claims no more than a theological "truth," are not reflected upon. It is clear, however, that if one presumes a monarchical organization of the church, a solid union, a disciplined submission, and a certain sociopolitical order, etc., theological reflection will be thoroughly configured to these practical interests in the election and exclusion of topics as well as the way of approaching and treating them. And even when one does not presume a practical end explicitly, it is clear that the theologian and his or her supposed academic work are configured by the desire to respond to certain challenges, even if the responses are quite distinct from the challenges. Think, for example, what conditions are necessary—whether for good or bad is another question—to understand theology as a university field of study that presumes the same academic credibility as other academic disciplines.

Therefore, it takes a more or less self-serving naivete to believe that theology enjoys a special status that immunizes it against all disfiguring conditions, at least when it does not explicitly refer to practical questions. Without entering into general considerations supported by the structure of human sentient intelligence (Zubiri) or by what is ultimately at the service of life, we can accept as a fact that theology, even as a pure exercise of reason, has all the characteristics appropriate to that exercise. Among others, it is carried out from a limited and self-serving perspective *[realidad]* and is at the service of certain interests. That this does not necessarily lead to a subjective anarchy should not prevent it from being recognized, but rather demands an examination of how to overcome it critically.

Moreover, insofar as theology is a special type of rational exercise, it contains special characteristics. This is a point where many criticisms of religious language have arisen, especially those of analytic philosophy (although not always justly, since they underline neither the real character of the symbolic nor the possibility of an indirect verification that can enter into conversation about a historically incarnate God). However, in the field of theological affirmations, we must face the fact that many of them are at least apparently unverifiable. As a result, they are more vulnerable to forces that disfigure and manipulate them in ways not always conscious. Many theologies, in effect, focus on especially "metaphysical" themes, the same themes that Kantian criticism severed from scientific knowledge (God, the soul and eternal life, the world in its totality). They insist on the impossibility of experiencing grace and the supernatural, and they absolutize and transcendentalize even the historical in such a way that they remove the possibility of its being verified.

This situation does not change substantially when recourse is made to revelation and the magisterium, as if these two instances guarantee objectivity beyond historical fluctuations. It does not change, in the first place because the same feature of free choice accompanies the sphere of faith both in its inception and throughout its exercise. But it does not change, above all, because revelation itself is historical in its very structure, such that it cannot have a single, univocal meaning for really distinct situations. And if this is so of revelation *qua* offer, it is even more so *qua* reception, in that the latter concerns selection within the sphere of revelation as well as hierarchical ordering among the topics selected to clarify a certain problem. Finally, the magisterium is also subject to historical conditioning, even in the extraordinary moments of its exercise, and without question in its ordinary exercise.

None of this absolutely relativizes—paradoxically speaking—either believing acceptance or theological reflection. It simply issues a warning not to fall into naive judgments. The most abstract affirmations can sometimes result in a religious expression of a situation whose truth is everything but religious. Religious discourse can be a mystification of economic and political discourse, not only when it makes a fetish out of certain historical realities, making them either divine or diabolical, but also when it supposedly speaks only of God or of the divine. While avoiding the exaggeration of thinking that all theological discourse is nothing but this, the question and the suspicion always remain regarding how much of this penetrates all theological discourse. Liberation theology, for example, very explicitly recognizes the political character of its discourse and its historical intention within social praxis. This being the case, in principle it avoids mystification, since it opens itself up to all kinds of criticisms and corrections. This is not the case with other types of theology that have failed to ask themselves about the political character of their affirmations.

And the biased use that sectors not only within but also outside the church make of theology cannot remain hidden. In these cases, the facts show that the theological affirmations have a political slant to them even if the theologians have not explicitly recognized it. And this happens not only when they are explicitly used but also when they are used as "pure" versions of faith among other affirmations that are "socially involved," as if the latter were horizontal while the former were vertical. We are tired of seeing the political use of vertical theology. One suspects, then, that there is no theological statement that is historically and politically neutral. As a result, the theologian should ask him/herself, "Who benefits and which behavior is favored by his/her reflections, or who feels welcomed by those reflections?" It is interesting from all angles—to say the least—that the politically and economically more conservative parties take as their banner a religion as subversive as Christianity is in principle. And it is suspicious that the richest and most powerful do not feel forcefully interrogated by the Christian message.

Nothing said up to now is new. Rather, these affirmations might be viewed as commonplace except that they continue to appear to be applicable to a vast body of theology that sees itself as official and academic. Although more creative theology habitually tries to critically overcome this problem, there still remains much contemporary theology that does not take this into account. It continues conveniently to affirm the existence of pure theological reason.

So as not to forget the historical context of theology, it is necessary to frame it in terms of ecclesial praxis, which is in turn framed in terms of historical praxis. Seeing theology as a moment in a certain praxis enables one to grasp its proper function more easily despite the complexity of the problem.

Establishing theology as the moment of ecclesial praxis highlights the fact that doing theology is not an autonomous, theoretical act, but is rather an element within a broader structure. Ecclesial praxis is taken here in the broad sense, which includes every historical action of the church, understood as a community of human beings that in some way realizes the Reign of God. The phrase "ecclesial praxis" is chosen to underline the aspect of praxis, that is, the transforming action that the church necessarily undertakes on its historical pilgrimage. To situate theology within the framework of ecclesial praxis implies that one consider theology not only in the most general way as being contextualized and determined but also as something essentially subsidiary to a historical praxis.

This subordination is not only a necessity but an ideal. Doing Christian theology—we are speaking here only of this kind of theology—is not conceivable in isolation from the church. Rather, maintaining all due autonomy, theology is at the service of the church insofar as the church is wholly devoted to the realization of God's Reign. But it is also a social necessity because doing theology, like any other action, is determined in any given moment precisely by historical praxis. The theologian could liberate herself from the ecclesial praxis in which she finds herself enveloped, but she must break from it and even then naturally runs the risk of finding herself enveloped in it anyway. Now, of course, not all ecclesial praxis is always fundamentally Christian, which places theology in danger of not being Christian as well.

Certainly, theology can in some way orient ecclesial praxis. But this does not mean that theology is not determined by it and should not see itself as determined by what is and what should be ecclesial praxis. One can never insist enough that the theological task be able to guarantee its full development: the theological task stems from an ecclesial praxis that is not always adequate, and it should always try to determine what its praxis should be in each case. This is a valid way to do theology in its totality, and it admits of degrees according to the tasks, which make up that totality. There is no doubt that in theology there are tasks that are predominantly technical, whose best contribution to the whole is the perfection of its technicality, which is valid not only in some areas of exegesis or history but also in its more theoretical development. But insofar as all these partial moments constitute the whole of doing theology, its orientation by and for ecclesial praxis should be recognized.

Now ecclesial praxis is a moment that depends on having a relative autonomy within the total historical praxis. Both points are important and should be maintained together: ecclesial praxis counts on a certain autonomy, and ecclesial praxis is only one moment of a historical praxis that is not only more general and encompassing but also truly more totalizing.

Ecclesial praxis has, in principle, a certain autonomy within the total historical praxis, although it cannot be realized in history. We understand autonomy here to mean the fact that, as a praxis, it is not—at least in principle—a mere mechanical reflection of other actions. Likewise, it indicates that it has its own capacity to reconfigure other nonecclesial actions. The criticisms of Christianity have not been able to show that—from the historical Jesus himself and the early community down to our day—all its activity is but a reflection of economic, social, and political conditions. Rather, a multitude of important facts prove the contrary. The theological foundation of this autonomy rests on the postulated presence of something "more" in history that is made effective in it, a postulated "more" that should receive some verification, however indirectly. The sociological foundation rests on the specialization of functions. For the Christian function does not become blurred, not even where it has empirical features verifiable by other distinct social functions. The epistemological foundation is supported by the singularity of its object and its method of reaching and realizing it. To announce and realize the Reign of God in history will have common points with other historical tasks, but as a living unity it has its own autonomy.

But however much we insist on the historical peculiarity and not merely the abstract quality of ecclesial praxis, we cannot fail to recognize that it is presented as a moment within a larger historical praxis that encompasses and totalizes it.

For one thing, this inclusion is a fact. It should be granted that each historical praxis has a certain unity. Each historical praxis and also the total praxis of present universal history, despite its many material, biological, economic, political, and cultural elements, despite its complexity, has a strict unity. This unity cannot be attributed factually to the moment of ecclesial praxis. Nor can ecclesial praxis be the whole of historical praxis, or even its totalizing element, or the element that "in the last resort" grounds and determines everything else in a real and effective way. What ecclesial praxis wants to be and to claim for itself—the source of all-embracing meaning and the final critical moment—does not confer to it the ability to "really" be that. To think otherwise is a purely idealistic illusion that confuses the fabrications of feeling with the operative reality of history. This is made even more clear if we move from the proclamation of principles and intentions to verifiable results of ecclesial praxis, its real practice. Not only are other moments of historical praxis more determinate of what occurs in history, but one could ask whether or not ecclesial praxis is more determined by other moments of history than these moments are by that praxis.

In addition, the inclusion of ecclesial praxis within the larger historical praxis is a necessity that follows from its own structure. Ecclesial praxis, by virtue of its own real nature, lacks the material conditions to be the dominant instance of the course of history, although at times it has tried to be such. Moreover, although in some places and circumstances it might appear that it could decisively intervene in history, it is clear that this intervention would become a ridiculous pretension when the real weight of other historical instances increased. Nevertheless, the social and historical situation of certain areas and the social weight that Christians have in these areas can lead to the mistake of wanting to constitute ecclesial praxis as a "power" alongside other powers. And where this fails to occur, one is led to believe that much of the received theology was elaborated when ecclesial praxis was wanting to exercise power over the course of history. That ecclesial praxis should influence history, and not only the souls of individuals or through conversation between persons, does not mean that it should or could be the determining moment in the historical process.

Finally, the inclusion of ecclesial praxis within the larger historical praxis is demanded by faith itself. Ecclesial praxis does not have its center within itself, or in a God who is foreign to history, but rather in a God who presents Godself in history. Ecclesial praxis has its center in the Reign of God and in the realization of this Reign in history, a Reign that presents itself in the gospel parable as the leaven in bread, as salt in food, etc., not the bread-dough or the food itself. And the bread-dough does not exist for the leaven, or the food for the salt, but just the opposite. Neither the transcendence of faith nor the necessity of its historical incarnation annul the power of history. Rather, they respect and support the distinctness of its autonomous moments.

This can all appear obvious and widely accepted. But it is necessary to underline it. The underlining refers itself, above all, to two aspects: ecclesial praxis is configured much more than is usually accepted by other moments of historical praxis, and ecclesial praxis should place itself at the service of historical praxis. We will now examine the consequences of these affirmations for the theological task (understood as a moment of ecclesial praxis encompassed in historical praxis).

Thus, theology represents, in a privileged way, the ideological moment of ecclesial praxis. We understand ideological moment here to mean the conscious and reflexive element of praxis. It is clear, then, that other activities pertain to that moment, like liturgy, art, devotional practices, etc., but theological reflection pertains to it in a special way. That magisterial activity has a greater ecclesiastical status in this line is not a problem for this notion, either because it generally could be considered as a theological practice or since it carries less weight from the strictly "ideological" point of view.

But before insisting on this ideological character, we should recall the primary consequence of the aforesaid. That ecclesial praxis is a moment in the totalizing historical praxis means that it is determined by the place that it holds in that total historical praxis. Because reality shows us that historical praxis is a divided and conflictive praxis, such that this is its overall actual form, ecclesial praxis is determined in large part by the position it adopts in the conflict. This denies neither the autonomy of ecclesial praxis nor its ideological moment, because either it does not take account of how it is being conditioned by one of the sides of the conflict, or it deliberately places itself on one of them. In the first case, autonomy is not exercised, and, in the second, this autonomy is consciously placed at the service of a particular historical praxis. One could object that the totality should be sought and that the autonomous way to overcome partiality would be to directly install oneself in the totality and not in one of the partialities. But this solution is hypothetical and idealistic. It is unrealizable given the reality of historical praxis. The historical mode of situating oneself in the totality involves incorporating oneself reflexively on one of its opposing sides in order to take on the opposition and in this way manage to overcome it. It is true that a Manichean division of history does not work, as if all the good resides in one opposing part and all the evil resides in the other. But it is possible to determine in each case where the principle of good or the principle of evil reigns more. The intention to escape from the conflict presupposes the intention to escape from history, when it is not indirectly increasing the power of one faction in the conflict. This proposal brings us one step closer to the ideological moment in ecclesial praxis.

As is well known, dogmatic Marxism or Marxist dogmatism attributes to the entire ecclesial praxis—the exceptions would be casual and occasional, true only *per accidens*—an ideological character. It attributes this because ecclesial praxis operates in the ideal sphere, as opposed to the economic and political-institutional and, above all, because it is a praxis that conceals (when it does not defend outright) the very domination and oppression of capitalistic exploitation. Such an approach simplifies the historical facts and does not use enough real experience of ecclesial praxis to make a correct judgment. When facing that dogmatic position, one should affirm two essential points from within ecclesial praxis. First, not all ecclesial praxis is alien to the material and productive development of history, since one material power can consist of different forms. Second, ecclesial praxis does not necessarily and in principle situate itself on behalf of oppression, but exactly the opposite. And in fact, it has not always been at the service of the oppressors. This brief allusion to the problem suffices in order to determine more precisely the ideological moment of theology, since historical analyses should prove or refute the Marxist thesis in each case.

To attribute an ideological character to the theological task does not necessarily imply an accusation. It does, however, imply a caution and a call to attention. It can be pejoratively ideological when it either does not attend to its character as a moment in ecclesial praxis, or when it consciously or unconsciously responds to an ecclesial praxis that in fact favors the oppressive side of historical praxis. Certainly this is the case with much theological work, and at least it will always be a point that calls for an examination of conscience and a discernment of spirits. But it can be ideological in a positive way when it intends to participate positively in ecclesial praxis, when it responds to, justifies, and supports the praxis that favors the side of the oppressed in the construction and establishment of a new earth. It constitutes, then, a fundamental part of ecclesial praxis insofar as it is both illuminating and critical, not only as an illumination of feeling, but as a transformative moment of historical reality.

To propose this rule for theology is not an irrational notion. If much of the usual theology of past centuries can make it appear that way, sociological reflection on the necessity that theology be that way and the reflection of believers on the fact itself of that necessity are more than sufficient to make that appearance go away. Revelation can be fundamentally understood as a theological reflection about a particular historical praxis that encompasses both individual experiences and collective experiences and events such that the reflection is inspired, and that it occasionally does not depend on a major critical and speculative apparatus, does not keep it from being considered a strictly theological reflection. The contents of that revelation are neither immediate transmissions, which have nothing to do with experience and the reflection of the sacred writer, much less are they pure theoretical reflections made at the margins of all praxis. They are, rather, theological readings of a specific historical praxis, which, in large part at least, is a historical praxis of liberation. As is known and recognized, even ideas like monotheism, the Trinity, creation, salvation, and the Reign of God, which are apparently not experienced, are reflexive expressions of a historical experience where the God of grace and revelation makes himself especially present both in the experienced historical event and in the experience and reflection upon that event.

What Ecclesial Praxis Gives Christian Legitimization to the Theological Task?

We have just seen that doing theology necessarily has to do with ecclesial praxis. It certainly also depends on the will and the psychological state of the theologian, but in its totality it responds to an ecclesial praxis according to the possibilities, limitations, interests, coordination of strengths, etc., that dominate in each moment. In addition, theology should place itself at the service of ecclesial praxis, whenever that praxis is Christian or in order that it be so. Theology is neither an end in itself nor does it have roots in itself; but neither can it simply subordinate itself to any ecclesial praxis. For although ecclesial praxis in its historical entirety cannot fundamentally separate itself from the following of Jesus, it can do so in particular moments and in large sectors of what makes up the ecclesial structure.

Because of this, the question arises as to which ecclesial praxis is the one that supplies the best conditions for theology to be as fully Christian as possible. It has already been suggested that this question cannot be answered easily by appealing to revelation and the magisterium, precisely because this appeal is only valid from within a certain ecclesial praxis and for a very precise ecclesial praxis. (Conversely, here we will not ask ourselves for the requisite conditions so that theology might have "academic weight" or in order that certain parts of the overall project be realized with the best techniques and rigor. This is another question entirely, one that will have to encompass the general theme of theory and praxis, where the praxical conditionality of a good theory should be discussed, especially a theory that refers to the kinds of themes with which theology works.)

The answer to the question at hand [which ecclesial praxis is the one that supplies the best conditions for theology to be as fully Christian as possible?] will line up what is the common opinion and general praxis of so-called Latin American theology. With different nuances, with consequences more or less advanced, and with different formulations, a common foundation can be found that will be presented here. In order to represent this common foundation (especially since it is the work of many authors, but, above all, since it is the need of many anonymous popular communities), we will leave aside all personal references and bibliographical data, which are also at the disposition of the readers of this journal.

A fundamental condition for encountering the most adequate ecclesial praxis is to conceive of the fundamental object of theology as the Reign of God, that is, to consider that the fundamental object of doing theology and, consequently, of theology itself is the realization of the Reign of God in history. This will appear to be only slightly different from other ways of conceiving theology. Nevertheless, the difference is fundamental.

To arrive at this thesis the Latin American theologian has proceeded according to the following fundamental methodological principle: *every ecclesial practice should be realized in order to follow the historical Jesus.* Applied to the principle in our case, it should be said that, if the fundamental object of the mission of Jesus was the Reign of God, it should also be the object of ecclesial praxis and of the ideological moment of that praxis. Although one subsequently needs to determine how Jesus understood the Reign of God and how the Reign of God that Jesus preached should be understood in each historical situation (two strictly theological tasks), it is resolutely affirmed as an adequate interpretation of the life and mission of Jesus that his fundamental objective is the Reign of God and that all other theological subjects should arise (not only in theoretical interpretation but also in projects and actions) within the framework of the Reign of God and in its historical realization. It evidently deals with what a Christian theology, not just any theology, should be. And what a Christian theology should be is not known by understanding it as one of the specific realizations of a presumptive general framework, but rather by taking the life of Jesus with absolute seriousness, be it innovative or not, whether it arises or not from an irreducible experience. The fundamental *Faktum* of Christian theology would be, therefore, the Reign of God as it appears in the New Testament, read and interpreted, as we shall later see, from the situation that Jesus himself proposes (and from the situation that his proclamation of the Reign proposes) as the privileged situation.

In other words, the Reign of God, which Christian theology has as its fundamental object, is the Reign of God announced by Jesus, read by an adequate ecclesial praxis, and carried on in history. Evidently that adequate ecclesial praxis will measure its adequacy by that which is the demand of the Reign of God in each case. There exists, therefore, a hermeneutical circle, which moves from the Reign to praxis but returns from praxis to the Reign, where both poles are gradually reinterpreted through the presence and influence of the Spirit of Christ. To want to begin from a generic concept of the Reign of God in order to arrive later at that which is the Reign of God announced by Jesus is not something that is adequate to Latin American theology. If a generic element is recognized, it arises out of the specific element and not vice versa, as if the general were a reality and not an impoverished abstraction of the different possible "reigns of God" that have been sought in history. It fundamentally deals with a concrete praxis that includes a plurality of elements in such a way that the Christian Reign of God is the terminus of a Christian practice begun in the name of Jesus and sustained in the active hope that flows from the resurrected Christ and from his new presence in history.

This Reign of God, the fundamental object of ecclesial praxis and of theology, is neither a verbal formula nor a stylistic evasion to speak no more about God. It formally includes God and God's reigning in history, but it includes them in intrinsic unity. Without wishing to develop this fundamental concept (which resolves the whole problem of dualisms and reductionisms, of verticalisms and horizontalisms), it is necessary to briefly show how it does not leave behind any subject of faith and how it demands (and in what sense it makes its demands in) a particular historical moment.

Precisely by being the Reign of *God* it appeals to the totality of God revealed by Jesus and in Jesus. But it appeals to this totality according to the very mode of the revelation of Jesus. In this way it loses nothing of what we call transcendence, although it does not necessarily retain everything about which human beings have waxed eloquent concerning this divine transcendence. Transcendence remains limited—in spite of its boundless openness—by the framework proposed by Jesus, just as this framework has been picked up but not closed by the tradition that constitutes revelation. It is one thing that systematic reflection categorizes in a more complex way the God revealed by Jesus and another that this God should be subordinated to that which autonomous speculation presupposes as essential characteristics of divinity.

But by being the *Reign* of God, it asks history and humankind to be the place of the presence and action of the God of Jesus Christ. It will not be easy for theology to show what this Reign should be in order really to be the Reign of God, but it is as fundamental a task as that of showing who the God of the Reign is. In this way we lose nothing of what we call immanence, although language about the Reign of God in no way exhausts the autonomy of the immanent, just as God is not exhausted in God's historical reigning, which will always be exceeded by a greater future that moves from the present to an ever greater presence and fulfillment.

Nevertheless, we are not dealing with two tasks, one that speaks of God and another that speaks of the Reign. If this were the case, we would once again be in the insuperable camp of dualisms, and we would be distancing ourselves from what was the life and mission of Jesus. There is only one fundamental object of theology: the Reign of God as reality and concept that is both historical and structural. For this reason, Latin American theology cannot agree with those who refer to its proper object as social praxis, such as the social doctrine of the church formulates it. In this there are multiple misunderstandings. Above all, Latin American theology, liberation theology, cannot be reduced to one part of the faith that has to do with social questions or social justice, as if it did not have as its object the totality of the faith. Liberation theology is concerned about historical praxis, but this does not mean that, formally, its object or theme is social justice. On the contrary, its theme and object is the Reign of God. And secondly, the area of Catholic social teaching is introduced by Latin American theology in the field of theological reflection on an equal footing with other subjects that refer to the *Reign* of God. Of course, this social teaching is treated in a very different way. Finally, the social teaching in some of its concrete answers to predominantly economic and political problems is subsidiary to certain mediations. They relativize it enormously, and that should be analyzed in each case by how they function technically and by how they cohere with the historical proclamations of the Reign of God.

What follows from this is that the very concept of the Reign of God is a dynamic concept, both on a historical and a transhistorical level. The reality of the Reign of God implies in itself the problem of its realization: it is a reality in the process of being realized. Theological reflection, therefore, has to concern itself directly with what constitutes the realization of the Reign of God. Since the fundamental object of theological reflection is not God but the Reign of God, the aspect of realization turns out to be decisive.

Theology, then, cannot be reduced to being a pure interpretation of the reality of the Reign of God. (Recognizing this would already be enough to put theological essays and their authors on new paths.) Nor can it be reduced to a mere search for the truth of the Reign, truth understood as the "meaning" of the reality of the Reign. Besides being all this, it also must be something that "has to be done," something that should orient a realization, which makes God present in the real conditions of this realization. On the one hand, this realization means putting into effect an economic and political project for which ecclesial praxis and theology have neither the vocation nor capacity (although there could be economic and political projects, just as there are personal or class-driven behaviors that cannot be reconciled with the Reign of God). On the other, this realization has to be interested in the moment of truth, and even in the ideal moment of behaviors, but understanding that moment of truth as a new reality that makes more transparent, in an objective way, the reality of God.

All of this demands that theology, through ecclesial praxis, insert itself in the totality of historical praxis. In the first part, it has already been shown that this insertion is the responsibility of theological reflection as a whole, and is only derivatively [the responsibility] of its integrated moments. The "immediatism" of the activist, which demands that every [pastoral] agent and theologian (and every theological product) have an immediate reference to action, or which attends only to a partial and superficial praxis, is the ruination of theological praxis, and ultimately of its relatively autonomous contribution to the whole of historical praxis. But, conversely, the partial elements of theology—be it what each theologian does or what one sector of systematic theology does—should be positively oriented toward that fundamental object of theology that is the realization of the Reign of God.

If one keeps in mind this point of realization and historicity that is the responsibility of the Reign of God, it is clear that the theological labor cannot be done apart from either historical experience or the social sciences. But we should not fall into scientific excesses in the manner of those who fell into metaphysical excesses, turning theology into a kind of absolute knowledge. But if theology is bringing about a historical realization of the Reign of God, it cannot carry out its mission without counting on historical praxis and the real conditions for a correct expression of its effort in historical praxis. The problem presents itself not only in the strategic actions and tactics that should be undertaken so that the historical course of human accomplishments can conform itself to the Reign of God but also with respect to the Reign of God itself as concrete history.

The question arises of how theology should limit itself to being a reflection and consequently a systematization of what is the historical praxis of each moment. It has been said, for example, that liberation theology should not be more than the reflective Christian contribution to a certain historical process of liberation. This affirmation is understood in a different way by those who favor liberation theology and by those who oppose it (the latter being those who speak of reductionisms both in the object of theology and in its supernatural dimension). Evidently, the former know better than the latter what they mean.

First of all, they think that all theology should be done from within a praxis and for a praxis, something that the realization of the Reign of God in history really demands. And in a certain way, this is reflective and critical. Of course, the divergences already begin with the different concepts held of the Reign of God and of its realization in history. The truth is that this divergence should be measured according to Latin American theology. Positively [it should be measured] in terms of its operative repudiation of injustice, and of the oppression and exploitation of some human beings by others. Negatively [it should be measured] in terms of the stances that oppressive and exploitative powers take with respect to it. A Reign of God that does not enter into conflict with a history configured by the power of sin, is not the Reign of the God of Jesus, however deeply spiritual it may appear (just as the Reign of God that does not enter into conflict with the malice and evil of personal existence is also not the Reign of God of Jesus). We have, thus, a historically verifiable criterion, a verification much more certain and profound than that of a presumed and partial conformity with theoretical formulas. This is not simply a problem of orthodoxy and orthopraxis, because the praxis that is sought here is the *true* and complete realization of the Reign of God.

But it can also be said that theology is a reflection on praxis, even on total historical praxis and not merely on ecclesial praxis. At first glance, this point of view may appear reductionistic because, although it could encompass the totality of historical praxis, it would leave aside those moments of faith that were not directly operative for the desired action. The appearance of reductionism increases if one takes as one's model the systematic results of classical theology and its claim to an absolute and total knowledge. In the face of these appearances, it can be pointed out that recent theological efforts are more focused on being systematic reflections, if not on all history, on the history of salvation, where this encompasses all history but under the aspect of "salvation." But this solution has the danger, above all, of making the history of salvation a parallel history that at best accompanies "profane" history and its real commitments.

But it has already been shown that there is nothing but one single history and that ecclesial praxis is one moment of historical praxis. It follows that one can focus upon history from distinct points of view. The important thing for theology is the realization of the Reign of God. Consequently, reflecting upon what is and ought to be the realization of the Reign of God in history does not imply any reductionism. Rather, it requires that we prune away false theological foliage and act with a sense of urgency to focus anew upon the most essential problems of the faith. To view history from the Reign and with an operative concern for its realization puts into life-giving contact two places pregnant with revelation. In their unity they give the Reign its historical plenitude and concreteness. I repeat that this cannot be adequately realized in terms of reflection without a well-developed theoretical apparatus but, above all, without a very precise ecclesial commitment.

One cannot say, therefore, that liberation theology has been only a reflection on a certain political praxis of liberation or that its fundamental intent has been a certain politicization of that praxis. It chose its subjects, and, above all, its way of focusing on them according to the historical necessity of the oppressed who are believing people and who expect their faith to decisively contribute to their struggles of liberation. This does not necessarily imply a reduction of the revealed message or a horizontalization of its contents. Whoever seriously knows the best contributions to this theology cannot reasonably make that claim. The insinuations of the International Theological Commission have an academic and elitist bent that weaken them, although they serve as a cautionary signal not to fall into excess. Let us not, however, forget that liberation theology could also offer cautionary signals to the writers of the document and to its representatives.

If historical praxis is a divided praxis, if in this divided historical praxis the Reign of God and the reign of evil become present and operative, if ecclesial praxis cannot remain neutral with respect to this division and this operative presence, if the theological task receives its truth, its verification, from its incarnation in the true ecclesial praxis, in a truly Christian ecclesial praxis, then it must be asked, in what form of ecclesial praxis should the ideological moment that is theology insert itself? Appealing to the Reign of God is not quite enough. Rather, it is necessary to determine the place in which the truth of the Reign of God is most accessible.

To encounter the privileged place of this access, one should begin from the principle that the privileged place of theology is the same as the privileged place of ecclesial praxis. There is no doubt that theology has theoretical requirements that cannot be replaced by anything. But theoretical requirements are not sufficient to capture the fullness of faith or the Christian understanding of a historical situation. They are not even self-sufficient enough to keep from going off course theoretically. Already the classical theologians spoke of a certain *connaturalitas* that makes theological assertions possible. But it is necessary to concretize the referents of that connaturality. They can no longer be divine things taken generically. Rather, they should be the realization of the kingdom of God, announced and made possible by Jesus. Because of the characteristics of this Reign and its realization, a fundamental commitment is required of theologians, along with an original praxis from where they can formally question *[interpelar]* what they have received in order to interpret and realize it.

Latin American theology does not hesitate to affirm that this commitment and praxis should be determined by the "church of the poor" or the popular church and by what is in each case the Christian need as is shown in the church of the poor who ceaselessly continue to produce Latin American theology. Anyone familiar with this subject knows that a new ecclesiology is being formed, whose two pillars are the Reign of God and the poor, as precisely defined by both sociology and theology. This has not been formed by moving from theory to praxis, but rather it has been the praxis of the believers and the committed ones who have been building together theoretical formulations.

It has been frequently recognized that what counts for Latin American theology is its real commitment to the liberating praxis of the oppressed. But what has not been seen with enough clarity is what this insertion represents as an essential methodological moment of the theological task. There is widespread approval for Latin American theology's contact with the daily lives of the people, its desire to render the cry of its suffering brothers and sisters audible, its goal of searching for efficacious principles of action, and even of procuring a spiritual experience of faith. But alongside this approval, what this insertion means and represents has not been adequately described. This insertion, in effect, is sought, not only for pastoral reasons, but because it also belongs inexcusably to properly theological work, since without this element it is impossible to adequately capture reality. In other words, without being inserted in the church of the poor, not only is one unable to contribute principles of action responsibly, but also one is not disposed to understand theoretically what is the Reign of

God—a Reign of God that is hidden from the powerful and from the wise who serve them and that nevertheless is open to the little ones and to those who, in the eyes of the world, have themselves "become little ones" in their service.

And so, the church of the poor is not being proposed as a possible pastoral alternative (or liberation theology as a form of pastoral theology for underdeveloped countries), but rather as the privileged place for theological reflection and for the realization of the Reign of God. If it is the privileged place for the realization of the Reign of God and for the full exercise of faith, hope, and charity, so, too, it is for the theoretical exercise that aims theoretically to purify that realization. This does not always guarantee its academic elaboration, but it does guarantee its correct orientation in the global recognition of the message of Christian praxis. But this academic elaboration is not even an indispensable condition for the profundity and rigor of its theoretical formulation. This is not to substitute pietistic practice for the necessary exercise of the intellect. It is precisely because the problems are so serious and complex that they require wise intellectual efforts. Let us not also forget that the detour of the unreal is often the necessary path to objectively and efficiently approaching the comprehension and transformation of reality.

This preference for the church of the poor as a privileged place of reality, ecclesial praxis, and theological reflection seems to prohibit the reality and praxis of those churches that exist amidst the wealth of developed countries. On the other hand, these developed countries and their people have their own problems. They should be recognized and responded to by their own theologians with their own way of doing theology. Is it not, therefore, a limitation and imposition of the third world to desire that ecclesial praxis and theology be ruled by the church of the poor?

The raising of this question is already a victory for the theology of liberation. It presupposes, in effect, that European theology is not theology *par excellence* (imposing itself with minor corrections and different applications on the rest of the culturally and economically diverse countries, even though its particular analyses and theoretical instruments can be used with caution anywhere). Likewise, it presupposes that, in a certain sense, theology needs to make its defense and justify both the theoretical and Christian relevance of its endeavors and results. Finally, it presupposes that it should look for ways to adjust its self-understanding and its work in accordance with the demands of the church of the poor.

There are two fundamental reasons for this. In the first place, it is clear that the privileged place of revelation taken in its entirety and, above all, the revelation of the New Testament, can be named the world of the poor and the oppressed. Not only is the historical context in which it emerges one of poverty and oppression, but the response that it offers with clear, historical universality is primarily a response whose privileged addressees are the poor and oppressed. Moreover, in the second place, it is also clear that the current situation of the great majority of humanity is a situation of poverty and oppression. Attending to that must be a priority if the church truly wants to be both catholic and universal. And so, if theology wants to aim for a certain universality, even though it be historical, it must go beyond whatever might be the situation of its local church and take careful account of that situation. I would add a third argument: the local context of the churches in developed countries includes, as a decisive factor, the necessity of attending to the element of sin in those countries, insofar as they are more or less directly responsible—by commission or omission—for what is happening in a tragic and massive way in the greater part of the world. The churches of the rich countries should seriously consider the parable of the Good Samaritan, so that they not be so focused on "more elevated and religious" concerns that they pass by Jesus himself crucified in history.

If theology understands itself as the ideological moment of ecclesial praxis, if ecclesial praxis takes part in the universal historical praxis on behalf of those who suffer the sin and injustice of the world, if this ecclesial praxis is that of a church of the poor that intends to realize the Reign of God in history on its own, then theology, whose fundamental object is the Reign of God and whose radical objective is the realization of this Reign, will generate the optimal conditions for realizing its own commitment in a Christian manner. This summarizes the thesis of this article in a few words, which, as was said in the beginning, only deals with one of the aspects of theological method.

—Translated by Anna Bonta Moreland and Kevin F. Burke, SJ

11

Christian Spirituality
(1983)

In the early 1980s the editors of a major Spanish theological dictionary invited Ignacio Ellacuría to contribute essays on three themes: "Pueblo de Dios" ("People of God"), "Pobres" ("The Poor"), and "Espiritualidad" ("Spirituality"). While the first two essays addressed concerns that surface overtly throughout his work and thought, spirituality emerges more quietly in both. As a Jesuit priest, Ellacuría was, of course, formed in Ignatian spirituality and later served as director of formation for the Society of Jesus in Central America (1968–75). In 1969, responding to the vision set forth by the Conference of Latin American Bishops (CELAM) at their meeting in Medellín, Colombia, Ellacuría helped guide the Central American Jesuits in a Discernment Retreat based on the Spiritual Exercises of St. Ignatius. In 1983, he represented his province at the Thirty-third General Congregation of the Society of Jesus. However, except for this essay, most of his notes and thoughts on spirituality were only published posthumously.

The roots of this essay reach deeply into Ellacuría's theological formation and ecclesial consciousness: his friendship with Karl Rahner (for whom the overcoming of the chasm between theology and spirituality was essential for the life of the church); his appreciation of Pedro Arrupe's leadership of the Society of Jesus; his growing sensitivity to the importance of spirituality for liberation theology; his passion for the liberation of the poor as crucial for any genuine Christian spirituality. The structure and content of this essay echo his philosophical and theological commitments. He grounds his understanding of Christian spirituality in the "differentiated unity" of the material and the spiritual dimensions of the human being, examines the biblical witness to the Spirit of God made present in history, and reflects on God's gift of the Spirit to individual believers, communities, and institutions. In the essay's final section he identifies several specific characteristics of Christian spirituality: its Christological focus on the mission of proclaiming and realizing the Reign of God in history; its option for the poor articulated in the beatitudes; its access to the triune life of God as manifested in the theological virtues of faith, hope and love.

The Spiritual and the Material:
Two Dimensions of the Person

A correct pastoral approach to spirituality ought to start from the assumption that "the spiritual" is nothing other than a dimension of the person considered individually and socially, as well as of the Christian, understood personally and institutionally. This dimension does not have an absolute autonomy, as spiritualists claim, such that it would be possible and necessary to cultivate it absolutely independently and separately from other dimensions of the person. Yet neither can it be reduced to a sort of quasi-mechanical reflection of specific material conditions, as the materialists claim. It has its autonomy, but only a relative autonomy, one that needs to be supported by conditions that are "not spiritual," conditions in which, moreover, spirituality must necessarily incarnate and express itself, and which it ought to illuminate and transform in turn. Said in other terms, a correct pastoral approach to spirituality ought to avoid both a dualist and a monist perspective, and should be framed in structural perspectives that are more or less dialectical, as the case requires, in such a way that a given dimension will not be what it is without being a codeterminant of another dimension and being codetermined by it. Each dimension would be a dimension of all the others and would be oriented toward constituting a whole, from which it receives its full reality and meaning.

Thus, the spiritual and the material; the individual and the social; the personal and the structural; the transcendent and the immanent; the Christian and the human; the supernatural and the natural; conversion and transformation; contemplation and action; work and prayer; faith and justice, etc.: none of these are identified one with the other in such a way that by cultivating one of the extremes the other is ipso facto cultivated, such that it is nothing but a reflection or accidental supplement. But neither are they separated one from the other in such a way that they could be cultivated without an intrinsic, essential, and efficacious mutual determination. Whatever separations it might be possible to make in the abstract, in concrete historical reality, just as God has effected it, these dimensions present themselves in unity and in mutual dependence.

This differentiated unity is not easy to maintain. It is not easy to maintain in the relative and requisite autonomy of the different dimensions or in the proportionate and appropriate connection. This is because not every historical situation can be united with given forms of spirituality. What is needed, thus, is an ongoing, alert, and committed discernment of the changing signs of the times and of the specific historical practices that would really be an appropriate response.

Toward a Correct Understanding of Christian Spirituality

From a Christian perspective, spiritual men and women are those men and women who are full of the Spirit of Christ, who are filled with this Spirit in a living and verifiable way, since the power and life of this Spirit invades the whole of their person and action.

The Spirit in the Bible

In the Old Testament the *Pneuma* of God was God's creative and saving power that acted both in the ordering of the natural universe and in the movement of history, empowering some exceptional men and women in a special way. The Spirit of God made itself present historically, and this presence of the Spirit, this efficacy of the Spirit, its spirituality, was more evident than the existence of the Holy Spirit per se as a person of the Trinity. The promise of the Spirit was a promise of new hearts, of a new people and of a new earth, in such a way that all would come to know this Spirit because the earth would be full of this spirituality as something historical, palpable, and transformative, something that could not be attributed to sinful men and women, but rather to a saving God.

In the New Testament we know more about the Spirit because the Spirit's presence has become more intense, above all, in Jesus but also in the primitive community, which is constituted and distinguished as a new community precisely due to the riches and fullness of the Spirit communicated to that community and received by it. We can even affirm that the Holy Spirit belongs to the Trinitarian mystery, not so much because of a direct revelation of the Trinity, but rather due to Jesus' resurrection and because of his action of sending us the Spirit. Real and palpable events transpire in the new community that compel a change in conceiving God, even when it comes to the unitarist bias. The complex reality of the divine life and its personal structure are discovered due to this new spirituality, which invaded Jesus and which, through his mediation and by virtue of him, his followers begin to receive.

What this shows is that Christian spirituality cannot be understood primarily as a constellation of spiritual practices (prayer, ascetic exercises, rules and norms of behavior, etc.), but rather as something so new, so unexpected, so vigorous and transformative that it brings us to affirm that God is becoming present among men and women in an exceptional way. It is clear that this spirituality makes no sense without the operative presence of the Spirit, which is not simply an abstract Spirit, but rather is the Spirit of Christ, which brings us to the Spirit of God. But one will not really perceive or believe in this Spirit except by starting from a living spirituality, from the reality of the Spirit's operative presence in the heart of the human being, in the Christian community, and even in the institutional character of the church and the movement of history. New words and deeds, unlooked-for and atypical ways of acting—these are the things that give rise to the question of who causes them and how they come to be inspired.

Nevertheless, there are not two different spirits—the Holy Spirit and the Spirit of Christ—even though their presentation in the New Testament has different characteristics and permits, even requires, that we make important distinctions and differentiations. What is important for pastoral purposes is to stress that the Spirit of Christ—which to begin with is the Spirit of the historical Jesus—is the one who brings us to the knowledge and possession of the Holy Spirit in its inner-Trinitarian moment. Thus, the Holy Spirit as Spirit of Christ is the one who opens up the creative path for history by teaching us with the Spirit's living presence what there is that is not fixed in advance, whether it be by the letter or by the law, that which is not finished in Jesus' redemptive and saving mission. This Spirit is the one who makes all things new, who presses on toward new heavens and a new earth, the one who orders the chaos of history as the Spirit of God ordered the chaos of nature in the beginning. We are introduced into the life of the Trinity itself by being enlivened by this Spirit of Christ, which Jesus merited for us and sent to us; we experience and believe that God's Holy Spirit is the Spirit of the Son, the Spirit of filiation: "If the Spirit has come from the Father through the Son, with that Spirit we are able to go to the Father through the Son. . . . If in coming down the Father loves us in the beloved Son, now in rising up we love the Father with the Son of the Father's love. . . . The Spirit actualizes in us the love that the Father has for us for all times in his Son" (Marcelino Legido).

Historical Presence of the Spirit

Christian spirituality is nothing other than the real presence of the Holy Spirit, the Spirit of Christ, self-consciously appropriated in the real life of persons, of communities, and of institutions that want to be Christian. Spiritual persons, then, are not those who do many "spiritual" practices, but rather those who, filled with the Spirit, attain to that Spirit's creative and renovating impetus, the Spirit's overcoming of sin and of death, the Spirit's power for resurrection and for more life. They are the ones who attain the fullness and liberty of the children of God, the ones who inspire and enlighten everyone else and bring them to live more fully and more freely. But all of this happens in conformity with the Spirit of Jesus, because Christian spirituality is essentially the spirituality of the Jesus crucified by our sins and raised up for our salvation. This is the Jesus who was born of Mary by the work of the Holy Spirit and whose prolongation will also happen by the work of the Holy Spirit coming over those today who are the continuations of Mary, the poor woman of Nazareth, the woman of the people, whose spirituality is reflected in the Magnificat. The Spirit of Christ has as a norm the historical life of Jesus, even though it is not exhausted by what that life was; that is why we cannot abandon the historical normativity of Jesus in the name of a disincarnate and de-historicized Spirit. Christian spirituality is of necessity a spirituality of the following of Jesus.

This does not mean that there cannot be different "spiritualities" within the one single Christian spirituality, that is, organic and totalizing ways of living the Spirit of Christ. There are several reasons why it is possible and necessary for there to be a pluralism of spiritualities of this sort. Above all, it is because there is no single historical form for expressing and making present the riches of the life of God in Jesus or the creative and renovating impulse of the Spirit of Christ. There is no individual, community, or institution that can presume to have exhausted in one specific historical form all that there is in the gift of the Spirit, which has been given to us in Jesus. In the second place, because of Christian spirituality's intrinsic historicity, it must reconcile itself by means of very profound changes to the profound changes of history. We can clearly see the historical enrichment of Christian spirituality that comes about because of historical changes, new demands of the times, and the subsequent appearance of men and women who are filled with the Spirit and achieve a new reading and appropriation of the person of Jesus. In the third place, it is because Christian spirituality has an ecclesial character, which guarantees that the church, as a people and as a body, will require a plurality of functions and comportments.

It is clear that not just any spirituality can be considered Christian, however much the name of Jesus is proclaimed in it. There are criteria for a Christian spirituality. Some are purely formal ones, but meaningful. Thus, we can disqualify those spiritualities that, being partial, want to present themselves as total and, in theory or in practice, as excluding other essential elements. It is certainly true that in the body of Christ there ought to be eyes and feet, hands and a head, and that the eye cannot say to the feet that they are not necessary. But there is no room within the extensive boundaries of Christian spirituality for eyes that prevent walking, authorities that prevent teaching, pastors who confuse administration with giving life to the sheep, spiritual people who make the rich pass easily through the eye of the needle, prophets who reject any kind of institutionalization and any hierarchy at all, etc. Other criteria have more in the way of content and bespeak the relationship to the fundamental criterion of following the historical Jesus, just as this is presented in the New Testament and just as it has been lived out by the great followers of Jesus in the Christian tradition.

Christian Spirituality as a Gift of God to the Poor

Christian spirituality, understood in this way, is fundamentally a gift of God the Father that continues the fundamental gift of God's self that the incarnate Son was. But this gift of God the Father itself tells us where and how it should be preferentially received. The gift is received in the world of the poor, in a praxis that responds efficaciously to the great task of ridding the world of sin, of death, so that the world and human beings might have more life. There can be little doubt that the poor are the preferential place for the revelation and living communication of the Christian God. The example of the Son himself, who, being rich, became poor, and the insistence of all the great reformers of the church that we take up poverty anew as the element that unleashes reform, ought to serve as proof. On the other hand, another thing that is essential to Christian faith and an indispensable condition for spirituality is that what is required is that there be a praxis that liberates from the sin of the world, that sin that is the great obstacle to the historical irruption of God's life among men and women—the Reign of God. This is because a spirituality that does not start from, and does not lead to, a liberative praxis from sin and from its consequences would not be a response to Jesus' life. This is *the* great spiritual practice, that is, an entire life that takes its start from the poor and is dedicated to the disappearance of sin—the negation of the Spirit of life—from the world, so that the Reign of God, a God who is a God of life, might irrupt into history.

This does not mean that fundamental spiritual practices, such as prayer in all its forms and sacramental celebrations, are not necessary. It has already been stated that the spiritual is not a mere mechanical or automatic reflection of a specific praxis. Not everything is sheer exteriority; there is an interiority to the human being and to the Christian that ought to be cultivated in a very explicit way. There is no full communication without solitude and seclusion. This is why other ascetic practices cannot be scorned or the use of methods that facilitate that moment of retreat and self-reflection that is essential in seeking and possessing the Spirit. Special care is required in seeking out adequate symbolic forms and practices that respond to the cultural level of the great popular masses, that need to express themselves, to be purified and to develop their great spiritual potential.

Specific Characteristics of Christian Spirituality

It is no easy thing to shed light on the problem of the specific contents of Christian spirituality. But what we can do is to indicate some features that cannot be absent.

As a fundamental presupposition of this spirituality, we ought to highlight what Jon Sobrino has characterized as honesty and fidelity to the truth of the real. Imprisoning the truth in injustice (Rom. 1:18) is what stands in the way of the revelation and communication of God and what becomes a source of condemnation. It is injustice that imprisons the truth of God, just as we find it happening in the reality of the world and in the reality of history. And it is, in turn, a great injustice to imprison this truth of God and to prevent it from speaking to us and challenging us. Starting from this presupposition, we can specify three fundamental trajectories that Christian spirituality ought to follow.

Christian spirituality ought to be centered Christologically on mission, which is the proclamation and realization of the Reign of God in history. With this principle we are highlighting the "missional" character of Christian spirituality. Christian spirituality is something that is received and cultivated in order to be transmitted. It is something that is actualized in the apostolic praxis of announcing and realizing the Reign of God. The spiritual moment cannot be separated from the missional; the moment of contemplation cannot be separated from the moment of action—as if the first ones were the truly spiritual moments and the second ones their mere results; as if the first were the place where God is encountered and the second the place where men and women are encountered. This is not to deny that one can distinguish methodologically between the moment of recollection and discernment and the moment of carrying something out, the moment of interior solitude and the moment of communication. But this does not entail privileging the moment of seclusion over the moment of commitment. Contemplation ought itself to be active, that is, oriented toward conversion and transformation; and action ought to be contemplative, that is, enlightened, discerning, reflective. The two great sources of this incarnate spirituality, each with its respective aids, are the word of God in scripture and tradition, and the word of God in the living reality of history and in the lives of men and women filled with the Spirit.

All of this moves forward guided by the aspiration that the Reign of God be established in history. The God whom Jesus proclaimed ought to be historicized among men and women, be made present and predominant in the world of men and women, so that God might be all in all, without annulling the specificity of particular structures and the identity of persons. It is not enough, then, that spirituality be missional, without this mission being oriented toward implanting the Reign of God.

We ought to understand the ecclesial character of Christian spirituality on the basis of this Reign of God, understanding the church primarily as the people of God gathered together in following Jesus. This is a church shaped in conformity with what the Reign of God proclaimed by Jesus requires, a Reign for which the church cannot substitute, with which it is not identified, and to which it should be subordinated. This ecclesial character also speaks to the communitarian and exterior character of Christian spirituality, which is not something merely individual and interior. The great celebrations and ecclesial action are not individualistic, but rather seek out personal fullness in a coming together that is not purely institutional but communal. The church as an institution ought not to smother this spirituality of the Reign of God, which is driven forward and supported by the Spirit of Christ, whose efficacious action does not necessarily pass through institutional channels. On the contrary, the institutional church ought to let itself be saturated with the Spirit, so that it does not let itself be carried along by social pressures that are inherent in its institutional character and the worldly pressures of the other institutions among which it moves. To want to substitute the spirituality of the institutional church for the spirituality of the Reign of God is to betray the Reign of God and the church. On the other hand, to want to produce a spirituality of the Reign of God outside of the institutional church ends up in manifestations that are dangerous to the Reign of God itself. What is necessary is to maintain the structural unity, a unity that can take on dialectical characteristics, even though the priority lies in the Reign of God and not in the institutional church.

Christian spirituality ought to be oriented by the spirit of the Sermon on the Mount and by the spirit of the Beatitudes in particular. The Sermon on the Mount and the Beatitudes do not, to be sure, express all the riches of the life and message of Jesus, but they give very specific guidelines of which we cannot be ignorant, on pain of abandoning something essential to Christian spirituality. And this ignorance happens very frequently, because these texts were written neither for institutional powers nor for civilizations of wealth, and today the Christians who are predominant in the processes of the world and of the church have too much to do with institutional powers and with the civilization of wealth. It is not that we should look for a mechanical reading of the Sermon on the Mount, as if its literal meaning could be spelled out and turned into a fixed law. What we must do is to live through this reading anew, taking the Spirit as one's starting point, as well as that of one's own historical situation. But the renovating and creative breath of the Spirit of Christ does not entail a rupture with the original and foundational word or forgetting it or mystifying it—because there are not two spirits or two Christs.

This is where we must locate that essential character of the Christian spirituality constituted by the preferential option for the poor and the struggle for justice (Medellín, Puebla). The Christian who is dismayed by the overwhelming presence of a poverty that is the fruit of inequality and of oppression; who is enlightened by the revelation that oppression, exploitation, and repression of one human being by another, of some classes by others, and of the majority of the people by a minority of them, is the great sin of the world; who is animated by the life and the word of Jesus; who for his or her part sees in the poor person the one preferred by the Father: this Christian will see it to be absolutely necessary that his or her spirituality be shaped so that it has as an essential characteristic the preferential option for the poor, which, given the universal historical context, takes on features of a liberative praxis.

Christian spirituality ought to be founded in faith, oriented by hope, and carried out in love. Christian spirituality ought to set in motion with all vigor three virtues, virtues that are not, however, understood only as virtues, but as virtues that are theologal in the strict sense, which is to say, virtues that put fundamental dimensions of the human person into close unity with the fullness of the triune God revealed in Jesus. Only in Jesus do we know that God is Father, Son, and Spirit; but at the same time, in Jesus we have discovered that the human being is faith, hope, and love: faith as the acceptance of the transcendent in the visible and the graced acceptance of the God who is given to us in Jesus; hope as the human person's openness and movement toward a future to be made, and as hope in a promise, made definitive in Jesus, that the Reign of God will come because in some way it is already here; love as a response to a God who loved us first and in whose originating love we can give ourselves totally to others within the framework of a dedication even unto death that brings with it the fullness of a new, resurrected life. These three are theologal virtues in which the triune God is made present in the most profound depths of the human person, in such a way that this presence opens up these depths to something that encompasses them, goes beyond them in the mediation of other men and women.

In some way mysterious, yet at the same time susceptible to experience, the triune life of God becomes the Christian's life in this triple dimension of faith, hope, and love, because the three are shaped in a clear way as they are referred to the Father, the Son, or the Spirit, and as they are referred to men and women and to the world, seen from the perspective of the Father, the Son, or the Spirit. What it all comes down to is that this triune life, taken up in this way, is what Christian spirituality is, a spirituality that is Trinitarian and incarnate, because, in short, there is no other spirituality, no other divine life for the human being, than the one that has been given to us in the life, death, and resurrection of the historical Jesus, whose life we follow because we live in his Spirit.

—Translated by J. Matthew Ashley

12

Monseñor Romero:

One Sent by God to Save His People
(1980)

The brutal assassination of Archbishop Oscar Romero on March 24, 1980, is without question the most important event in modern Salvadoran history. It precipitated an unprecedented period of violent repression, directly triggering a civil war that lasted thirteen years. It became a flashpoint for different interpretations of Salvadoran reality. It continues to ripple and resonate three decades later, not only in El Salvador and Central America, but throughout the church and all over the world. Ignacio Ellacuría, like many other theologians, church people, political commentators, and historians moved quickly to take stock of Archbishop Romero. He wrote several later essays where he interpreted the church and the Christian university in the light of Romero's witness, but in this early, important reflection—written just eight months after Romero's shocking murder—he produces his most eloquent elaboration of the theological significance of Archbishop Romero.

"With Monseñor Romero, God passed through El Salvador," Ellacuría said famously shortly after Romero's martyrdom. The theological symbol woven through this chapter—one sent by God to save His people—corresponds to and elaborates the truth of that saying. Romero was not so much an exemplar of liberation theology, as some have said, but an example of how to historicize the gospel as a historical force. His "conversion" was the fruit of an honest encounter with historical reality: "It was not that he transformed, and then he was able to see something that he had not seen before; rather he saw something new, something objectively new, and this transformed him." Prior to Romero's conversion, it was as if the "poor" were "something else he had to attend to"; they now became "the orienting center of his pastoral work." And Romero never stopped appealing to transcendence or criticizing false absolutes: he witnessed to the God who breaks into human history to redeem and transform it, to save and convert people. Ellacuría even speaks of "the salvation of the historical process" of El Salvador resulting from Romero's vibrant witness.

"The word, life, and example of Monseñor Romero made the Christian message credible to a larger and larger part of the Salvadoran people because he opened them to a hope that was always greater and more pure."

It has been eight months—since March 24—that Archbishop Romero was killed on the altar while saying Mass. It took only one bullet to the heart to end his mortal life. Even though he had been threatened for months, Romero never sought out the least bit of protection. He drove his car himself and lived in a small apartment adjacent to the chapel in which he was assassinated. Those who killed him are the same ones who kill the people, the same ones who in this year of Romero's martyrdom have exterminated almost 10,000 persons. The majority of these persons are young peasants, workers, and students, but also elderly women and children, who are taken from their homes and appear shortly thereafter: tortured, destroyed, and often unrecognizable.

It is not important to determine who shot Romero. It was evil; it was sin; it was the anti-Christ. However, it was a historical evil, a historical sin, and a historical anti-Christ, which have been incarnated in unjust structures and in those who have chosen to take on the role of Cain. Romero had only three years of public life as archbishop of San Salvador. They were enough to sow the seeds of God's word and to make present the countenance of Jesus to his people. This was too much for those who cannot tolerate the light of truth and the fire of love.

What was the ministry and testimony of this man who, in three years, passed from anonymity and ineffectiveness to a universal public renown and the height of social effectiveness without ever ceasing to be a Christian, a pastor, a prophet, and a priest?

The Historical Force of the Gospel

The theology of liberation has striven to demonstrate that the gospel is a historical force, at the same time as being a salvific force, and it is so most authentically when it is most authentically Christian. Liberation theology sees this coming to be a historical force as an intrinsic exigency of Christianity, not by way of Christendom or by similar forms of historicization, but rather as pure gospel incarnated in the historical reality of human beings.

Archbishop Romero is an eminent example of this historical force of the gospel. There is no doubt, and no one would dare dispute, that in the last three years of his life he became an extremely powerful figure in the Salvadoran social process. Yet, what is important is to underscore the fact that he achieved this, not by abandoning his episcopal duties, but by realizing them fully. Clearly, the mere fact of being bishop, regardless of the social weight that it still carries in El Salvador, does not explain his tremendous social impact. The other Salvadoran bishops do not have this impact. What explains it is his way of being bishop, of being a Christian, of being a priest.

This conclusion becomes even clearer if we examine the relative ineffectiveness of his prior years as a priest and bishop. Wasn't he the same person, with the same qualities and preparation, both before and after being named archbishop of San Salvador? Weren't there the same circumstances of oppression and repression? Then what new thing occurred during those last three years of his ministry?

The new thing was that Romero sought to historicize properly the force of the gospel. His worth and his greatness, the ultimate cause of his unprecedented influence does not come from his being a political leader, an intellectual, or a great orator. The ultimate cause is that he announced and realized the gospel in its fullness and with a full incarnation. In his previous phase, Romero was a priest and a bishop of good will, a pious man of prayer, and an eager pastor. He was considered a spiritual type, and consequently, he was reluctant to interfere in temporal matters. He dealt with the wealthy but did not scorn the poor. Yet with all this, he hardly represented anything in the church of El Salvador. Rather, he was considered an opponent of the new ecclesial movement awakened at Medellín. Interested above all in orthodoxy, Romero distrusted the new formulations of liberation theology and even tagged with the label of Marxist contagion those who denounced the structural injustice of the country.

His pastoral message spoke to the small elite, those who belonged to Opus Dei, and to groups of the Christian family movement. However, the pain and misery of the people scarcely said anything to him, and he did not signify anything to the people. Here is the key, as we will see later, but for now it should be clear that before his conversion, Romero did not know how to historicize adequately that which is most true and vital in the gospel.

The Conversion of Monseñor Romero

Monseñor Romero did not change because of being named archbishop of San Salvador. Rather, he was chosen in order to contain the incipient preferential option for the poor in the archdiocese and to redirect it into more traditional channels. That incipient option had already driven many sectors of the archdiocese into new pastoral directions and the first prophetic confrontations with the country's authorities and dominant class. In order to avoid this, Bishop Romero was named ahead of the candidate of the more committed part of the archdiocese, Bishop Rivera y Damas.

Nevertheless, Monseñor Romero converted into what was God's great gift to the archdiocese, contrary to the arrangement successfully forged by the government and the ecclesiastical authorities. Monseñor Romero was not chosen so that he would become what he did become; he was chosen almost for the opposite reason. Yet, the Holy Spirit empowered him and shattered all human plans and perspectives, including the plans and perspectives of Romero himself. Romero became the great gift of God because he himself was totally converted. It did not occur in one blow, though his initial change was sudden. The assassination of Father [Rutilio] Grande, the first of the martyr priests that he would have to bury, shook his conscience. It tore the veil that had hidden the truth, and the new truth began to empower his entire being. Initially, it was not a subjective change, but an objective one. Something was discovered that had not been seen in him, in spite of his good will and purity of intention, his hours of prayer, his repeated orthodoxy, and his fidelity to the Magisterium and the Vatican hierarchy. The light empowered him, and this is what transformed him. It was not that he transformed, and then he was able to see something that he had not seen before; rather he saw something new, something objectively new, and this transformed him.

At a first moment, that something new was the dazzling truth of a priest who had dedicated himself to evangelizing the poor, a priest who, in that evangelization, had encouraged the poor to historicize salvation, to give historical flesh to the eternally new word of God. For that reason, he was assassinated by those who felt threatened by that evangelizing word and by the people who had given it historical flesh and, to a certain point, made with it a political project. Other bishops and Christians saw the martyrdom of Father Grande as a political act and even gave unbelievable and blind interpretations to it. Not Monseñor Romero. His cleansed eyes saw the truth, and it was revealed to him what it means to be an apostle in El Salvador today—what it means to be a prophet and martyr. From that point, he began down the path of prophet and martyr, not because he would have chosen it, but because God filled him with the historical voices of the suffering of his chosen people and with the voice of the blood of the first innocent to die as a martyr in El Salvador today, so that all could have more life and that the whole church could regain that prophetic pulse it had lost.

The Historical Specificity of His Conversion

After this initial conversion, which is merely the beginning of something that could have ended right there, Monseñor Romero enters a new phase. He enters into a deep conversion of his mission, and it is this mission, the faithfulness to this mission, that ends up transforming his life and that makes him become a fundamental factor in the salvation history of El Salvador. His mission, his new sense of mission, sanctifies him more and more. He does not accommodate his mission to what he would have liked, but rather he accommodates his entire life to his new mission.

Until then, Romero had occupied himself with the poor and oppressed "also." However, from this moment on, they become the orienting center of his pastoral work. He makes a preferential option for an oppressed people, not in light of theoretical considerations, but in light of his fidelity to the gospel and because he begins to see in that oppressed people the historicized Jesus that summons him and makes demands from him. This option saves him and puts him in a condition to save. When the people represented hardly anything to him, he hardly represented anything to the people, we used to say. Now we can add that when the people finally did become important to him, his announcement of the gospel finally had force; it was finally credible. It was not any force but the evangelical force of salvation, the historical force of liberation.

Romero comes to understand, once and for all, that the mission of the church is the announcement and realization of the Reign of God, but he understands at the same time that the announcement and realization of the Reign of God pass inescapably through the proclamation of the good news to the poor and liberation to the oppressed. But all of this is so that these can take their proper place in the church—the church of the poor—and that they can take their proper place in the task of the historical realization of the people. Romero desired and sought that his word of salvation would be operative and that it would be received joyfully and with hope by the primary and principal addressees of that word of salvation. He took this conviction to its ultimate consequences when he saw in the voiceless people, the very voice of God; in the crucified people,

God the savior; in the struggle for liberation, the path to arriving at a new heaven and a new earth.

The gospel is always read from a location, always read contextually, and faith is also lived out in a particular situation. That reading and that living out will never be adequate if the location and context are not, in a preferential way, that of the oppressed. Monseñor Romero's apostolic conversion is based on this. He changed locations, changed contexts, and what was once an opaque word, amorphous and ineffective, became a torrent of life to which the people approached to quench their thirst. The people without a voice made his voice, that of the archbishop and the church, resound not only throughout the country but throughout the world. Through Monseñor Romero, the crucifixion and death of a people became resurrection and life. Through him, the struggles for liberation found a transcendent meaning that served to strengthen and challenge the immanent dimensions of the political task.

For doing all of this, Romero took on the same fate as his people. He lived with calumny, defamation, and persecution. They accused him of being in politics instead of being the church; they accused him of fomenting class struggle instead of proclaiming love; they accused him of preaching violence instead of spreading love. Like Jesus, they accused him of agitating the people and opposing paying tribute to Caesar. The wise and prudent of this world, ecclesiastical, civil, and military, the wealthy and powerful of this world felt this and said this. But the people of God, those who hunger and thirst for justice, the pure of heart, the poor of spirit knew that all of this was false; they knew and felt that the word of Monseñor Romero was pure gospel. They had never felt God so close, the Spirit so operative, Christianity so true, so full of meaning, so full of grace and truth. Because of this he was killed. Because of this he was assassinated. Because of this he is a martyr. Because of this he lives so deeply in the hearts of the people. If one day the people really take power and initiate the painful march in search of total liberation, the church will not be seen as extraneous because, for this people, the church would continue to be the church of Monseñor Romero. This church could never be extraneous to a people that loved him, trusted him, and expected to hear from him the words of eternal life.

Salvation of the Historical Process

Monseñor Romero never tired in repeating that political processes, as pure and idealistic as they may be, can never be enough to bring integral liberation to men and women. He understood perfectly that saying of St.

Augustine that to be human, one must be "more" human. For Romero, history that was only human, that only attempted to be human, would promptly cease to be so. Neither humanity nor history are self-sufficient.

For that reason, Romero never stopped appealing to transcendence. This theme emerged in almost all of his homilies: the word of God, the action of God breaking through human limits. It was a transcendence that was never presented as an abandonment of the human, as flight from the human, but as humanity's improvement and perfection. It is a "beyond" (*más alla*) that does not abandon the "closer" (*más acá*), but rather opens it up and propels it forward.

This is why Romero sought an authentic *salvation* of the historical process and salvation of a *process* that, as a historical process, has its own autonomous laws. Said another way, he did not de-historicize the process of reality with its concrete, intramundane conditions. What Romero did was attempt to remove from it the weight of sin and open it up to its best transcendent possibilities. He did so from a Christian perspective, as much in the identification and condemnation of what was sin, as in the identification of what were the best transcendent possibilities.

From this perspective he raged—although in his heart there was not a bit of rage—against injustice, above all, against the injustice of the powerful against the oppressed majority. From here, Romero would fight against any absolutization of the finite and human, above all, against the absolutization of power and wealth, but also of one's ideas (dogmatism) and one's own organization (sectarianism). From here, he would speak in favor of the people so that he himself would critically contribute to a new earth in which the dominant values would be justice, love, solidarity, and freedom. From here, he would, time and again, set his eyes on Jesus as the principle of Christian faith and Christian transcendence.

The people opened to this Christian transcendence. The word, life, and example of Monseñor Romero made the Christian message credible to a larger and larger part of the Salvadoran people, because he opened them to a hope that was always greater and more pure. From Romero, the people received a new strength to hope, to struggle with hope, to offer their lives, filling their heroic sacrifice with a sense of meaning. The church, for its part, received a credibility and strength from this people that trusted in its new stage, now not naively but critically.

For this reason, one can say that with Romero, there began to be realized, in a surprisingly effective manner, the salvation of the historical process that is being carried out in El Salvador. He fostered this process in its concrete historical reality because he saw in it more light than darkness, more life than violence, and he took sides in this process for that which favored the oppressed people. However, he did not simply identify himself with this process, because the gospel requires incarnation "in," but not identification "with" a specific historical process. This evangelical incarnation permitted him to contend with very real political projects without the easy escape of principles, as if the Christian prophet need only announce abstract generalities. That incarnation gained him the love of the oppressed people and the hatred of the oppressors. It earned him persecution, the same persecution that the people suffered. That is how he died, and that is why they killed him. That is why, likewise, he became an exceptional example of how the power of the gospel can become a historical power of transformation. That is why he continues to live after his death, not only because there are many who still remember him, not only because there are many that had the veil that obscured the truth of the gospel removed from their eyes, but because, above all, there are many who are ready to follow his path, knowing that Monseñor Romero, in the last three years of his life, was an exemplary follower of Jesus of Nazareth.

—Translated by Michael E. Lee

Publication Histories

1. The Latin American Quincentenary: Discovery or Cover-up? (1989)

This first full English translation of "Quinto centenario de Ameríca Latina ¿descubrimiento o encubrimiento?" appeared as one in a larger series of lectures organized by the *Associació per al diàlog amb les cultures* (OSMI) and the *Comissió Internacional de la Crida*. Shortly after the UCA massacre in November 1989, this transcription of Ellacuría's lecture was published in Spain in the pamphlet-series *Cuadernos Cristianisme i justicia* (Barcelona, 1990); in El Salvador, *Revista Latinoamericana de Teología* 21 (1990): 271–82; in Mexico, *Christus: Revista de Teología, Ciencias Humanas y Pastoral* 638 (1990): 7–13; and in a publication of the Society of Jesus in Central America, *Diakonía* 56 (1990): 15–32. It appears in *Escritos teológicos,* vol. 2 (2000), 525–39.

2. On Liberation (1989)

Ellacuría penned this essay in 1989 and published it under the title "En torno al concepto y la idea de liberación" [literally "Around the Concept and the Idea of Liberation"] in a collection entitled *Implicaciones sociales y políticas de la teologia de la liberación* (Madrid: Escuela de Estudios Hispanoamericanos, Instituto de Filosofía, 1989), 91–109. It appears in his collected works under that same title: *Escritos teológicos,* vol. 1 (2000), 629–957. Several years after its initial publication, the UCA published this essay under the one word title "Liberación" ["Liberation"] in *Revista Latinoamericana de Teología* 30 (1993): 213–32; it also appeared with this title as an entry in the Spanish theological dictionary, *Conceptos fundamentales del Cristianismo,* edited by C. Floristán and J. J. Tomayo (Madrid: Trotta, 1993), 690–710. The current translation utilizes a title in English that combines elements of both Spanish titles.

3. Laying the Philosophical Foundations of Latin American Theological Method (1975)

First published as "Hacia una fundamentacíon filosófica del método teológico Latinoamericano," in E. Ruiz Maldonado, ed., *Liberación y cautiverio: Debates en torno al metodo de la teología en América Latina,* las comunicaciones y los debates del Encuentro Latinoamericano de Teología, Mexico City (August 11–15, 1975), 609–35, Ellacuría also published it in the same year in *Estudios Centroamericanos* 322–23 (1975): 409–25. The critical edition of the essay appears in his collected theological writings, *Escritos teológicos*, vol. 1 (2000), 187–218.

4. The Liberating Function of Philosophy (1985)

"The Liberating Function of Philosophy" is the first full English translation of "Función liberadora de la filosofía" which initially appeared in *Estudios Centroamericanos* 435–36 (1985): 45–64. In his collected works, it appears in *Veinte años de historia en El Salvador (1969–1989): Escritos políticos,* vol. 1 (1991), 93–121.

5. The Christian Challenge of Liberation Theology (1987)

"El desafío cristiano de la teología de la liberación" is the transcript of Ellacuría's 1987 presentation to the conference organized by the *Fundación Banco Exterior* in Madrid, Spain, around the theme *"Lo temporal y la religioso en el mundo actual."* The talk was first published after Ellacuría's death in three installments in *Cartas a las Iglesias* 263 (1992): 12–15; 264 (1992): 11–13; 265 (1992): 14–16. It is included in Ellacuría's collected works: *Escritos teológicos*, vol. 1 (2000), 19–33.

6. The Historicity of Christian Salvation (1984)

The original text of "Historicidad de la salvación cristiana" first appeared in *Revista Latinoamericana de Teología* 1 (1984): 5–45. Ellacuría later published it in the Catalonian journal *Selecciones de Teología* 101 (1987): 59–80. The year after the UCA massacre it appeared in *Mysterium liberationis: Conceptos fundamentales de la teología de la liberación*, coedited by Ellacuría and Jon Sobrino and jointly published in Madrid (Editorial Trotta, 1990) and in San Salvador (UCA Editores, 1991), vol. 1, 323–72. It appears in his collected writings, *Escritos teológicos,* vol. 1 (2000), 353–96. This essay is an abridged and emended version that was first translated into English by Margaret D. Wilde and can be read in its entirety in *Mysterium Liberationis: Fundamental Concepts of Liberation Theology* (Maryknoll, NY: Orbis Books, 1993), 251–89.

7. Salvation History (1987)

Ellacuría first wrote "Salvation History" in 1987, but he was assassinated before he would see it published. It appeared in 1993 in two different venues under similar but different titles, as "Historia de la salvación" in *Revista Latinoamericana de Teología* 28 (1993): 3–25 and as "Salvación en la historia" in the theological dictionary *Conceptos fundamentales del Cristianismo*, C. Floristán and J. J. Tomayo, eds. (Madrid: Trotta, 1993), 1252–74. The essay appears among Ellacuría's collected works under the first title: "Historia de la salvación," *Escritos teológicos,* vol. 1 (2000), 597–628.

8. The Crucified People: An Essay in Historical Soteriology (1978)

"El pueblo crucificado, ensayo de soteriología histórica" appeared in 1978 in I. Ellacuría, et al., *Cruz y resurrección: Anuncio de una iglesia nueva* (Mexico City, CTR), 49–82. Two years later, it was published in Barcelona in the journal *Selecciones de Teología* 76 (1980): 325–41. It appears as a chapter in Ellacuría's book, *Conversión de la iglesia al reino de Dios: Para anunciarlo y realizarlo en la historia* (Santander, Spain: Editorial Sal Terrae, 1984), 25–63, and, in the year he was assassinated, the UCA published it in *Revista Latinoamericana de Teología* 18 (1989): 305–33. It is one of four major essays by Ellacuría to be included in *Mysterium liberationis: Conceptos fundamentales de la teología de la liberación*, vol. 2 (Madrid: Editorial Trotta, 1990), 189–216. It appears in Ellacuría's collected works: *Escritos teológicos*, vol. 2 (2000), 137–70. "The Crucified People," the English translation by Phillip Berryman and Robert R. Barr, first appeared in *Mysterium Liberationis: Fundamental Concepts of Liberation Theology* (Maryknoll, NY: Orbis Books, 1993), 580–603 and also in *Systematic Theology: Perspectives from Liberation Theology* (Maryknoll, NY: Orbis Books, 1996), 257–78. The current essay is an emended version of the Berryman-Barr translation.

9. The Church of the Poor, Historical Sacrament of Liberation (1977)

Among Ellacuría's most frequently republished essays, "La iglesia de los pobres, sacramento histórico de la liberación" first appeared in *Estudios Centroamericanos* 348–49 (1977): 707–22. Subsequently it appeared in the Catalonian theological journal *Selecciones de Teología* 70 (1979): 119–34, the journal of the Centro de Proyección Cristiana in Lima, Peru, *Encuentro: Selecciones para Latinoamérica* 1 (1980): 142–48, and Ellacuría's book, *Conversión de la iglesia al reino de Dios: Para anunciarlo y realizarlo en la historia* (Santander, Spain: Editorial Sal Terrae, 1984), 179–216. After his death it appeared in *Mysterium liberationis: Conceptos fundamentales de la teología de la liberación*, vol. 2 (Madrid: Editorial Trotta, 1990), 127–54. It is included in his collected works: *Escritos teológicos*, vol. 2 (2000), 453–85. It first appeared in English in *Mysterium Liberationis: Fundamental Concepts of Liberation Theology* (Maryknoll, NY: Orbis Books, 1993), 543–64, translated by Margaret D. Wilde; this chapter includes emendations of the Wilde translation.

10. Theology as the Ideological Moment of Ecclesial Praxis (1978)

Ellacuría published "La teología como momento ideológico de la praxis eclesial" in 1978 in a prestigious Spanish theological journal, *Estudios Eclesiásticos* 207 (1978): 457–76. In his collected writings, it is found in *Escritos teológicos*, vol. 1 (2000), 163–85.

11. Christian Spirituality (1983)

"Christian Spirituality" was first published as "Espiritualidad" in C. Floristán and J. J. Tomayo, eds., *Conceptos fundamentales de pastoral* (Madrid: Trotta, 1983), 304–09. The following year it appeared in a publication of the Society of Jesus in Central America under the title used in this translation: "La espiritualidad Cristiana," *Diakonía* 30 (1984): 123–32. Four years after Ellacuría's martyrdom, the Spanish theologians, Casiano Floristán and Juan José Tomayo, republished this entry under its original title in their new dictionary of Christianity, *Conceptos fundamentales del Cristianismo* (Madrid: Trotta, 1993), 413–20, along with the same two essays that appeared in the 1983 volume and two newer essays that appear in this present collection, *Liberación* (see chapter 2) and *Salvación en la historia* (see chapter 7). In Ellacuría's collected writings, it appears as "Espiritualidad," *Escritos teológicos*, vol. 4 (2002), 47–57.

12. Monseñor Romero: One Sent by God to Save His People (1980)

"Monseñor Romero, un enviado de Dios para salvar a su pueblo" appeared first in the Spanish periodical *Sal Terrae* 811 (1980): 825–32 and then the Central American Jesuit publication, *Diakonía* 17 (1981): 2–8. After the UCA massacre, this essay by one martyr about the theological witness of another martyr appeared in the UCA's two primary publications: *Estudios Centroamericanos* 497 (1990): 141–46 and *Revista Latinoamericana de Teología* 19 (1990) 5–10. Among Ellacuría's collected works, it is found in *Escritos teológicos*, vol. 3 (2002), 93–100.

Index